PORTRAITS
FROM LIFE

PORTRAITS FROM LIFE
FORD MADOX FORD

Memories and criticisms of

HENRY JAMES

JOSEPH CONRAD

THOMAS HARDY

H. G. WELLS

STEPHEN CRANE

D. H. LAWRENCE

JOHN GALSWORTHY

IVAN TURGENEV

W. H. HUDSON

THEODORE DREISER

A. C. SWINBURNE

A GATEWAY EDITION

HENRY REGNERY COMPANY   CHICAGO

Copyright 1936 and 1937, by Ford Madox Ford

*First American edition published 1937
by Houghton Mifflin Company. Man-
ufactured in the United States of
America, 6-60.*

TO PAUL PALMER, ESQ.

My Dear Palmer,

You will have to accept the ascription of this book, for, if there is any shame attaching to it, you, as accomplice before the act, must incur one half or more of that shame. When, as you will remember, you fixed your Rhadamanthine eye upon me and ordered me to write for you these sketches of strong men who lived before today's Agamemnons, I, as you will remember too, protested strongly. I did not want to write about these people. I have written more than I want about these people. My mind was fixed on other peoples and places.

You simply answered monosyllabically:

'Sit down. Take your pen and write.'

I then decided that if I were to be forced to write a book I did not want to write, I would emphatically see that when it came from the press it would be something that I *did* want to write. I determined, that is to say, to erect to my—nearly all dead—friends not so much a monument more sounding than brass, but an, as it were, intimately vignetted representation that should force the public to see that circle of strong personalities as I want them to be seen. I am, that is to say, a novelist, and I want them to be seen pretty much as you see the characters in a novel . . . as if one should see the frequenters of the Mermaid Tavern in an historical romance. . . . Ford with his melancholy hat, Jonson with his learned sock, and the Shakespeare who had once bitten off the heads of chickens prior to roasting them outside the Globe Theatre for the clients whose horses he held . . .

A great deal has been written about my characters. But the official biographer, the literary executor, the cooks, sluts, and bottle-washers who plentifully surround the Great during their lives—these all as a rule want their props to fortune and glory seen in one way . . . aloft on a pedestal surrounded by rosebud garlands, one hand raised, the other inserted in the upper opening of their waistcoat, and, on their faces, fatuous and nearly imbecile smiles.

Naturally executors, cooks, and the rest, sometimes, having been harassed beyond bearing by their various patrons, will turn and not only rend but render, the deceased as anything from benign and imbecile bell-wethers, to town bulls and malignant, tottering pantaloons. That, however, happens rather rarely. And in the meanwhile the young lions, anxious to sit in their still warm seats, call them *vieux-jeu*, Henrietta-Maria-ish . . . what you will.

For myself I wanted them to be seen by posterity as I had seen them—the strong, strongly featured men whose little weaknesses they themselves were prone to exaggerate, since they knew very well that it is because of your little weaknesses that your life is preserved for your Art. Agamemnon cannot be for ever bending his bow; his arm and its string will slacken. If you are really wrapped up in your life's task your strengths alone will make too much call on you.

At any rate, so it seems to me and so it must have seemed to you—for you knew too much about my work and mental slant not to see the sort of contribution to the gaiety and quarrelsomenesses of the literary of two great nations that would result. So, when the bricks are beginning to be heaved at me, get you ready your arnica, opodeldoc, and court plaster. You shall need them.

I have one fear. If you have read much of me you will see that I here repeat myself from time to time. I never know what is the exact ethics of self-quotation—but a good many esteemed writers have amended themselves not merely once but many times, and I am ready to follow in the footsteps of my betters. I haven't, that is to say, so much quoted myself as tried to make my renderings clearer, sharper, more—aesthetically—exact. For factual exactitudes I have never had much use. I have, I repeat, been trying to make you see these people whom I very much loved—as I want them seen.

And there is the other aspect. I cannot hope for immortality. I have aimed at it. But there being only about some fifty authentic immortals to X billions of billions of people who have existed since creation, the doctrine of chances would seem to be against one's own immortality. If one were immortal one might expect one's books to be pored over for ever. But I can hardly expect you or any other man to go through my books for the separated traces I have hitherto put down as to the demigods of whom I here treat. So for the convenience of the reader it seemed to me to be expedient to group them all together under one cover.

In any case I hope you will permit me to include amongst the names of those who subscribe themselves your humble, obliged, and obedient servants that of, by these presents,

FORD MADOX FORD

CONTENTS

PORTRAITS
FROM LIFE

HENRY JAMES

THE MASTER

I WILL begin this work with a little romance in the style of the Master—for *what* an intrigue he would have made of it if he had heard it at one of the hospitable boards where he so continually picked up what 'I have always recognized on the spot as "germs" '—the central ideas from which sprang his innumerable stories. . . . And it is the innumerability of his stories rather than the involutions of his style and plots that most have struck me in re-reading the works of him who must, whether we like to acknowledge it or not, be called the great master of all us novelists of today.

I hasten to avert thunders from my head by saying that I know that there are thousands of novelists of today and here who will swear that they never read a word of Henry James—just as the first words that Mr. H. M. Tomlinson ever said to me were, 'Never heard of the fellow!'—the 'fellow' being Conrad. But one's master is far more an aura in the air than an admonitory gentleman with uplifted forefinger, and one learns as much by reacting against a prevailing tendency as by following in a father's footsteps. . . .

Well, then . . . I was sitting one day in my study in Winchelsea when, from beside the window, on the little verandah, I heard a male voice, softened by the intervening wall, going on and on interminably . . . with the effect of a long murmuring of bees. I had been lost in the search for one just word or other so that the gentle sound had only dreamily penetrated to my attention. When it did so penetrate and after the monologue had gone on much, much longer, a certain irritation took hold of me. Was I not the owner of the establishment? Was I not supposed by long pondering over just words and their subsequent transference to paper to add at least to the credit, if not to the resources of that establishment? Was it not, therefore, understood that chance visitors must *not* be entertained at the front door which was just beside my window? . . . The sound, however, was not harsh or disagreeable and I stood it for perhaps another ten minutes. But at last impatience overcame me and I sprang to my door.

Silhouetted against the light at the end of the little passage were the figures of one of the housemaids and of Mr. Henry James. And Mr. James was uttering the earth-shaking question:

'Would you then advise me . . . for I know that such an ornament decorates your master's establishment and you will therefore from your particular level be able to illuminate me as to the . . . ah . . . smooth functioning of such, if I may use the expression, a wheel in the domestic timepiece—always supposing that you will permit me the image, meaning that, as I am sure in this household is the case, the daily revolution of a really harmonious *chez soi* is as smooth as the passing of shadows over a dial

. . . would you then advise me to have . . . in short to introduce into *my* household and employ . . . a . . . that is to say . . . a Lady Help?'

I advanced at that and, as the housemaid with a sigh of relief disappeared amongst the rustlings of her skirts, in the strongest and firmest possible terms assured Mr. James that such an adornment of the household of an illustrious and well-appointed bachelor was one that should very certainly not be employed. He sighed. He appeared worn, thin for him, dry-skinned, unspirited. His liquid and marvellous dark eyes were dulled, the skin over his aquiline nose was drawn tight. He was suffering from a domestic upheaval—his household, that for a generation had, indeed, revolved around him as quietly as the shadows on a dial, with housekeeper, butler, upper housemaid, lower housemaid, tweeny maid, knife-boy, gardener, had suddenly erupted all round him so that for some time he had been forced to content himself with the services of the knife-boy.

That meant that he had to eat in the ancient hostelry, called The Mermaid, that stood beside his door. And, his housekeeper having for thirty years and more sent up, by the imposing if bottle-nosed butler who was her husband, all Mr. James's meals without his ever having ordered a single one—being used to such a halcyon cuisine the Master had not the slightest idea of what foods agreed with him and which did not. So that everything disagreed with him and he had all the appearance of being really ill. . . . The cause of the bottle-nose had been also the occasion of the eruption, all the female servants having one day left in a body on account of the 'carryings-on' of the butler, and the butler him-

self, together, alas, with his admirable wife, the
housekeeper, having, twenty-four hours later, to be
summarily and violently ejected by a sympathetic
police sergeant.

So the poor Master was not only infinitely worried
about finding an appropriate asylum for the butler
and his wife, but had had to spend long mornings
and afternoons on what he called 'the benches of
desolation in purgatorial, if I may allow myself the
word, establishments, ill-named, since no one appeared there to register themselves . . . eminently
ill-named: *registry-offices* . . .' And there would
be a sound like the hiss of a snake as he uttered the
compound word. . . .

He would pass his time, he said, interviewing ladies
all of a certain age, all of haughty—the French
would say *renfrognée*—expressions, all of whom
would unanimously assure him that, if they demeaned
themselves merely by for an instant considering the
idea of entering the household of an untitled person
like himself, in such a God-forsaken end of the
world as the Ancient Town of Rye, they having
passed their lives in the families of never anyone
less than a belted earl in mansions on Constitution
Hill in the shadow of Buckingham Palace . . . if
they for a fleeting moment toyed with the idea, it was
merely, they begged to assure him . . . 'forthegood-
oftheirhealths.' Mr. James having dallied with this
sentence would utter the last words with extreme
rapidity, raising his eyebrows and his cane in the
air and digging the ferrule suddenly into the surface
of the road. . . .

How they come back to me after a quarter of a
century . . . the savoured, half-humorous, half-de-

precatory words, the ironically exaggerated gestures, the workings of the closely shaved lips, the halting to emphasize a point, the sudden scurryings forward, for all the world like the White Rabbit hurrying to the Queen's tea-party . . . along the Rye Road, through the marshes, from Winchelsea. . . . I walking beside him and hardly ever speaking, in the guise of God's strong, silent Englishman—which he took me really to be. . . .

To give the romance, then, its happy ending . . . One of the matrons of Rye had conceived the idea of lodging a dependant orphan niece in poor Mr. James's house and so had recommended him to employ a Lady Help, offering to supply herself that domestic functionary. He had consulted as to the advisability of this step all the doctors', lawyers', and parsons' wives of the neighbourhood, and in addition one of the local great ladies—I think it was Lady Maude Warrender. The commoners' ladies, loyal to the one who wanted to dispose of the dependant niece, had all said the idea was admirable. Her Ladyship was non-committal, going no further than to assure him that the great ladies of the neighbourhood would not refuse to come to tea with him in his garden—that being their, as well as his, favourite way of passing an afternoon—merely because he should shelter an unattached orphan beneath his roof. But she would go no further than that.

So, in his passion for getting, from every possible angle, light on every possible situation—including his own—he had walked over to Winchelsea to consult not only me, but any female member of my household upon whom he should chance, and had kept the appalled and agitated housemaid for a full half hour on the doorstep whilst he consulted her as to the advisability of the step he was contemplating. . . . But I soon put a stop to *that* idea. In practical matters Mr. James did me the honour to pay exact attention to my opinions—I was for him the strong, silent man of affairs.

How long his agony lasted after that I cannot say. His perturbations were so agonizing to witness that it seemed to be a matter of years. And then, one day, he turned up with a faint adumbration of jauntiness. At last he had heard of a lady who gave some promise of being satisfactory. . . . The only shadow appeared to be the nature of her present employment.

'Guess,' he said, 'under whose august roof she is at the moment sheltering? . . . *Je vous le donne en mille.* . . .' He started back dramatically, rolling his fine eyes, and with great speed he exclaimed:

'The Poet Laureate . . . no less a person!'

Now the Poet Laureate occupies in England a position that it is very difficult to explain on this side of the water. By his official situation he is something preposterous and eminent . . . and at the same time he is something obsolescent, harmless, and ridiculous. Southey, Tennyson, and Doctor Bridges have commanded personally a certain respect, but I cannot think of anyone else who was anything else than ridiculous . . . rendered ridiculous by his office. And at the time of which I am speaking the whole literary world felt outragedly that either Swinburne or Mr. Kipling ought to have been the laureate. As it was, the holder of the title was a Mr. Alfred Austin, an obscure, amiable, and harmless poetaster who wrote about manor-houses and gardens and lived in a very beautiful manor-house in a very beautiful garden.

And, two days later Mr. James turned up, radiant. He lifted both hands above his head and exclaimed:

'As the German Emperor is said to say about his mostachio, *"it is accomplished."* . . . Rejoice—as I am confident you will—with me, my young friend. All from now onwards shall, I am assured, be with me gas and gingerbread. . . . Halcyon, halcyon days. In short, ahem . . .' And he tapped himself lightly on the breast and assumed the air of a traveller returned from the wintry seas. 'I went,' he continued, 'to the house of the Poet Laureate . . . to the back door of course . . . and interviewed a Lady who, except for one trifling—let us not say defect but let us express it "let or hindrance" to what I will permit myself to call the perfect union, the continuing *lune de miel* . . . except for that, then, she appeared the perfect, the incredible, the except for the pure-in-heart, unattainable She . . . But upon delicate enquiry . . . oh, I assure you, enquiry of the *most* delicate . . . for the obstacle was no less than that on reckoning up the tale of her previous "situations" . . . as twenty years with the Earl of Breadalbane, thirty years with Sir Ponsonby Peregrine Perowne, forty with the Right Honourable the Lord Bishop of Tintagel and Camelot . . . on reckoning up the incredible tale of years it appeared that she must be of the combined ages of Methuselah and the insupportable Mariner—not of your friend Conrad, but of the author of *Kubla Khan*. But upon investigation it appeared that this paragon and phoenix actually was and in consequence will, to the end

of recorded time, remain, exactly the same age as'
. . . and he took three precise, jaunty steps to the
rear, laid his hand over his heart and made a quick
bow . . . '*myself*. . . .'

'And,' he resumed, 'an upper housemaid and her
sister, the under-housemaid, who had left me in circumstances that I was unable to fathom but that
today are only too woefully apparent to me, having
offered to return and to provide a what they call
tweeny of their own choosing . . . all shall for the
future be as I have already adumbrated, not only gas
and gingerbread, but cloves and clothes pegs and
beatitude and bliss and beauty . . .' And so it
proved.

I have taken some time over that Romance because the whole of James, the man, could be evolved
from it—and a great deal of James, the writer. For
me the strongest note of all in his character was expressed in his precautions. Not his cautions, for in
action, as in writing, he was not in the least cautious.

Whether for his books or life he studied every
aspect of the affair on which he was engaged with
extraordinary elaboration—the elaboration which he
gave to every speech that he uttered. And he was a
man of the most amazing vitality, inexhaustible, indefatigable. He consulted everybody from the conductor of the tram from Rye Harbor to Rye golf
links, to the chauffeur of a royal automobile who,
having conveyed his august master to call on the
local great lady, spent a disgusted afternoon in The
Mermaid expressing rancour at the fact that the
stone-deaf old lady who kept the local tollgate should
have refused to let her Sovereign pass through except

after payment of a shilling. What exact treasures of information Mr. James can have extracted as to either the passengers to the golf links or the travelling habits of Edward VII, or what use he expected to make of that information, I do not know. But he had an extraordinary gift of exacting confidences and even confessions so that his collection of human instances must have been one of the vastest that any man ever had. It made him perhaps feel safe—or at least as safe as it was in his nature to feel. He could feel, that is to say, that he knew his own *milieu*—the coterie of titled, distinguished, and 'good' people in which he and his books moved and had their beings. And in the special English sense the words 'good people' does not mean the virtuous, but all the sufficiently well-born, sufficiently inconspicuous, sufficiently but not too conspicuously opulent, sufficiently but very certainly not too conspicuously intelligent and educated, that supply recruits to the ruling classes of the British Isles. . . .

Of that class he knew the lives and circumstances, at first perhaps rather superficially and with enthusiasm, and at last profoundly and with disillusionment as profound as his knowledge. . . . And it comforted him to know 'things' about the lives of the innumerable not-born that surrounded the manors or the De Vere Street apartments of the people he really knew, in the sense of having them on his calling list—and being on theirs. . . . He saw the 'common people' lying like a dark sea round the raft of the privileged. They excited his piqued wonder, his ardent curiosity, he built the most elaborate theories all over and round them, he observed enough of them to be able to give characteristics, phrases, and

turns of mind to the retainers of the Privileged, but
he never could be brought to think that he knew
enough about them to let him project their lives onto
paper. He noted admirably the very phraseology of
Mrs. Wicks, the faithful attendant of Maisie who
lived forever in fear of being 'spoken to,' and with
equal admirableness the point of view of poor Brook-
smith, the gentleman's valet who 'never *had* got his
spirits up' after the loss of his one wonderful master.
But if, as happens to us today, he had been confronted by a Radical Left clamouring that he must
write about the proletariat or be lost, he would just
for ever have dismissed his faithful amanuensis and
relapsed into mournful silence.

He had that conscientiousness—or if you will,
that pre-cautiousness . . . and that sense of duty to
his public. He set himself up—and the claim was no
little one—as directing his reader as to the fine
shades of the psychology of a decorative and utterly
refined world where it was always five o'clock. He
makes the claim with the utmost equanimity again
and again in his Prefaces, only abandoning it to say
that if the world did not in fact contain any creatures
of such hypersensibility and sensitiveness as those he
rendered in his later work, the world ought, if it was
to lay claim to being civilized, to contain nobody
else. . . . Yet he actually knew so many details of
the lives of the poorer people about him in Rye that,
as I have elsewhere related, I once asked him why
he did not for once try his hand at something with
at least the local peasantry for a *milieu*. The question
was prompted more by wonder at the amazing
amount he did know than by any idea that he would
possibly consider having a try at it. After all, in

masterpieces like *The Spoils of Poynton*, which remains for me the technical high-water mark of all James's work—and can't I remember the rapturous and shouting enthusiasm of Conrad over that story when we first read it together so that that must have been the high-water mark of Conrad's enthusiasm for the work of any other writer? In masterpieces, then, like *The Spoils of Poynton*, James, who fifteen years or so before must have been utterly foreign to the *milieu*, had got completely and mercilessly under the skin of the English ruling classes. So that if he could penetrate one foreignness, why not another? And I cited his other great and impeccable masterpiece, *The Real Thing*, which shows members of the ruling classes reduced by financial disaster to complete pennilessness. He replied, pausing for a moment whilst the heights of Iden with its white, thatched farmhouses formed a background to his male and vigorous personality—for it was always on the Winchelsea Road that we conversed . . . he replied then:

'My dear H, you confuse the analogies. You might say that I came to this country *from* comfortable circumstances *into* comfortably circumstanced circles. Though no further uptown than Washington Square, the Washington Square of my youth was almost infinitely divided, by gulfs, chasms, canyons, from the downtownnesses round Trinity Spire where, you understand, they worked—mysteriously and at occupations as to which we of Washington Square hadn't the very ghost of an inkling. . . . And if, as you have heard me say, the comfortably circumstanced of that day were not by any manner of means luxuriously—or even hardly so much as comfortably caparisoned or upholstered or garnished at table or horse-furnitured when they rode in their buggies . . . or, if in the mecca of good society, internationally of the highest cultivation and nationally of all that the nation had of the illustrious to offer . . . if, then, on descending the steps of the capitol *on trébu-chait sur des vaches* as the Marquis de Sabran-Penthièvre remarked in the seventies, . . . if they still, at Washington, D.C., not Square, they still, to the embarrassment of the feet of visiting diplomatists, pastured cows on the lawns outside the White House, nevertheless the frame of mind . . . the frame of mind, and that's the important thing, was equally, for the supporters of the initials as for those of the Square, that of all the most comfortable that the world had to offer. . . . I do not suppose that, with the exception of the just-landed relatives of my parents' Nancies or Biddies or Bridgets in the kitchen visiting their kinsmaids, I ever saw to speak to a single human being who did not, as the phrase is— and Heaven knows, more than the phrase is and desperate and dark and hideously insupportable the condition must be—the verb's coming now . . . didn't know where their next day's meals were coming from . . . who were, that is to say, of that frame of mind, that, as the lamentable song says: "They lived in a dive and sometimes contrived to pick up a copper or two." . . . For of course, as you were kind enough to say, in *The Real Thing* I have sufficiently well rendered the perturbations of the English comfortable who by financial disaster were reduced, literally, to complete vagueness as to the provenance of their next day's breakfast, lunch, tea, and dinner. . . . Or, as in the sketch—it isn't sufficiently complete of the more than reduced circumstances of the fathers of Kate Croy in m . . . mmm. . . .' He stopped and surveyed me with a roguish and carefully simulated embarrassment. For it was established sufficiently between us that in the longish, leanish, fairish Englishman who was Morton Densher of *The Wings of the Dove*, he had made an at least external portrait of myself at a time when he had known me only vaguely and hadn't imagined that in the ordinary course of things the acquaintance would deepen. . . . So he began again:

'Consider,' he said with a sort of appalled vehemence, 'what it must be—how desperate and dark and abhorrent—to live in such tenebrousness that all the light that could fall into your cavern must come in through a tiny orifice which, if it were shuttered by a penny, would give you light, warmth, sustenance, society, even . . . and that, if it were absent, that penny would disclose nothing but unmeasured blackness that penetrated to and pervaded your miserable lair. . . . All light, all hope, all chance in life or of heaven dependant from that tiny disk of metal . . . Why, how could you enter into a frame of mind similar to that, and still more, if you were a writer, how could you render such circumstances and all their circumambiences and implications? . . . And you ask me, who *am*, for my sins, of the same vocation as the beautiful Russian genius—who am, I permit myself to say, a renderer of human vicissitudes . . . of a certain conscience, of a certain scrupulousness . . . you ask *me* to mislead my devotees by the rendering of caves as to which I know nothing and as to the penetration or the mere imagination of which I truly shudder? . . . Perish the thought . . . I say perish, perish the damnable thought. . . .' He walked on for some time in a really disturbed silence, muttering every two or three seconds to himself—and then turned on me almost furiously.

'You understand,' he said, 'the damnable thought is not that I might be poor. If I had to be poor I should hope to support the condition with equanimity. . . .' And he went on to explain that it wasn't even the idea of contemplating, of delving into the poverty of others. What he shrank from was the temptation to treat themes that did not come into his province—the province that he considered the one in which he could work assuredly and with a quiet conscience.

Once he stopped suddenly on the road and said, speaking very fast:

'You've read my last volume? . . . There's a story in it. . . .' He continued gazing intently at me, then as suddenly he began again: 'There are subjects one thinks of treating all one's life. . . . And one says they are not for one. And one says one must not treat them . . . all one's life. All one's life. . . . And then suddenly . . . one does . . . *Voilà!*' He had been speaking with almost painful agitation. He added much more calmly: 'One has yielded to temptation. One is to that extent dishonoured. One must make the best of it.'

That story was *The Great Good Place*, appearing, I think, in the volume called *The Soft Side*. In it he considered that he had overstepped the bounds of what he considered proper to treat—in the way of his sort of mysticism. There were, that is to say,

mysticisms that he considered proper to treat and
others whose depths he thought should not be probed
—at any rate by his pen. For there were whole regions of his character that he never exploited in
literature, and it would be the greatest mistake to
forget that the strongest note in that character was a
mysticism different altogether in character from that
of the great Catholic mystics. It resembled rather a
perception of a sort of fourth dimensional penetration of the material world by strata of the supernatural, of the world of the living by individuals
from among the dead. You will get a good inkling
of what I mean if you will read again *The Turn of
the Screw* with the constant peepings-in of the ghosts
of the groom and the governess with their sense of
esoteric evil—their constant peepings-in on the
haunted mortals of the story. For him, good and
evil were not represented by acts; they were something present in the circumambience of the actual
world, something spiritual attendant on actions or
words. As such he rendered them and, once convinced that he had got that sense in, he was content
—he even took an impish pleasure in leaving out the
renderings of the evil actions.

Of that you can read sufficiently in his enormous
and affrighting Prefaces. . . . He never specifies in
The Turn of the Screw what were the evil deeds of
the ghostly visitants, nor what the nature of the corruption into which the children fell. And, says he in
the Preface to the story:

Only make the reader's vision of evil intense
enough, I said to myself—and that is already a
charming job—and his own experience, his own

sympathy (with the children) and horror (of their false friends) will supply him quite sufficiently with all the particulars. Make him *think* the evil, make him think it for himself, and you are released from weak specifications.

It is an admirable artistic maxim. But it did not—and that is what I am trying to emphasize as the main note of this paper—dispense him, in his own mind, from having all the knowledges, whether of esoteric sin or the mentality of butlers, that were necessary to make him feel that he knew enough about his subject to influence the reader's vision in the right direction. As far as I know—and if diligence in reading the works of James gives one the right to know, I ought to have that right—not a single rendering of esoteric sin, sexual incidents, or shadowing of obscenities exists in all the works of the Master, and his answer to D. H. Lawrence or to Rabelais would, for him, have been sufficiently and triumphantly expressed in the sentences I have just quoted.

But that did not prevent him—when he considered the occasion to serve—from making his conversation heroically Rabelaisian, or, for me, really horrific, on the topics of esoteric sin or sexual indulgence. I have attended at conversations between him and a queer tiny being who lay as if crumpled up on the stately sofa in James's magnificent panelled room in Lamb House—conversations that made the tall wax candles seem to me to waver in their sockets and the skin of my forehead and hands to prickle with sweat. I am in these things rather squeamish; I sometimes wish I was not, but it is so and I can't help it. I don't wish to leave the impression that these conversations were carried on for purposes of lewd stimulation or irreverent ribaldry. They occurred as part of the necessary pursuit of that knowledge that permitted James to give his reader the 'sense of evil.' . . . And I dare say they freed him from the almost universal proneness of Anglo-Saxon writers to indulge in their works in a continually intrusive fumbling in placket-holes as Sterne called it, or in the lugubrious occupation of composing libidinous Limericks. James would utter his racy 'Ho-ho-ho's' and roll his fine eyes whilst talking to his curious little friend, but they were not a whit more racy and his eyes did not roll any more than they did when he was asking a housemaid or a parson's wife for advice as to the advisability of employing a Lady's Help, or than when he was recounting urbane anecdotes at tea on his lawn to the Ladies So-and-So and So-and-So. It was all in the day's work.

Exactly what may have been his intimate conviction as to, say, what should be the proper relation of the sexes, I don't profess to know. That he demanded from the more fortunate characters in his books a certain urbanity of behaviour as long as that behaviour took place in the public eye, his books are there to prove. That either Mr. Beale Farange or Mrs. Beale committed in the circumambience of *What Maisie Knew* one or more adulteries must be obvious, since they obtained divorces in England. But the fact never came into the foreground of the book. And that he had a personal horror of letting his more august friends come into contact through him with anyone who might be even remotely suspected of marital irregularities, I know from the odd, seasonal nature of my relations with him. We met during the winters almost every day, but during the summers only by, usually telegraphed, appointment. This was because during the summer Mr. James's garden overflowed with the titled, the distinguished, the eminent in the diplomatic world . . . with all his *milieu*. And, once he had got it well fixed into his head that I was a journalist, he conceived the idea that all my friends must be illegally united with members of the opposite sex. So that it was inconceivable that my summer friends should have any chance to penetrate onto his wonderfully kept lawns. I do not think that I knew any journalists at all in those days, and I am perfectly certain that, with one very eminent exception, I did not know anyone who had been so much as a plaintiff in the shadow of the divorce courts. I was in the mood to be an English country gentleman and, for the time being, I was. . . . It happened, however, that the extraordinarily respectable wives of two eminent editors were one week-end during a certain summer staying in Winchelsea—which was a well-known tourist resort— and they took it into their heads to go and call on James at Rye.

I had hardly so much as a bowing acquaintance with them. But the next day, happening to go into Rye, I met the Old Man down by the harbour. Just at the point where we met was a coal yard whose proprietor had the same name as one of the husbands of one of those ladies. James stopped short and with a face working with fury pointed his stick at the coal man's name above the gate and brought out the exasperated words:

'A couple of jaded . . . WANTONS! . . .' and, realizing that I was fairly quick on the uptake, nothing whatever more. . . . But, as soon as the leaves fell, there he was back on my doorstep, asking innumerable advices—as to his investments, as to what would cure the parasites of a dog, as to brands of cigars, as to where to procure cordwood, as to the effects of the Corn Laws on the landed gentry of England . . . And I would accompany him, after he had had a cup of tea, back to his Ancient Town; and next day I would go over and drink a cup of tea with him and wait whilst he finished dictating one of his sentences to his amanuensis and then he would walk back with me to Winchelsea. . . . In that way we each got a four-mile walk a day. . . .

No, I never did get any knowledge as to how he regarded sexual irregularities. . . . I remember he one day nearly made me jump out of my skin during a one-sided discussion as to the relative merits of Flaubert and Turgenev—the beautiful Russian genius of his youth.

Turgenev was for him perfection—in person, except that his features were a little broad, in the Slav manner; in his books; in his manners; in his social relations, which were of the highest; in what was aristocratic. But Flaubert, James went on and on hating and grumbling at to the end of his days. Flaubert had, as I have elsewhere related, once been rude to the young James. That James never mentioned. But he had subsequently received James and Turgenev in his dressing-gown. . . . It was not, of course, a dressing-gown, but a working garment—a sort of long, loose coat without revers—called a

chandail. And if a French man of letters received you
in his *chandail,* he considered it a sort of showing
honour, as if he had admitted you into his working
intimacy. But James never forgave that—more perhaps on account of Turgenev than himself. . . .
Flaubert for ever afterwards was for him the man
who worked, who thought, who received, who lived
—and perhaps went to Heaven in—his dressing-
gown! . . . In consequence he was a failure. All his
books except one were failures—technical and material . . . and that one, *Madame Bovary,* if it was a
success in both departments . . . well, it was nothing to write home about. And Flaubert's little *salon*
in the Faubourg Saint-Honoré was 'rather bare and
provisional,' and Flaubert cared too much for 'form,'
and, because he backed bills for a relation, died in
reduced circumstances. . . .

Flaubert was in short the sort of untidy colossus
whom I might, if I had the chance, receive at Winchelsea, but who would never, never have been received on the summer lawns of Lamb House at Rye.

And suddenly Mr. James exclaimed, just at the
dog-leg bend in the road between the two Ancient
Towns:

'But Maupassant!!!! . . .' That man apparently
was, for him, the real Prince Fortunatus amongst
writers. I don't mean to say that he did not appreciate the literary importance of the author of *La
Maison Tellier*—who was also the author of *Ce
Cochon de Morin* and, alas, of *Le Horla,* so that
whilst in 1888 James was writing of him the words I
am about to quote, that poor Prince was already
gravitating towards the lunatic asylum. But, writes
Mr. James:

What makes M. de Maupassant salient is two facts: the first of which is that his gifts are remarkably strong and definite and the second that he writes directly *from* them. . . . Nothing can exceed the masculine firmness, the quiet force of his style in which every phrase is a close sequence, every epithet a paying piece. Less than anyone today does he beat the air; more than anyone does he hit out from the shoulder . . .

sentiments which seem—but only seem—singular in view of the later convolutions of epithet that distinguished our Master. . . .

And those considerations in his conversation Mr. James completely omitted. On the Rye Road, Maupassant was for him the really prodigious, prodigal, munificent, magnificently rewarded Happy Prince of the Kingdom of Letters. He had yachts, villas on the Mediterranean, 'affairs,' mistresses, wardrobes of the most gorgeous, grooms, the entrée into the historic salons of Paris, furnishings, overflowing bank balances . . . everything that the heart of man could require even to the perfectly authentic *de* to ally him to the nobility and a public that was commensurate with the ends of the earth. . . . And then, as the topstone of that edifice, Mr. James recounted that once, when Mr. James had been invited to lunch with him, Maupassant had received him, not, be assured, in a dressing-gown, but in the society of a naked lady wearing a mask. . . . And Maupassant assured the author of *The Great Good Place* that the lady was a *femme du monde*. And Mr. James believed him. . . . Fortune could go no further than *that!* . . .

Manners, morals, and the point of view have so

changed since even 1906 when Mr. James must have recounted that anecdote that I am not going to dilate upon it. And you have to remember that some years after the 1888 in which he wrote the words I have quoted, Mr. James underwent an experience that completely altered his point of view, his methods, and his entire literary practice. His earlier stages, Mr. James the Second contrived entirely—or almost entirely—to obscure in a sort of cuttlefish cloud of interminable phrases. Until the middle nineties nothing could have exceeded the masculine firmness, the quiet force of his writing, and of no one else than himself could it more justly be written that 'less than anyone did he beat the air, more than anyone did he hit out from the shoulder.'

That is amazingly the case. I have more than once proclaimed the fact that there were two Jameses. And yet no one could be more overwhelmed than I at re-reading in their earliest forms, after all these years, his early masterpieces as they were written and before he went over and elaborated their phrases. Thus to re-read is to realize with immense force that more than anyone else, in the matter of approach to his subjects, Maupassant rather than Turgenev must have been the young James's master. *Daisy Miller;* the most wonderful *nouvelle* of all, *The Four Meetings; The Pupil; The Lesson of the Master; The Death of the Lion,* and all the clear, crisp, mordant-stories that went between, right up to *The Real Thing* and *In the Cage*—all these stories are of a complete directness, an economy, even of phrase, that make James one of the great masters of the *nouvelle,* the long or merely longish short story.

But at a given date, after a misfortune that, for

the second time, shattered his life and convinced him
that his illusions as to the delicacies of his 'good'
people of a certain *milieu* were in fact . . . delu-
sions; after that he became the creature of infinite
precautions that he was when I knew him best. I
had, that is to say, a sight—two or three sights—of
him in the previous stage. Then he resembled one of
those bearded elder statesmen—the Marquis of Salisbury, Sir Charles Dilke, or the Prince who was to
become Edward VII. He was then slightly magis-
terial; he cross-questioned rather than questioned
you; he was obviously of the *grand monde* and of the
daily habit of rubbing, on equal terms, shoulders
with the great.

But about the later James, clean-shaven, like an
actor, so as to recover what he could of the aspect of
youth; nervous; his face for ever mobile; his hands
for ever gesturing; there hung continually the feeling
of a forced energy, as if of a man conscious of failure
and determined to conceal mortification. He had had
two great passions—the one for a cousin whom he
was to have married and who died of consumption
while they were both very young, and the other for
a more conspicuous but less satisfactory personage
who in the end, at about the time when the break
occurred, let him down mercilessly after a period of
years. And the tenacity of his attachments was singular and unforgetting.

The Wings of the Dove [he writes in his Preface
of 1909 to that novel], published in 1902, represents to my memory a very old—if I shouldn't
perhaps say a very young—motive. I can scarcely
remember the time when the motive on which this

long-drawn fiction mainly rests was not vividly present to me. The idea, reduced to its essence, is that of a young person conscious of a great capacity for life, but early stricken and doomed, condemned to die under short respite while also enamoured of the world. . . . She was the last fine flower—blooming alone for the fullest attestation of her freedom—of an old New York stem, the happy congruities thus preserved being matters that I may not now go into, although the fine association . . . shall yet elsewhere await me. . . .

I do not know anywhere words more touching. . . . And I do not think that, in spite of the later obscuration, the image of the Milly Theale of that book was ever very far away from his thoughts. I remember that when, in 1906, I told him that I was coming to this country, his immediate reaction was to ask me to visit his cousins, the Misses Mason at Newport, Rhode Island, and to take a certain walk along the undercliff beneath Ocean Avenue and there pay, as it were, vicarious honour to the spot where, for the last time, he had parted from his dead cousin. It was the most romantic—it was the only one that was romantic—of the many small jobs that I did for him. . . . And in one of the fits of apologizing that would occasionally come over him—for having physically drawn myself in the portrait of Morton Densher, who was, to be sure, no hero if he wasn't more than only very subterraneously discreditable —he once said:

'After all you've got to remember that I was to fabricate a person who could decently accompany, if only in the pages of my book, another person to whom I was—and remain, and remain, Heaven knows—let us say, most tenderly attached. . . .' As if to say that, in fabricating such a person, his mind would not let him portray someone who was completely disagreeable.

The other attachment was completely detrimental to him. Its rupture left him the person of infinite precautions that I have here rather disproportionately limned. It was as if, from then on, he was determined that nobody or nothing—no society coterie, no tram-conductor, no housemaid, no *femme du monde*—should ever have the chance, either in life or in his books, to let him down. And it was as if he said the very same thing to the phrases that he wrote. If he was continuously parenthetic, it was in the determination that no word he wrote should ever be misinterpreted, and if he is, in his later work, bewildering, it was because of the almost panicked resolve to be dazzlingly clear. Because of that he could never let his phrases alone. . . . How often when waiting for him to go for a walk haven't I heard him say whilst dictating the finish of a phrase:

'No, no, Miss Dash . . . that is not clear. . . . Insert before "we all are" . . . Let me see. . . . Yes, insert "not so much locally, though to be sure we're here; but temperamentally, in a manner of speaking." ' . . . So that the phrase, blindingly clear to him by that time, when completed would run:

> So that here, not so much locally, though to be sure we're here, but at least temperamentally in a manner of speaking, we all are.

No doubt the habit of dictating had something to do with these convolutions, and the truth of the matter is that during these later years he wrote far more for the ear of his amanuensis than for the eye of the eventual reader. So that, if you will try the experiment of reading him aloud and with expression, you will find his even latest pages relatively plain to understand. But, far more than that, the underlying factor in his later work was the endless determination to add more and more detail, so that the exact illusions and the exact facts of life may appear, and so that everything may be blindingly clear even to a little child. . . . For I have heard him explain with the same profusion of detail as he gave to my appalled and bewildered housemaid—I have heard him explain to Conrad's son of five why he wore a particular hat whose unusual shape had attracted the child's attention. He was determined to present to the world the real, right thing!

I will quote, to conclude, the description of myself as it appears in *The Wings of the Dove* so that you may have some idea of what was James's image of the rather silent person who walked so often beside him on the Rye Road.

He was a longish, leanish [alas, alas!], fairish young Englishman, not unamenable on certain sides to classification—as for instance being a gentleman, by being rather specifically one of the educated, one of the generally sound and generally civil; yet, though to that degree neither extraordinary nor abnormal, he would have failed to play straight into an observer's hands. He was young for the House of Commons; he was loose for the

Army. He was refined, as might have been said, for
the City and, quite apart from the cut of his cloth,
sceptical, it might have been felt, for the Church.
On the other hand he was credulous for diplo-
macy, or perhaps even for science, while he was
perhaps at the same time too much in his real
senses for poetry and yet too little in them for art.
. . . The difficulty with Densher was that he
looked vague without looking weak—idle without
looking empty. It was the accident possibly of his
long legs which were apt to stretch themselves;
of his straight hair and well-shaped head, never,
the latter neatly smooth and apt into the bargain
. . . to throw itself suddenly back and, supported
behind by his uplifted arms and interlocked hands,
place him for unconscionable periods in commun-
ion with the ceiling, the tree-tops, the sky. . . .

That, I suppose, was the young man that James
rather liked.

STEPHEN CRANE

IF IT were desired to prove that supernatural beings pay rare visits to this earth, there could be no apparition more suited to supporting the assertion than was Stephen Crane, whose eclipse is as fabulous as was his fabulous progress across this earth. . . . One awakened one morning in the nineties in England and *The Red Badge of Courage* was not; by noon of the same day it filled the universe. There was nothing you could talk of but that book. And, by teatime, as it were, this hot blast of fame had swept back across the Atlantic and there was nothing they could talk of in New York and its hinterlands but that book.

There was no doubt a non-literary reason for the phenomenon. The middle nineties and the twenty years that succeeded them formed together a period of war consciousness and war preparation such as the world has seldom seen, and it came after a quarter century of profoundly peaceful psychology. From the end of the Franco-Prussian War in 1871 to about 1895, no one thought of organized bloodshed as affording a solution for human problems—no one except perhaps Bismarck—and he regarded his army only as an instrument for policing the French. The strife of 1870-71 had for the moment exhausted the human appetite for blood in the gutters. Yet the next twenty years saw nothing, the world over, but preparations for conflict. The United States prepared and brought off a war against Spain after very nearly bringing off, over Venezuela, a war against Great Britain. Greece and Italy prepared several wars against Turkey, China against Japan, Japan against Russia. Great Britian, after equally preparing for war against this country, over Venezuela, brought off one of great difficulty against the South Africans. . . . And all the while, in every state of the globe, went on the sabre-rattling that ended in the late Armageddon. It was universal.

There was thus no man below a certain age who had not at one time or another to think of how he would behave in the case of his participation in a feast of bloodshed. For already it was manifest that in any considerable war all the manhood of the countries engaged must be called upon. And there was nothing to show him how he, the ordinary milkman or bank clerk, would probably behave when bullets were flying. There was nothing. No book; no memories; no pictures except those of poorly invented posturings. Bewhiskered major generals had written about campaigns; historians had dug accounts of strategy out of documents; dryly admirable staff officers had recorded the movings of wedges labelled 'infantry' or 'gunners' here and there on the escarpments of hills or against embrasures or redans. The young officer had his nose held down, *ad nauseam*, to the ordnance orders of Grant at Vicksburg or to the minutiae of Pickett's charge. I dare say that, at twenty, I knew more about the tactics of the battles of the Civil War than did Crane. Occasionally the writers added a few reflections as to the morale of this or that wedge of humanity on a special battle-field distinguished by concentrated shell-fire, or during rear-guard actions. But few had given any picture at all of post-medieval warfare, and absolutely none had introduced us behind the foreheads of the units who made up those moving wedges.

And suddenly there was *The Red Badge of Courage* showing us, to our absolute conviction, how the normal, absolutely undistinguished, essentially civilian man from the street had behaved in a terrible and prolonged war—without distinction, without military qualities, without special courage, without even any profound apprehension of, or passion as to, the causes of the struggle in which, almost without will, he was engaged. (And is it beside the mark to note that this was exactly how we all did take it twenty years later, from the English Channel to the frontiers of Italy?) The point was that, with *The Red Badge* in the nineties, we were provided with a map showing us our own hearts. If before that date we had been asked how we should behave in a war, we should no doubt have answered that we should behave like demigods, with all the marmoreal attributes of war memorials. But, a minute after peeping into *The Red Badge*, we knew that, at best, we should behave doggedly but with weary non-comprehension, flinging away our chassepot rifles, our haversacks, and fleeing into the swamps of Shiloh. We could not have any other conviction. The idea of falling like heroes on ceremonial battle-fields was gone forever; we knew that we should fall like street-sweepers subsiding ignobly into rivers of mud.

It was none the less convincing that those secrets of the heart in battle were revealed by a boy hardly out of his teens—and a boy who had never seen a war. The book was a revelation so miraculous that the more of the wonderful there was in its inception and preparation, the more profoundly convincing it seemed. Saint Rumwold of Bonnington was very properly canonized. He contributed immensely to converting the heathen who surrounded his cradle, because at the moment of his birth he began the recitation of the Creed and died at its conclusion. So with Crane. . . . It was fitting that this apparently miraculous being should be the first really American writer.

When he descended on me in the troglodytic cottage on Limpsfield Chart where I lived severely browbeaten by Garnetts and the Good generally, though usually of a Fabian or Advanced Russian variety, I took him at once to be a god—an Apollo with starry eyes. I have never had this feeling about any other man but Hudson, and Hudson's divinity was of a more hidden, woodland order. Crane had a way of dropping lightly down the stairs that I have always envied; and I see him now, descending with accurate feet the rough stones that formed my porch —coming out swiftly, holding a long-handled spade which, a minute later, he showed that he could use as swiftly and as accurately.

Don't imagine that I had tried to impress him into the ranks of the Small Producers of the world. It was merely that someone—not myself but probably Mr. Edward Garnett—had persuaded him to plant a rosebush beside my porch—with the confident belief that it would rival eventually, in fame, Shakespeare's mulberry tree and the laurels of Dante. It perhaps will. At any rate, when I last saw it, it had hidden all the harsh stones of that cottage front.

I dig back into the detritus of half-forgotten things, against which only the figure of Crane stands out with any bright light on it. . . . I dig back in my memory to find the date. It must have been in the late fall of 1897. The Cranes must have been married in Athens in the late summer of that year and drifted by way of Paris to Limpsfield Chart, attracted there, no doubt, by the Edward Garnetts, and they must have taken the hideous and disastrous villa called Ravensbrook at Oxted, which is next door, by Michaelmas. . . . It does not, of course, really matter, only I was wondering why I should have had an unplanted rosebush lying about if it was not the fall.

In any case Crane left on me an impression of supernaturalness that I still have. It was perhaps the aura of that youth that never deserted him—perhaps because of his aspect of frailty. He seemed to shine —and perhaps the November sun really did come out and cast on his figure, in the gloom of my entry, a ray of light. At any rate, there he stands, poising the spade and radiating brightness. But it was perhaps more than anything the avenging quality of his brows and the resentful frown of his dark blue eyes. He saw, that is to say, the folly and malignity of humanity—not in the individual but in committees. For Providence has ordained that if you take four or five of the most inspired, benevolent, farseeing, and practical of men, and form them into a committee, their enactments will make the angels laugh and ruin will stultify their achievements. The committee formed by the thirteen most distinguished men and women of France to devise measures for increasing the birth-rate of that country has—perhaps fortunately—not yet succeeded in finding or propagating any pronouncements—and not only that, but the whole baker's dozen have produced only three children. . . . And when such committees expand to form parliaments, senates, legislatures, what further stultification, oppression, imbecility, malignity, bloodshed; and from offices of War, Commerce, the Marine (whether commercial or military), or Agriculture or Music or the Arts, what corruption and foolishness! . . .

It is the province of a godhead to chastise all these, so Crane had avenging eyes. He had by then seen one imagined war; off the coast of Cuba, the makings of another; in Athens, the happenings in the rear of actual fighting. He had experienced the banalities of critics and censors of morals, and, once he had discovered with wonder that they 'did not want' the presentation of truths about war, or heaven or hell or the Bowery, wrath had descended into his heart. This was a thing he never got over. He had to chastise. He had to chastise me.

After he had planted that rosebush he had to tell me that he had been privileged indeed to be allowed to visit my 'bully baronial relic.' That troglodytic cottage was indeed unfinished, with immense stones jutting out of it towards the south, so that a west wing might one day be added. So he had really taken it to be a relic of baronial splendour. . . . He considered that writers should not take refuge amongst relics of medieval splendour—or in what it is for the moment the fashion to call Ivory Towers. He thought they ought to face life—which was what I thought I was doing by turning some acres of sandy hillside

and thistles into cultivable soil—making two blades
of corn grow where none had grown before. I was
at the time in a severely Small-Producer frame of
mind and nothing could have been further from my
thoughts than baronial relics. . . .

He continued the chastisement shortly afterwards
during a whole-night sitting. It was when he had been
up to town from Oxted, and Pinker had promised
him, after a lean period, twenty pounds for every
thousand words he chose to write. So he had returned
with hampers of *foie gras* and caviar and champagne,
and desperately wanted someone to share his good
fortune. So, till breakfast next morning, he went on
passionately telling me that he didn't give whatever
it was the then fashionable slang not to give for corner lots and battle-fields; that I ruined, ruined, ruined
my verse by going out of my way, in the pre-Raphaelite manner, to drag in rhymes which made *longueurs*
and diluted the sense. He told me that he was the son
of an Episcopalian bishop and had been born indifferently in the Bowery or in Wyoming or on Pike's
Peak. There were thus no flies on him, whereas I was
simply crawling with them. . . . And he produced
from the hip pocket of the riding-breeches into which
he had changed from his town clothes, a Colt re-
volver, with the foresight of which he proceeded to
kill flies. . . . He had spilt a little champagne over
a lump of sugar on the table and flies had come in
companies. He really did succeed in killing one, flick-
ing the gun backhanded with his remarkably strong
wrists. Then he looked at me avengingly and said:

'That's what you want to do instead of interring
yourself amongst purple pre-Raphaelite pleonasms.
. . . That's what you learn out in the West. . . .'

But even I knew that in Wyoming or Leadville or other places where you gunned, you filed the fore-sight off the barrel so that it should not stick in your holster when you wanted to draw quickly. . . .

He got that note out of his system on that occasion —at any rate, as far as I was concerned—and found that our ideas about life and letters were pretty similar. So that I never jeered at him when—so very little later, because his life was so short—he found himself occupying a real baronial manor-house on the site of the battle of Hastings, with his wife in medieval dress and with, on the floors of the ban-queting-hall, rushes amongst which the innumerable dogs fought for the bones which the guests cast them. . . . And with what a crowd of retainers!

It occurs to me that all this is so far away and so long ago that the present generation may know noth-ing about the circumstances of Crane. . . . 'The present generation' is the right phrase because they say it takes thirty years to make—and exhaust—a generation, and all this happened from 1897 to 1900, Crane having been born in 1871 and just living to see the twentieth century and his thirtieth year.

Crane, then, arrived in England in 1897 on his way to the Greco-Turkish War. He came back to-wards the end of the year and occupied furnished rooms on Limpsfield Chart, a breezy, uplifting hilltop completely surrounded by Fabians. He then moved to Oxted, which lies in a bottom, his house having a spring flowing through its basement. After that he moved to Brede Place. That ill-fated mansion lies also in a damp hollow. It is partly Elizabethan, partly even medieval. I had known it before Crane occupied it because William Hyde, a black-and-white artist who made illustrations for my book on the Cinque Ports, had inhabited all alone the room over the porch where Crane afterwards worked. Hyde was a mysterious and, with his black beard and his secret processes, a ferocious, gipsy-like figure. He was of the opinion that local smugglers objected to his occupying the place which had long stood empty and had been handy for their purposes, and he was always full of stories of how they tried to thwart him in his work. There were mysterious noises in the cellars, remote explosions, rumblings, sounds resembling gunfire. But Hyde stuck it out until he had finished the illustrations and I dare say longer.

I used to go and watch him at work and I formed a very disagreeable impression of Brede. It seemed to be full of evil influences, to be very damp, and to be hopelessly remote. You have to know that up and down East Sussex country with its deep hollows, dank coppices, and precipitous hop-fields to appreciate how hopelessly remote it could seem and how full of hobgoblins and miasmas. It was, alas, not remote enough. . . .

I don't know why Crane's then advisers should have induced him to go to Brede. It was, of course, very cheap as far as rent went, for I believe the Moreton Frewens let him have it for nothing; but it would have needed the resources of an American millionaire or a non-depressed English great land-owner to keep it up, and poor Steevie's twenty pounds a thousand words were like straws against the intolerable tide of expenses into which he was gradually pushed.

In his life of Crane, which was written ten or a dozen years ago and which, for a man who did not

know Crane, was a very difficult and creditable labor
of love, Mr. Thomas Beer said that Crane did not
have a very tumultuous reception in England. He
was wrong, for that was exactly the type of reception
that poor Crane did get once he was settled at first in
Oxted and afterwards in Brede. Before that he had
the reception that any serious man of letters should
have wanted at that date to have in England. He
was, that is to say, accepted at once, on his achievements and personality, as a serious and distinguished
human being by practically all the serious people in
England. Obviously the steamer in which he went
over was not met in Gallions' Reach by tugboats full
of interviewers, nor did the Queen in a drawing-room
step two paces forward to clasp him by the hand.
. . . But a young foreigner of twenty-five coming
into a country as suspicious, reserved, and toughly
conservative as was the England of that date, and
being received at once as an equal into the intimacies
of Conrad and Henry James, and Mr. Edward Garnett and all the intensely highbrow Fabians of Limpsfield, and Mr. Shaw and Professor Hobson, and the
more distinguished members of the Savile, the
Devonshire, and the Savage Clubs, was done about
as well as highbrow England could do him. And for
the matter of that, he had what is called the entrée
into aristocratic circles which would be closed as if
against the breath of infection to the most brilliant
young English writers. So that, at first, I found his
reflections on England a little trying because of the
titled qualifications of his informants. He seemed to
have been received by half the Cabinet and a perfect
galaxy of Irish peeresses. And his manners were so
quiet and unmarked that there was no reason why he

should not have climbed to Jamesian heights and have had Lady Maude Warrender to tea on his lawn every other afternoon. It might, really, have been better for him if he had.

For Crane was scarcely established in his Oxted villa before the tumultuous note began. Literary London of that day—I do not know how it may be now—was filled to about capacity by the most discreditable bums that any city can ever have seen. They pullulated mostly about the purlieus of the Savage Club, but you would find them in Bedford Park and you would find them in Limehouse. And no sooner did the word go round that there was in Oxted, and afterwards in Brede, a shining young American of genius, earning twenty pounds for every thousand words that he wrote, and ready to sit up all night dispensing endless hampers of caviar, *foie gras*, champagne, and oysters in season . . . ah, then there was tumult indeed in the twenty miles that separate Limehouse from Bedford Park.

The reverberations were terrific. London was at that time full of American reporters. It was the fat time for war correspondents and they all went through the Savage Club—to the Balkans, to Athens, to Vladivostok by the Trans-Siberian; and innumerable lame ducks, bad hats, *tristes sires,* and human detritus from New York to Tin Can, Nevada, were left by the tide between Fleet Street and Adelphi Terrace, which was the Mecca of the Bohemian out-at-elbows. And, merely to be reputed to have known that Fortunate Youth was to have parcels of that flotsam drift onto one's doorstep. I was never myself in the Savage Club but once in my life; that sort of conviviality always rather frightened me. But my brother was there a good deal. I don't think he knew who Crane was, but he knew I knew him, and if dim shapes floated up to him and asked for an introduction to the Hermit of Brede, he would send them down to me. I had moved before that to Winchelsea, the next parish to Brede.

I was naïve in those days, but not so naïve as to send them on to poor Steevie—but they bothered me a good deal. One hero stole two short stories of mine and sold them in Chicago as his own; another wrote articles in my name—about America—and sold them in Boston to gilt-edged periodicals. A lady from a Toronto paper was rather troublesome. She said she had heard that I had collaborated with Conrad and she did not see why she should not collaborate with Henry James or Crane if I would give her introductions. She had not found it necessary to have an introduction to me. She wore, I remember, a scarlet pilot jacket and a dun-coloured tam-o'-shanter, and she said something remarkable had happened on her voyage over. A young lady on board the boat had had occasion to go into a gentleman's stateroom to return a book and the wind had slammed the door so that she had been a prisoner all the afternoon. Wasn't that exactly the sort of story Henry James would want to collaborate on? Or perhaps, better still, the author of *The Red Badge of Courage?* . . .

I avoided Brede Place during that period, but Crane used to ride over, perched on the top of one of his two enormous carriage horses which gave him the air of a frail eagle astride a gaunt elephant, and would talk with discouragement of the revival of medieval places of sanctuary. I didn't avoid Brede because I was afraid of the company there. Amongst a perfect wilderness of cats and monkeys there would always be at least one just soul who was really devoted to Steevie—Conrad, or occasionally the Old Man himself, or Mr. Garnett, or Harold Frederic, or Robert Barr, all strong and good men in their day. But I could not stand the sunlight there. It filtered down into those dank green places and was ghastly.

An Elizabethan manor's ground plan is that of an E—out of compliment to the Virgin Queen—and Brede Place conformed exactly to that plan. . . . Two longish wings, one at each end; in the centre a shorter wing which held the arched porch and the entrance hall. All the mass of the building of grey stone with mullioned, leaded windows, offering a proud and sinister front to sunlight coming through lowering clouds. On the bank which supported it played all the things in the world that nobody wanted —unwanted children, dogs, men, old maids—like beachcombers washed up on green sands. And behind the façade, a rabbit warren of passages with beer barrels set up at odd corners, and barons of beef for real tramps at the kitchen door, and troops of dogs and maids and butlers and sham tramps of the New York newspaper world and women who couldn't sell their manuscripts. . . .

And poor, frail Steevie, with all the organs of his body martyred to the waters of Cuba, the mosquitoes of the swamps around Athens, the cold Caribbean, the dusts of Wyoming or Nevada or Colorado, the stenches of Bowery slums, the squalor of New York hall-bedrooms . . . Heaven knows where he really had or hadn't been; he might, like Cyrano, have come sliding from the moon to the earth down a sunbeam. . . . Poor, frail Steevie, in the little room over the porch in the E, writing incessantly—like a spider that gave its entrails to nourish a wilderness of parasites. For, with his pen that moved so slowly in microscopic black trails over the immense sheets of paper that he affected, he had to support all that wilderness. That was the thought I could not bear.

I drove over several times, behind a pony that for some reason detested the Udimore highroad so that the driving was a weariness—several times from Winchelsea to Brede, and then turned back because I was unable to bear the prospect of seeing that little figure perched, as if at the foot of a mountain, before those great sheets, in that Elizabethan cave, with an untasted glass of very small beer, gone flat beside him.

The last time I drove that way was on the second day of January, 1900, and that time I did not see him in his workroom. I was led instead by an imposing maid to a hide-hole in a summer house up the bank behind that lugubrious place. It seemed a singular spot for a consumptive to choose on a January afternoon. But when I approached him, he sprang out, his face radiant, and exclaimed:

'Hueffer, thank God, it's you! . . . I always say you bring me luck. . . .'

The luck I had brought him was that of not being the tax collector from whom he was hiding. He had the theory that if, in England, you did not pay your taxes on New Year's Day, you went to prison.

I certainly had happened upon him usually at his more fortunate moments—on the occasion of his glorious visit to Pinker, the agent; on that day when

I had certainly brought him all the good wishes of
the season; several times when he had received un-
expected payment checks—and once that he certainly
regarded as miraculous. I had been driving along the
Udimore road which was unduly domed and with a
glassy perfection of surface. At a little distance I
saw him coming along on one of his immense horses
and a second later I saw him on the ground with the
horse lying on his leg. The horse's legs had shot out
sideways on the treacherous surface. I suppose they
were both a trifle stunned; for he said I had all the
aspect of a fabulous deliverer, appearing in a dogcart
and dragging him forcibly from under his horse. . . .

On that second of January, after I had assured
him that he need not fear the tax collector for two
or three months . . . and alas, a more grim visitor
reached him before that functionary . . . on that
second of January he led me delightedly into his
drawing-room where there was someone rather nice
talking to Mrs. Crane and Mrs. Rudy. . . . It might
have been Robert Barr or James or Conrad—or possibly Owen Wister. I suppose an English visitor
would have reassured him as to the habits of the
collectors of Her Majesty's revenue. . . . At any
rate, it was someone nice and probably American,
and we sat and had tea and muffins before blazing
logs and talked composedly about the house party
which had so lately been swept out of the place that
the drawing-room was as yet the only habitable
apartment in the house—a great room with warm
shadows and rather good bits of furniture that Mrs.
Crane had picked up here and there. It might have
been the tea hour at Henry James's Lamb House. . . .

But when I was getting into my dogcart on the

steps before the arched porch, Crane took hold of my arm suddenly; with an air of the deepest gravity, his avenger's face lit by my cart lamps against the January darkness, he exclaimed:

'Mr. Hueffer, you have been intimate with me in several places: in Limpsfield; in Oxted; in London a little . . . and here. . . . Now tell me on your honour . . .'

He asked me whether I had ever seen him drunk; or drugged; or lecherously inclined; or foul-mouthed; or quarrelsome even. He said—and that struck me as shrewd—that we had lived in the same villages for several years; our servants knew each other. Had I ever heard a word of housemaids' or village gossip against him? In any particular or on any occasion?

Poor Steevie; poor dear fortunate youth. . . . If you nourish broods of vipers for long periods in your bosom, it is likely that you will be stung. He had been.

Of course I had never heard a word said against him. If it did not seem so fantastic I should be inclined to say that I am certain that he was as pure in heart—and almost as naïve—as his mother, the wife of a Non-conformist minister.

I don't know. I wonder which is the better mode of life for a writer—of the two modes followed by those two Americans in that old corner far away and long ago. There was James, with his carefully calculated life in a Georgian treasure-house—with his lawns and his Ladies and his flowers and his old, mellow, brick garden walls and his smooth-running household—and all his suavities. And with all his passionate inner life for ever concealed so that you would have sworn he had never lived at all. . . .

And there was Crane, for ever stuffed in somewhere
as waste paper is stuffed into any old drawer—in an
Oxted villa; on a Cuban hillside; in a hut in Tin Can,
Nevada; in an Athens hospital; in an Adirondack
tent; in a New York rooming-house; in an open boat;
in an Elizabethan manor—and in a grave in Elizabeth, New Jersey, of all places in the world to have
chosen for you. . . . But the point really was that
these places were all chosen for him or dictated by
circumstances. Someone took rooms for him on
Limpsfield Chart—and if he had gone on living there
he might have been alive to this day. Then someone
shoved him into Ravensbrook, Oxted, and if he had
gone on living there he would have been dead in
three months. Then someone shoved him into Brede
and he died of it—of that and of Havana and Athens
and lower Seventh Avenue and Little Rock, Arkan-
sas, and Lincoln, Nebraska, and the Alamo and Fort
Sam Houston, where he was refused for the army
. . . or so he said . . . and the Painted Desert of
Arizona, and Jacksonville, Florida, and the Open
Boat. . . . I don't in fact know where-all he went,
but I have heard him claim to have been in those
places . . . not of course that that meant anything.
Crane would assert that he had been in all sorts of
improbable spots and done all sorts of things, not
vaingloriously lying, but in order to spin around his
identity a veil behind which he might have some
privacy. A writer needs privacy, and people talked so
incessantly about poor Steevie that he had to keep
his private life to himself.

No, I don't know. The main job of a writer is to
write—to have circumstances favourable to his writing at the best. I suppose that if Crane had settled

down in the cottage on Limpsfield Chart, he might have gone on writing till today—or if he had evolved all the hide-holes from contact with the life of Lamb House. . . . But perhaps his writing would have grown thinner.

He had a curious deference for the opinions of those older than himself and a curious necessity for their approval. So that, because he knew I approved of him and his work, he had to regard me as vastly his senior, though actually I entered the world two years and forty-five days after he did. But I wore in those days a beard and was known as the last of the pre-Raphaelites, and Crane insisted that to be the last of a race one must be tremendously aged and dim-eyed and wise. So except on moments of deep emotion he always called me Mr. Hueffer and insisted that his friends should be silent so that I could speak.

I appear once to have offended one of his Canadian friends and, as I am never tired of repeating, in almost his last letter Crane wrote to him:

> You must not be offended by Mr. Hueffer's manner. He patronizes Mr. James. He patronizes Mr. Conrad. Of course he patronizes me and he will patronize Almighty God when they meet, but God will get used to it, for Hueffer is all right. . . .

That is almost like having the Victoria Cross of the long sad battlefield that is a writer's life.

Crane's work is the most electric thing that ever happened in that struggle—it was and so remains. His influence on his time, and the short space of time that has succeeded his day, was so tremendous that if today you read *Maggie,* it is as if you heard a number of echoes, so many have his imitators been; and you can say as much of *The Red Badge.* That is simply because his methods have become the standard for dealing with war scenes or slum life. Until there comes a new Homer, we shall continue to see those things in that way.

His technique was amazing and extraordinarily contagious. How many stories since its day have not opened with a direct imitation of the marvellous first sentence of *The Open Boat*:

None of them knew the colour of the sky.

Haven't a thousand stories, since then, opened with just that cadence, like a machine-gun sounding just before stand-to at dawn and calling the whole world to attention? And of course there is more to it than just the cadence of the eight monosyllables to the one dissyllable. The statement is arresting because it is mysterious and yet perfectly clear. So your attention is grasped even before you realize that the men in the boat were pulling or watching the waves so desperately that they had no time to look up. That is skill, and when it comes, as it did with Crane, intuitively, out of the very nature of the narrator, it is the pledge of genius. It is the writing of somebody who cannot go wrong . . . who is authentic.

I have spoken of Crane as the first American writer. The claim is not new, though I do not know who made it first. I dare say I did because I must certainly have been one of the first to think it. It remains perhaps a little controversial. But all Ameri-

can writers who preceded him had their eyes on
Europe. They may have aped Anglicism in their
writings, like the Concord group; or, like Mark
Twain—or even if you like, O. Henry—they were
chronic protesters against Europeanism. At any rate,
the Old World preoccupied them.

There was nothing of this about Crane. To say
that he was completely ignorant of Zola or Maupassant would probably be untrue. He would state at one
moment, with expletives, that he had never heard of
those fellows and, at the next, display a considerable
acquaintance with their work. Indeed, he said that it
was after dipping into Zola's novel about the Franco-
Prussian War that he determined to write a real
war novel, and so sat down to *The Red Badge*.

No, he was the first American writer because he
was the first to be passionately interested in the life
that surrounded him—and the life that surrounded
him was that of America. Don't believe that he was
in the least changed by his residence at Brede. He
paid, as it were, a courteous attention to Oxted or
London or Brede, but he moved about in them an
abstracted and solitary figure . . . and he footed the
bills. I don't mean to say that he was homesick for a
bench in Union Square. He didn't have to be; he
was always there, surveying the world from that hard
seat. He picked his way between dogs snarling over
their bones in the rushes of the medieval hall, but
he was thinking how to render the crash of dray
horses' hooves and the rattle of the iron-bound
wheels on the surface of Broadway where it crosses
Fourteenth Street. Or he was lost in the Bowery.
Or Havana. Or the Oranges. He had been shoved
into Brede because his friends thought that he needed

a little medievalizing to rub off the rough edges of his merciless thought—and because Mrs. Crane wanted to be a medieval lady of the castle with her long sleeves brushing with their tips those same rushes.

I was reading my *Congressional Record* this morning and I came upon this pious opinion in a speech of the Honorable Byron N. Scott:

> What does America stand for to the world? We have no Gothic cathedrals; no Rembrandt, no Shakespeare. We do not stand for art and culture, but we stand for the greatest experiment ever made in government. . . . If we ever have a high place along with Greece and Rome and the Italy of the Middle Ages, it will be for this contribution to history.

It won't. It will be because Crane discovered and gave a voice to America. . . . And you can spare a thought, too, to James and Whistler and Hudson. There is a hall in Washington hung with bluish pictures that need not fear comparison with *The Night Watch* or *The Lesson in Anatomy*, and before honourable congressmen claim that by their labours they are raising monuments such as the Age of Pericles alone could show, they might remember, a little shamefacedly, if congressmen can know shame, a certain stone in the cemetery of Elizabeth, New Jersey.

I had occasion to go through that town a dozen times a month or so ago and I remember saying to one of my companions that I couldn't imagine any reason in the world why one should want to stop off in Elizabeth, New Jersey. That was before I knew that Crane was buried there, for, not taking much interest in necrologies, I did not know that Steevie lay there until I read again, the other day, Mr. Beer's painstaking biography. . . . Well, then, if America is to be saved—America of the typewriting machine, of the libraries, of the universities, of the paint brushes and music paper and plumb line, which is the only America that counts, *pace* Congress and its labours—that day will come when as many pious pilgrims go to Elizabeth as to Stratford itself.

At present the only book of Crane's that you can buy in all New York is a cheap reprint of a random collection that happens to contain *The Open Boat* and *Maggie*, and when I asked his publisher with what volumes he could supply me, he very amiably sent me his file copies of a work containing *Maggie*, *George's Mother*, and *The Blue Hotel*—and Mr. Beer's *Stephen Crane*. But he had none for sale. . . .

Congress should do something about it—so that at least a footnote may for certain remain concerning the greatest experiment ever made in government!

W. H. HUDSON

In the days when there were still gods—and that was indeed far away and long ago, for if you ran a thousand years with the speed of the victor of Atalanta you would never discover that vanished place or overtake those receding minutes—in those days, then, there was Hudson. And also in London, in Gerrard Street, Soho, there was a French restaurant called the Mont Blanc where, on Tuesdays, the elect of the city's intelligentsia lunched and discussed with grave sobriety the social problems of the day . . . under the presidency of Mr. Edward Garnett, who has for so long been London's literary—as if Nonconformist—Pope that I cannot remember when he was not. But now and then imaginative writers would drop in at the Mont Blanc and the atmosphere would grow more excited. There would be Conrad and Galsworthy and W. B. Yeats and Mr. Hilaire Belloc and Muirhead Bone, the etcher, and Sturge Moore, the poet, and others that the world has forgotten and yet others whom I have forgotten. Then voices would begin to raise themselves a little. For the thin beer or barley water of ordinary days gave place to a Bordeaux that had never seen the slopes of the Bordelais—a sort of *pinard,* from, I should think, the Canton de Vaux in Switzerland but labelled Saint

Emilion, which is the drink *par excellence* of the English literati and gentry. It was heady, too, and when a little of it had there been consumed you would begin to hear the shouted names of Flaubert and Maupassant and Huysmans and Mendès and Monet and Manet and Maeterlinck and Sisley and Turgenev. And if Belloc came bustling in and Conrad was there, the noise would grow to exceed the noise of Irish fairs when shillelaghs were in use. Because Mr. Belloc with his rich brogue and burr would loudly assert that his ambition was to make by writing four thousand pounds a year and to order a monthly ten dozen of Clos Vougeot or Château Brane Cantenac . . . and this to Conrad who would go rigid with fury if you suggested that anyone, not merely himself, but any writer of position, could possibly write for money. So they would go to it: you might have imagined yourself for the moment at the famous Thursdays at Brébant's with Flaubert shouting abuse at the young Henry James for speaking disrespectfully of Mérimée, and Turgenev doing his best to divert the thunders from the young American. And then suddenly, in a silence, you would hear the song of birds, the wind in the green boughs of the New Forest in Hampshire. . . .

An immensely long form would be leaning in the doorway that separated the upper rooms of the Mont Blanc, and the effect was just the same as that which was said to be produced when Turgenev came into the dining-room of Brébant's. After a pause of almost breathlessness we would all of us exclaim 'Hud . . . son'—all except Mr. Garnett who, as his discoverer, permitted himself to say 'Huddie!' and Mr. Belloc who, respecting nobody, would permit himself to say: '*Tiens, le voilà encore,*' and go on eating his soup. . . .

One day Mr. Belloc was recounting the fabulous legends of his service in the French Army. Mr. Belloc was in those days—as I do hope he remains still—the spoiled child of the fortune-bearing fates who look after the garden of the muses. Orator, poet, tragedian, comedian, censor of manners, guardian of public finances, Defender of the Faith, and Geographer Royal to His Majesty's Army, he was possessed of at least ten birthplaces, thus exceeding Homer. He was also Member for Salford and *enfant trois fois terrible* of the House of Commons. Ah, you should have seen the Mr. Belloc of those days! Well, with his golden, burred, and triumphant organ and with his impassioned gestures that were accompanied by the tinkle of glasses as he swept them off the table, Mr. Belloc was telling what he said to the *adjudant*. An *adjudant* is not the same as an adjutant, but something much worse . . . worse than the toughest sergeant-major you ever imagined. And Mr. Belloc had gone on to tell of how, when on parade, the troop-horse threw him . . . and here Mr. Belloc made as if to disappear under the table . . . threw him with such violence that he vanished into the dust of the parade ground and was not discovered for several days. That necessitated another dramatic interview with the virulent *adjudant,* the charge being absence from parade. . . . Though how, I remember wondering, could he be charged with absence if he was actually present and why, since as we all understood he honoured with his service the *Diables Bleus,* the famous Alpine regiment, could he have been drilling on a horse?

Then Mr. Belloc made as if to emerge from under the table, brushed the hair from his eyes, and with a new voice exclaimed:

'Glorious county, Sussex. Most glorious county in the world!'

Someone made a protest in favour of the Rhondda Valley.

'Nonsense,' said Mr. Belloc. Hudson had just come in behind his back. 'Sussex, my birthplace. The only glorious county. Glorious. . . . More and more glorious!' and swept his hair in several different directions whilst he drank a bumper of *pinard* from the only remaining flower vase.

All the while, towering above him, with his air of looking into a strong wind, his eyes all screwed up and his beard-point sticking forward . . . all the while Hudson watched that Sussex-born French-mounted Alpinist with the expression of an Atlas Mountain lion, inspecting from a high boulder the gyrations below him of an acrobatic precursor of Mr. Charles Chaplin. I don't mean that Mr. Belloc resembled Mr. Chaplin, but that Hudson looked like a lion looking at that star.

'Glorious county,' Mr. Belloc began again. 'Not another like it in the world. The Downs, the sea . . . why, when I am in the Midlands and the day is left behind . . . only think . . . you can ride from the Crystal Palace to Beachy Head with only four checks.'

Then for the first time the voice of Hudson, solemn like a great bell, boomed across that place of inferior refection.

'Five!' it said.

Mr. Belloc spun around with intense energy and cried out:

'Nonsense. You're wrong. Four. Four only.' And he began with the violence of a man who wishes to mutilate himself to bend back with his right the fingers of his left hand. 'There's Cucking and Wucking. And Hitching and Fitching.'

'Five.' In the deep silence, where we all listened fascinated, boomed the voice of the watcher of birds.

'Good God, fellow!' shouted Mr. Belloc with the desperate energy of a strong man who is being drawn into a bottomless pit by an irresistible force. 'You're a Yankee, or a Guatemalan, or a Tierra del Fuegoan; you never came to England till you were ninety-seven. . . . And you propose to dictate to me, a Sussex man! . . . Why, when I am in the Midlands . . .'

That silent, stone figure from Sunday Island continued to lean a little forward with the fixed expression at once good-humoured and sardonic of the Atlas lion that is *going to eat* Mr. Chaplin!

'I tell you; I tell all these good people . . . Only four. . . . There are Cucking and Wucking, and Hitching and Fitching . . .'

Again the breathless pause. Hudson's level, remorseless voice brought out the syllables:

'West,' and after a long time, 'Dean!'

A death rattle sounded from Mr. Belloc's throat; he threw up his hand with the gesture of a dying gladiator; his almost maniacal voice exclaimed:

'By God! . . . This man comes from Quilmes in the Argentine. I know all about Quilmes. It is a country of an ineradicable inaccuracy of mind. . . . Yet he comes from there and looks like a don of the sixteenth century and talks to me about Sussex!

. . . And I . . . I who was born on Chanctonbury
Ring which is the highest point in Sussex; from it you
can see the whole of Sussex; I who have galloped a
thousand times from the Crystal Palace the sixty
miles to Beachy Head . . . with only four checks;
I who have hunted the red fox in the storms of winter, the freshets of spring, the torrid heats of summer
when the mirage runs all along those Sussex Downs
. . . I who was born in Lewes Castle and have never
in my life been out of Sussex . . . I, *moi qui vous
parle,* must needs forget West Dean!'

My sympathies, I must confess, were all with Mr.
Belloc, for I am equally capable of being inspired
with such enthusiasms for certain parts of the earth
so that I can work myself up to the belief that,
morally at least, I was born there. Indeed, when I
come to think of it, in my last book I proved to my
own satisfaction—and I am sure to that of my
readers—that I was almost born in Arles. . . . And
I could do as much for Colmar in Alsace, or Bettws-
y-Coed in North Wales, or Vienna, or Cracow. Or
even Staunton, Virginia. And no good man can tell
how many steps lead up to his front door which he
goes down from ten times a day in a complete calm-
ness, much less can he tell how many checks there
will be in a good gallop when he is excited.

But Hudson had that type of tranquil mind. He
once proved to me that he knew better than I what
bushes I had in my own hedges, though I had brushed
them over and over again and I did not know that
he had seen them at all, he having called on me when
I was out. And similarly he proved to the *gauchos*—
who, though they can tell a man from an ostrich at

seven miles' distance, are singularly unobservant in small matters and can never be brought to see the difference between an *m* and an *n*—he proved to the *gauchos* of the pampas that the grass of the plains over which they galloped all day and the *ombu* trees under which they spent all their siestas and night hours, were not solid masses of green, like billiard cloths or the painted leaden trees that shelter tin soldiers. They had never noticed that and could not see it until he lent them his reading spectacles. Then they fell off their horses in amazement. So Hudson appeared to be full of the queerest knowledges, and, as he penetrated into the most unusual and dissimilar places, his range of those knowledges was extraordinary and disconcerting and made him a person very dangerous to argue with.

You walked beside him, he stalking along and, from far above you, Olympianly destroying your theories with accurate dogma. He was very tall, with the immense, lean frame of an old giant who has for long stooped to hear men talk. The muscles of his arms stood out like knotted cords. He had the Spanish face and peaked grey beard of a Don Desperado of the Spanish Main; his features seemed always slightly screwed together like the faces of men looking to windward in a gale. He paused always for an appreciable moment before he spoke, and when he spoke he looked at you with a sort of humorous anticipation, as if you were a nice cockatoo whom he expected to perform amusing tricks. He was the gentlest of giants, although occasionally he would go astonishingly off the deep end, as when he would exclaim violently, 'I'm not one of you damned writers: I'm a naturalist from La Plata.' This he would put over with a laugh, for of course he did not lastingly resent being called the greatest prose writer of his day. But he had a deep, dark, permanent rage at the thought of any cruelty to birds.

Hudson was born of American parentage in a place called Quilmes in the Argentine, about 1840, and coming to London in the eighties of the last century, he was accustomed to declare—in order to account for his almost impassioned love for the English countryside—that no member of his family had been in England for over two hundred and fifty years. After his death his industrious and devoted biographer, Mr. Morley Roberts, ferreted out that Hudson's father had been born in the State of Maine about 1814, his paternal father having gone there from the West of England a little before the Declaration of Independence. On his mother's side he was, however, of very old United States descent. In any case his youth and young manhood had been passed in Spanish-American countries and that no doubt gave him his gravity of behaviour . . . and of prose. For he remained always an extraordinarily closed-up person and the legends that grew up about him could hardly be distinguished from the little biographical truths that one knew. The truths always came in asides. You would be talking about pumas. For this beast he had a great affection, calling it the friend of man. He would declare that the puma would follow a traveller for days over the pampas or through the forest, watch over him and his horse whilst he slept, and drive away the jaguar . . . who was the enemy of man. He said that this had happened to him many times. Once he had been riding for two months on the pampas, sleeping beneath the *ombu* trees that

seem to cover half a county, and three times a puma
had driven off a jaguar. It had been a period of
drought. For a whole week he had not been able to
wash his face. One asked what it was like not to wash
one's face for a week and he would reply: 'Disagreeable. . . . Not so bad . . . as if cobwebs touched
you here and there.' You would say that that must
have been a disagreeable week all the same and he
would slip out: 'Not so bad as a week I've known
. . . when Mrs. Hudson and I passed a whole ten
days in a garret with nothing but a coupe of tins of
cocoa and some oatmeal to eat.'

And gradually it would reach your consciousness,
by means of a lot of such asides, that, after he first
came to England, there had been a long, dragging
series of years in which he had passed through periods
of near starvation, trying to make a career. It was
almost impossble to realize; he seemed so remote
from the usual vicissitudes, with his hidalgo aloof-
ness and his mind set on birds. And there was no one
—no writer—who did not acknowledge without question that this composed giant was the greatest living
writer of English. It seemed to be implicit in every
one of his long, slow movements.

When his life was nearly done, his book *Green
Mansions* had an enormous sale in the United States.
I was astonished to hear from Mr. Alfred Knopf
the other day how great that sale was. It kept Hudson
in comfort for the rest of his life. But one never heard
about it from him and it made no difference in his
manner of living. . . .

He was, at any rate in England, a writer's writer.
I never heard a lay person speak of Hudson in London, at least with any enthusiasm. I never heard a

writer speak of him with anything but a reverence
that was given to no other human being. For as a
writer he was a magician. He used such simple means
to give such gorgeous illusions. It was that that made
him the great imaginative writer that he was. If you
read his *Green Mansions* you feel sure that he had an
extraordinary intimacy with the life of tropical forests
and, indeed, once you had read it you couldn't, when
you met him next, fail to believe that he was the
child of some woodland deity. You could not rid
yourself of the belief even when he snapped at you
half contemptuously that he had never been in a
forest in his life. That was probably a fact, for he said
over and over again that, until he came to London
at the age of forty, he had never been off the pampas
except to go—but very rarely—to Buenos Aires.
. . . And this because of a weakness, real or supposed, of a heart that nevertheless contrived to do
its work until he was eighty.

> *Buenos Aires—patria hermosa—*
> *Tiene su Pampa grandiosa:*
> *La Pampa tien' el Ombu.*

The pampas . . . that is to say, an immense plain
of rolling grassland which has no forest, its only
trees being the *ombu*, which, however, in its solitude,
appears as large as a forest by itself . . . and Hudson had certainly never been in the hinterland of
Venezuela. Nevertheless, it was in the hinterland of
Venezuela that the scene of *Green Mansions* was
laid. But *Green Mansions* differs from Hudson's other
masterpieces—*The Purple Land, El Ombu, Nature
in Downland,* and *Far Away and Long Ago*—in that

it is a projection of a passion. *The Purple Land* is Romance; it is Romance as it was never before and never again will be put into words. But, like *El Ombu*, its situations are got in by rendering redolences of the soil, of humanity and humanity's companion, the horse, and of man's plaything, woman. It is full of laughter and broad stories and the picaresque spirit and hot youth and reckless fugitive passions.

If I have heard one, I have heard twenty of Hudson's rivals, from Conrad to Maurice Hewlett, or from Galsworthy to the much-too-much-forgotten George Gissing, say that *The Purple Land* is the supreme—is the only—rendering of Romance in the English language; and if I have heard one I have heard twenty say that *Green Mansions* is Anglo-Saxondom's only rendering of hopeless, of aching passion. There was, therefore, as Hudson felt with his sure instinct, no need for localization; indeed, topographical exactitudes would have been the fifth wheel on a coach that was the story of a man's passion for a voice that sang in the green house of a tree's boughs . . . and nothing else. And his instinct for covering his tracks, for retaining a veil of secrecy over his past, was also a motive for setting his story in a wilderness of forest that had never been explored. And no doubt there were material reasons for the change of the locale because there is also no doubt and no reason for preserving secrecy as to the fact that Hudson had once, far away and long ago, nourished an intolerable passion for a being who had had a beautiful voice and sang from the gleaming shadows of the green mansion of an *ombu*. It had eaten into his life; it had made him take to expressing himself; it had driven him from the limitless plains of his manhood and youth to the sordid glooms and weeping gaslit streets of . . . Bayswater!

The Purple Land, on the other hand, was a projection rather of other people's reckless lives in a revolutionary South. He was obviously not old enough to have ridden with Bolivar, but in his boyhood all South America rang with fables of the exploits of the Liberator. And his anecdotes of that heroic theorist were so vivid that you actually saw him galloping a black horse into the smoke from the lines of the Royalists. You saw it yourself and, as not until long after his death was the date of his birth ever established, you thought him a hundred years of age. And it all added to the romantic Hudson legend of the frequenters of the Mont Blanc.

Actually Bolivar the Liberator was an inspiring theorist of liberty, rather than a hat-waving horseman —a thin, nervous, Spanish revolutionary of genius. And his personal ambition was so small that when by the middle eighteen-twenties he had liberated the whole of South America from the European yoke and was going on to the founding of the confederation of Latin America, he suddenly resigned his power. He was too sensitive to stand the possible accusation that he aimed at dictatorship. He was born in 1783—about the year when Hudson's paternal grandfather came to the State of Maine and died in 1830, eleven years before Hudson was born. But such a man leaves after him such an aura of legends that it was no wonder that, brought up amongst peons and peasants who had all seen the Liberator in the flesh, Hudson should be able to convey to you the idea that he too had ridden with Bolivar and known the rollicking life of a heroic spurred-and-saddled pampas era.

And it was that faculty above all that made Hudson take his place with the great writers. He shared with Turgenev the quality that makes you unable to find out how he got his effects. Like Turgenev he was utterly undramatic in his methods, and his books have that same quality that have those of the author of *Fathers and Children*. When you read them you forget the lines and the print. It is as if a remotely smiling face looked up at you out of the page and told you things. And those things become part of your own experience. It is years and years since I first read *Nature in Downland*. Yet, as I have already said somewhere or other, the first words that I there read have become a part of my own life. They describe how, lying on the turf of the high sunlit downs above Lewes in Sussex, Hudson looked up into the perfect, limpid blue of the sky and saw, going to infinite distances one behind the other, the eye picking up one, then another beyond it, and another and another, until the whole sky was populated . . . little shining globes, like soap bubbles. They were thistledown floating in an almost windless heaven.

Now that is part of my life. I have never had the patience—the contemplative tranquillity—to lie looking up into the heavens. I have never in my life done it. Yet that is I, not Hudson, looking up into the heavens, the eye discovering more and more tiny, shining globes until the whole sky is filled with them, and those thistle-seed globes seem to be my globes.

For that is the quality of great art—and its use.

It is you, not another, who at night with the stars shining have leaned over a Venice balcony and talked about patines of bright gold; you, not anyone else, saw the parents of Bazarov realize that their wonderful son was dead. And you yourself heard the voice cry *Eli, Eli, lamma sabacthani!* . . . because of the quality of the art with which those scenes were projected.

That quality Hudson had in a supreme degree. He made you see everything of which he wrote, and made you be present in every scene that he evolved, whether in Venezuela or on the Sussex Downs. And so the world became visible to you and you were a traveller. It is almost impossible to quote Hudson *in petto*. He builds up his atmospheres with such little, skilful touches that you are caught into his world before you are aware that you have even moved. But you can't, just because of that, get his atmospheres fully without all the little touches that go to make them up. The passage that follows I selected by a process akin to that of the *sortes Virgilianae* of the ancients. I went in the dark to the shelf where my Hudsons are kept, took the book my hand first lighted on, and pushed my index finger into the leaves until it stopped on the passage I have written down here. It is from *Hampshire Days* and it is appropriate that it should be about his beloved birds. For Hudson watched birds with a passion that exceeded anything that he gave to any other beings . . . except to Rima of *Green Mansions*.

The old coots would stand on the floating weeds and preen and preen their plumage by the hour. They were like mermaids for ever combing out

their locks and had the clear stream for mirror.
The dull-brown, white-breasted young coots, now
fully grown, would meanwhile swim about picking
up their own food. The moorhens were with them,
preening and feeding, and one had its nest there.
It was a very big and conspicuous nest, built up on
a bunch of weeds, and formed, when the bird was
on it, a pretty and curious object; for every day
fresh, bright green sedge leaves were plucked and
woven round it and on that high, bright green
nest, as on a throne, the bird sat. . . . And when
I went near the edge of the water . . .

Don't you wish you knew what came next! . . .
And don't you see the extraordinary skill with which
the picture is built, and won't that picture be a permanent part of your mind's eye from now on? I
don't suppose you would ever take the trouble to
wade through rushes to the edge of clear water and
stand for hours watching water birds in their domes-
ticities. I know I never should, though I am never
happy if I have not wild birds somewhere near me.
But I have that picture and know now how water
birds comport themselves when, like men after work
sitting before their cottage doors, they take their ease
in the twilight. And indeed, before I had half-finished
transcribing that passage, I knew what was coming.
I cannot have re-read *Hampshire Days* since just after
it was republished in 1923, a year after Hudson's
death. But when I had got as far as 'and had the
clear stream for mirror' I knew what was coming—
the high mound of the moorhen's nest decked out
with bright green leaves.

Conrad—who was an even more impassioned ad-

mirer of Hudson's talent than am even I—used to
say: 'You may try for ever to learn how Hudson got
his effects and you will never know. He writes down
his words as the good God makes the green grass
to grow, and that is all you will ever find to say
about it if you try for ever.'

That is true. For the magic of Hudson's talent was
his temperament, and how or why the good God
gives a man his temperament is a secret that will be
for ever hidden . . . unless we shall one day have
all knowledge. It is easy to say that the picture is
made for you when those words 'and had the clear
stream for mirror' are written. But why did Hudson
select that exactly right image with which to get in
his picture? His secrets were too well protected.

I once or twice went through his proofs for literals
after he had gone through them himself and was not
feeling well, when I had called to take him for a
walk in the park. And you learned nothing from
his corrections. He would substitute for the simple
word *grew* the almost more simple word *were*. *When
the hedges were green* for *when the hedges grew
green,* not so much with the idea of avoiding allitera-
tion as because there is an actual difference in the
effect produced visually. You do not see hedges grow,
but you do see that they are green. And I suppose
these minute verbal alterations, meticulously attended
to, did give his projected scenes their vividness. I
fancy, too, that his first manuscript drafts may have
been rather florid, as if he made in them a sort of
shorthand of his thoughts immediately after seeing
something that interested him. But I was never able
to make out even a few words of his first drafts. From
a whole scratched-out page one cannot discern a

single whole phrase . . . *As to art my feeling is that* . . . and then three lines scratched out and two illegible; then the words *money value,* and, in the middle of the last paragraph on the page, *in August,* and three lines lower, *may develop,* which I know he afterwards changed into *may become,* because I saw it in the proofs of the article which he wrote for one of the heavier magazines. . . . And the curious thing is that I can hardly remember at all what the article was about, except that it contained on the side some reflections on the value of the arts to the public: yet I remember perfectly well his making that change—or rather seeing that he had made that change.

I am glad that the question of Hudson's attitude towards the Arts has come in thus almost accidentally, for most writers about Hudson—and Hudson gave them ground enough for the idea—have written that he cared nothing about the Arts as arts, but considered himself, as so many Anglo-Saxon writers do, a man of action before he was a writer. I am convinced that this is wrong. It was with him a sort of humility; he was, as it were, as astonished that the writers of the Mont Blanc should take him seriously as a writer as they were that he should notice anything as dingy as that poor imitation of a Paris *bistrôt* and its occupants. Because one's astonishment every time that he appeared there gave place in the end always to the feeling that he would surely never come there again. But if at the end of three or four hours' conversational labour one had convinced him that he was really a very great writer, he would express a sort of grim and sardonic satisfaction, wrinkling up his nose more than ever and from far above your head letting out humph-humphs and well-wells. And would then contentedly listen to a great deal of praise. It would go like this:

'It's the simplicity of your prose,' I would protest. 'It's as if a child wrote with the mind of one extraordinarily erudite.'

He would answer: 'You've hit it. I've got the mind of a child. Anyone can write simply. I just sit down and write. No doubt what I write about is important. I try to make it so. It's important that the chough should not be exterminated by those Cornish brutes. The chough is a beautiful and rare bird and it's important that beauty and rareness should not be driven from the world. But it's simple enough to write that down.'

'You know it isn't,' I would protest. 'Look how you sweat over correcting and recorrecting your own writing. Look how you went all through *Green Mansions* before it was published again. You took out every cliché . . .'

'Why, I was a very young man when I wrote the book. It was full of sham genteel words. I took them out. That isn't difficult.'

'It is,' I said, 'so difficult that if you can do it, you become an artist in words.'

He exclaimed still violently, but weakening a little: 'That's not reasonable. I'm not an artist. It's the last thing I should call myself. I'm a field naturalist who writes down what he sees. *You're* a stylist. You write these complicated things that no one else could. But it's perfectly simple to write down what one has seen. You could do it if you wanted to. With your eyes shut.'

I answered: 'I can do it for an hour. An hour and a

half. Then simplicity bores me. I want to write long, complicated cadences . . .'

'Well, that's art,' Hudson brought out triumphantly. 'I told you so long ago.'

I said: 'It isn't. Art is clarity; art is economy; art is surprise. Hang it, suppose you want to drive an ox. You tickle his hide with a sharpened stick; you don't stand away off from him and flick a fly off him with a twenty-yard sjambok.'

He would reply: 'I should have thought that that was what art was . . . showing off in some sort of way. But I never want to show off. That's why I'm not an artist. . . .' And I would throw up my hands in despair and begin all over again.

I used to write him tremendously long letters as to points in technique and he would answer them by letters as long. It must have been a nuisance to him. Heavens, the letters I used to write in those days when I was trying to get the English to take some interest in how to write! . . . I have just been shocked by reading in print a letter I wrote about that date to Galsworthy, who was then a neophyte. It occupied three pages of a very large book and the writing is like that of the proverbial *cocher de fiacre*. He bore it like a hero.

But the longest and most voluminous correspondence I had with Hudson was about caged birds. I was then emerging from a nervous breakdown and, acting on the advice of the nerve specialist in Butler's *The Way of All Flesh*, I had had the glass taken out of my bedroom window and replaced by small meshed wire netting and I had let loose in the room a half-dozen African wax-billed finches and parakeets. They seemed to flourish and to be quite happy, and my nerves were immensely soothed by lying in bed and watching them fly about. I won't go into the argument. It was the usual one between bird-lovers and those who find solace from keeping birds in captivity. And finally I brought it to an end by saying that I should keep the birds and go on keeping them. Besides: what would be the sense of turning African waxbills and parakeets loose in London? . . . At that he came to see me and stumped up the stairs to inspect my bedroom. He looked for a long time at the birds which were perfectly lively. Then he recommended me to have some large mirrors set into the walls with perches in front of them. And to hang about bright silvered balls from Christmas trees, and scarlet ribbons. Birds, he said, loved all bright objects, and the mirrors gave them the illusion, with their reflected images, that they were in great crowds of birds. Then he said, 'Humph,' and stumped down the stairs and never to me mentioned the subject of birds in captivity again.

Well, that was Hudson the writer. As a great, tall, Spanish-looking man he had his legends of a romantic past; and he had them, as I have said, in the most disparate atmospheres, for he penetrated into the most dissimilar households. You would meet him one afternoon at Sir Edward Grey's, where he was regarded as an impassive don with a past of lashings of women and cavalcades, now become a bird-watcher; for Sir Edward Grey, whilst holding the balance of all Europe, loved birds almost as passionately as Hudson. And next day you would meet him at the Mont Blanc, where other legends gathered about him. The legends were deduced rather than set about for the most part by Mr. Garnett, but in-numerable verificatory details would be added by Conrad, who had sailed the seas, by Charles Doughty, who wrote *Arabia Deserta,* by Wilfred Scawen Blunt, who bred the Arab mares, by Mr. Robert Bontine Cunninghame Graham, who besides being the legiti-mate King of Scotland is—alas, I must now write 'was'!—an incomparable writer of English and an unsurpassed rider of the plains, whether of Maghreb el Aqsa or the pampas itself. And as all these people had about them, too, the airs of romantic adventures and loves and gallopings, the odd bits of information that they communicated about Hudson enormously enhanced his aura of forests, romantic loves, lianas . . . and a fantastic longevity.

Conrad would dilate with enthusiasm about this *capataz* of the Revolution who had a wife as tiny as he was romantic. 'You know,' he would say, 'she's so tiny that when she stands on the floor she cannot look over the edge of the dinner table. Extraordinary!' And Mr. Garnett would add information about Mrs. Hudson's exquisite voice; about her having been the rival of Jenny Lind and of Malibran of Her Majesty's opera, and of her having wilfully refused to sing a note after Hudson married her . . . so that there was the tragedy of Rima of *Green Mansions* all over again . . . and there was the legend of the Mont Blanc.

And a day or two later you would go and spend a night or two under the thatched roof of his hide-hole on Salisbury Plain in that curious long village of thatched cottages where, on one side of the street, all the women were dark as Spaniards and beautiful and blue of eye, and on the other they were all blonde

Anglo-Saxons, buxom and high-coloured and slow.
And there he was, as legendary and as much at home
as on Carlton House Terrace and Gerrard Street,
Soho, where the imitation French restaurants swarm.
. . . There he was a gipsyish man who had been in
foreign parts, but knew the pedigree of every shepherd's dog on the Plain and the head of game that
every coppice carried and the hole of every vixen and
the way every dog fox took when at night he went
ravaging at a distance . . . for the fox never takes
poultry near his home. Not he! For fear of retribu-
tion. And you may see the fox cubs play in the
sunlight with the young rabbits from the next bur-
row. . . . Hudson had told the villagers that and
they recognized how true it was. And he knew all
about all the dead and gone folk of the Plain, and
all the living good-looking women, and he was a
healer who brought you good luck merely by looking
at you. . . .

And there that great tall man would sit by the
shepherd's table, drinking the terribly strong tea
out of the thick cups and eating the fleed-cake and
the poached rabbits. And the tiny little black-haired,
blue-eyed girls caressing their insteps with their shoe
soles and visiting his great gamekeeper's pockets for
the candies they were confident of finding there . . .
as confident as the tame squirrel of finding nuts . . .
and there were always orange flowers in an earthen-
ware mug on the table, the flower that is just a weed
in English gardens, but is cherished above all others
in the winter flower beds above the Mediterranean.

And then the great, long figure would arise, brushing the beams of the cottage ceiling with his hair,
and stroll down the broad valley. And stay for many

minutes watching the colony of rooks in the trees that still stood a hundred years after the manor-house that they had sheltered had fallen to the ground. And so to the station and back to the strangest home of all those that sheltered him.

How the townsman, town born and bred, regards this flower—the marigold [he says in *A Shepherd's Life*]—I do not know. He is in spite of all the time I have spent in his company a comparative stranger to me. . . . A pale people with hurrying feet and eager, restless minds who live apart in monstrous, crowded camps like wood ants that go not out to forage for themselves—six millions of them crowded together in one camp alone! I have lived in these colonies, years and years, never losing the sense of captivity, of exile, ever conscious of my burden, taking no interest in the doings of that innumerable multitude. . . .

His wife then—and it was at least true that in her day she had been a celebrated singer—kept a boarding-house. She was twenty years older than Hudson and did not come up to his elbow. And it was more or less true that after her marriage to him she sang very little, because her voice was leaving her. But otherwise she was very normal and quick-witted, if a little quick-tempered and not a good business woman. For all the great money she had earned in her day had gone and shortly after their marriage her boarding-house went bankrupt too. It was then that they had known days of real starvation and it is not the least romantic part of Hudson's career, the desperate and courageous efforts he made to keep them going. He was a stranger in London with nothing to earn a living by but his pen; and it is curious to think that one of the ways by which he did earn money was by ferreting out genealogical tables for Americans of English origins. Then he also did hack-work descriptions of South American birds for scientific ornithologists who had never seen a bird. And then magazines began to commission him for articles about birds; his wife inherited a fantastically gloomy house in the most sooty neighbourhood of London and a small sum of money with which she set up a boarding-house that this time did not fail. And it was touching to see how Hudson made another gentle legend for himself amongst Shetland-shawled old maids and broken-down Indian colonels. And then he was granted a pension on the King's Civil List, and then fame came to him in London and money from New York. And he and his wife lived together until she died, a little before him, at the great age of a hundred years. . . . That, too, was Romance.

I am ashamed to say that I did not see it at the time, and I disliked the atmosphere of the boarding-house so much that whenever I could I used to insist on Hudson's coming out with me to Kensington Gardens. He was not a good walker in those days in spite of the fact that he had spent the greater part of his life on his feet, watching birds. We used to pace very slowly up and down beneath the tall elms of the Broad Walk and in front of the little palace, amongst the children of the wealthy. We would watch the grey squirrels that had come from New York and that were monstrously at home in the Gardens, having bitten off the tails of all the aboriginal red squirrels. And he would talk of how the Liberator carried his whip and reviewed his troops; and of the birds and herds and great trees of the pampas, far away and long ago. And *Far Away and Long Ago* is the most self-revelatory of all his books.

I do not think that I would much like to recapture many of the atmospheres of my own past. The present days are better. But I would be glad, indeed, if once again I could walk slowly along the dingy streets that led from that Bayswater boarding-house to Paddington Station . . . slowly beside Hudson and his wife who would be going away towards English greennesses, through the most lugubrious streets the world could imagine, let alone know. And Huddie would be expressing theories as to the English rain and far below him his tiny wife would be incessantly telling him that he was going the wrong way.

Hudson had lived in that district for forty years, continuing to stay there after fortune had a little smiled on him—because it was near the great terminus of Paddington and they could slip away from there to the country without attracting attention by their singular disproportion in size. In spite of this they never could go to that exit from London without her telling him that he was going the wrong way . . . I suppose because she had lived there for nearly a century. And she would keep on and on at it, bickering like a tiny wren threatening some great beast approaching her nest in the gorse. Her great age only affected her colouration so that she seemed to recede further and further into the mists of Saint

Luke's Road until she was almost invisible. But her vivacity was unconquerable, and appropriate. It was as if, having framed that romantic giant, the force of nature could go no further, and to frame a fitting mate must compound for him that singular and elfish humming-bird.

CONRAD AND THE SEA

I<small>T IS</small>, singularly enough, *The Secret Agent* that most affects me when, ten years after the death of Joseph Conrad, I sit in New York and read his works—and the other books that are not about the lives of seamen: *The Arrow of Gold, Under Western Eyes, Nostromo,* and *Heart of Darkness.* Should this come to be the final verdict on the work of that great and romantic poet, it would singularly appease his poor ghost. For he never tired of protesting that he was not a writer about the sea; he detested the sea as a man detests a cast-off mistress, and with the hatred of a small man who has had, on freezing nights of gales, to wrestle with immense yards and dripping cordage; his passion became to live out of sight of the sea and all its memories; he never tired of repeating Christina Rossetti's last written words:

> *A little while and we shall be,*
> *Please God, where there is no more sea.*

The curious, Oriental courtiership in Conrad's disposition led him to greet the humblest of human beings with gestures of servility, with strokings of the hand, with bendings of the back, and with verbal eulogia that would have added glory to a czar on his

throne—and I have seen him, I emphasize, behave
with an identical Oriental display before an old labourer's wife; his child's nurse; myself; a peer of the
realm; Messrs. Gosse, Garnett, and Galsworthy; his
own son, aged twelve; or the deaf, grizzled, tangled-
bearded old farmer who farmed the land of the Pent;
so that, if he was a respecter of persons, he respected
all persons alike. Acting then on the conviction that
every Briton liked to think of himself as having veins
filled with Viking blood, that curious Oriental spirit
of courtiership also led him during six-elevenths of
his writing life to shower bouquets all over the sea
from Tilbury Dock to Palembang and back by way of
Sydney Heads. . . .

He had that curious half-misconception of the
English character. So that he must needs begin his
matchless *Youth* with the statement:

> This could have happened nowhere but in Eng-
> land where men and sea interpenetrate, so to
> speak—the sea entering into the life of most men
> and the men knowing something or everything
> about the sea . . .

Actually, the sea in England enters more into the
consciousness of the average Englishman than into
the consciousness of inhabitants of Illinois or Central
Russia—but not very much more. Most English boys
of my generation read, like Conrad himself, the
novels of Marryat, and from ten years of age till
twelve we all imagined ourselves captains of seventy-
fours or admirals of the fleet. But it stopped pretty
well there, and the English boy of today does not
read even *Peter Simple*. But still, flogged into it by

Conrad's carefully simulated enthusiasm, the Englishman of the second, and perhaps a little of the first, decade of this century, when he had a book of Conrad's in his hand, would puff out his chest and remember that he was a hardy Norseman, a son of Drake, a companion in arms of Lord Nelson, or the first mate of an Australian wool clipper. And, in revenge, that same Englishman exacted that Conrad should write exclusively about the sea.

It was a curious and wanton nemesis. For many years of his life almost all the English whom Conrad met were men connected with the sea. And, with his highly developed sense of nationalities, Conrad was almost superaware of the immense part that the sea has played in the history of the English race—of the Anglo-Saxon congeries of nations.

Most men enter London by way of Charing Cross or Victoria, railway stations about sixty miles away from the sea and its ships. Therefore, for them, London is the City of London. If you questioned them, and they were at all knowledgeable men, they might confess to a dim awareness that, somewhere in that city, there were some ships tucked away in a negligible corner, much as an inhabitant of Minneapolis coming to New York might agree that somewhere near the Battery seagoing craft would probably be found. . . . So either might agree that it would be appropriate to speak of the City and Port of London, or New York, as the case might be.

But Conrad first approached London from its amazing other end, going up a great, silver-grey estuary between sixty miles of docks, all with seagoing ships lying shoulder to shoulder, like fish in thick shoals. And he was confronted with grandiosities, evidences of wealth, of steadfastness, courage, enterprise, and justice, in a world where the first and last of the virtues is the quality of shipshapeness. So for Conrad that metropolis was the Port of London and, as an afterthought, he might have conceded that you might reasonably style it the Port and City of London. For some years that remained his naïve psychology.

For, when he wrote, 'This could have happened nowhere but in England,' and the rest, he was expressing what for him was the God's truth . . . of the moment. And even when he had left off from following the sea, and while he was writing *Youth* and *Heart of Darkness,* he still lived within sound of the steamer sirens and within hail of the tides—in a dreary hamlet called Stamford-le-Hope, in among the Essex mud flats, on the edge of Thames Estuary. And perhaps his finest passage of prose of those, his early and as if virgin days, is precisely the last paragraph of *Heart of Darkness*:

'We have lost the first of the ebb,' said the Director suddenly. I raised my head. The offing was barred by a black bank of clouds and the tranquil waterway, leading to the uttermost ends of the earth, flowed sombre under an overcast sky— seemed to lead into the heart of an immense darkness.

I will pause here to make some annotations. *Heart of Darkness* is a tale told *viva voce* by a ship's captain on the deck of a cruising yawl, to a Director of Companies, a Lawyer, and an Accountant, all of whom followed the sea to the extent of taking week-end cruises in the *Nellie*—the cruising yawl. They formed the society in which Conrad lived at Stamford-le-Hope while, having left the sea but living near its verge, he was still quivering with his attempt, with the aid of the Director, the Lawyer, and the Accountant, to float a diamond mine in South Africa. For Conrad had his adventures of that sort, too—adventures ending naturally in frustration. And since, while waiting for that financial flotation to mature, he floated physically during week-ends in the company of those financiers on the bosom of that tranquil waterway, he really believed that all the bankers, lawyers, and accountants of the obscure square mile of city upstream were also seamen, or so near it as made no difference. He emerged, of course, from that conviction, but the tragedy was that, by the time he came to see life more collectively and less as a matter of Conway-trained and steadfast individuals heroically fighting august northwesters, the unseeing and malignant destiny that waits on us writers set him in such circumstances as robbed him of the leisure in which *Youth* and *Heart of Darkness* could be written. For those two stories were written and re-written and filed and thought over and re-thought over and re- and re-thought over by a leisured mind of a rare literary common sense.

With his later work, it was different, since the leisure mood was gone; he thought, as it were, continually under a cloud of panic and finally in moods of despair broke the backs of his books . . . 'Broke the back' was his own phrase. By it he meant that, after months and months, or even years and years, of desperate and agonized thinking, despairingly and at the dictates of Pinker or Pawling or old Mr. Blackwood or some other cheque-withholding minister of destiny, he contrived any old end for his book and let it go at that, such a book remaining for ever after in his mind as a record of failure and of the futility of human effort. For obviously the buildings-up of such an immense fabric as the earlier pages of *Nostromo* were meant to lead to an impressive, protracted, and dwelt-upon end. Yet, actually, the book, as was the case with *Chance,* with *Under Western Eyes,* with *The Secret Agent,* and with how many more, is finished off with the quick, deft touches of a de Maupassant *conte* and the rapid invention of any efficient writer of short stories.

So that, ironically, while he was still under the spell of sea-following and the hypnotism of mariners, he did his best and, as it were, cleanest work. For I think it is to *Youth, Heart of Darkness,* and the matchless *Nigger of the Narcissus* that those epithets must be ascribed, leaving *Almayer* and *The Outpost of Progress* to be considered as his prentice work.

I will add some further notations as to the passage I have quoted from *Heart of Darkness*. It has always seemed to me—and still seems—one of the most perfect passages of prose in the language and it has for me a certain added significance from the fact that it must have been the first passage of Conrad's prose to which I ever paid minute and letter-by-letter consideration. He had come to stop with me at the Pent, and had there received the proofs of the story in one or another of its stages. And being worried over—and above all having the leisure to attend to—his closing passages, it was the last paragraph to which he first invited me to pay attention.

We must have argued over it for three whole days,

going from time to time over the beginning and the body of the story, but always at the back of the mind considering that last paragraph and returning to it to suggest one or another minute change in wording or in punctuation.

If you will take the trouble to look back to the passage as I have quoted it, you will see that it begins, 'We have lost the first of the ebb.' Actually, in the copy from which I am quoting—Doubleday, Doran's Malay edition of 1928—the last paragraph begins, 'Marlow ceased and sat apart, indistinct and silent, in the pose of a meditating Buddha. Nobody moved for a time,' and then continues with the Director's speech.

In the original version, those last two sentences stood apart, the word 'time' ending the paragraph. And we tried every possible juxtaposition of those sentences, putting 'No one moved for a time' in front of Marlow's ceasing; running that sentence up to the end of the last paragraph of speech; cutting it out altogether—because the first principle of the technique of Conrad and myself at that time was that you should never state a negative. If nobody moves, you do not have to make the statement; just as, if somebody is silent, you just do not record any speech of his, and leave it at that.

However, that negative statement got itself left in at the end, I suppose as a matter of cadence, though I remember suggesting the excision of 'for a time'— a suggestion that Conrad turned down because that would have made the statement too abrupt and dramatic. The last paragraph of a story should have the effect of what musicians call a coda—a passage meditative in tone, suited for letting the reader or hearer gently down from the tense drama of the story, in which all his senses have been shut up, into the ordinary workaday world again.

In the interest of that tranquillity, either Conrad or I suggested the use of the adjectival-participle form in the last clause of the paragraph. I can't remember which of us it was, because we changed our position morning by morning, according as the one or the other of us had got up feeling the more French. We never read anything but French in those days, but sometimes Conrad, and less often I, would have a British reaction. . . . And to make that passage classic English prose, you would have to put it:

. . . the tranquil waterway, leading to the uttermost ends of the earth, flowing sombre under an overcast sky, seemed to lead into the heart of an immense darkness.

Or, since Conrad—or, in the alternative, I—might object to the assonance of 'flowing' and 'leading':

the tranquil waterway, leading to the uttermost ends of the earth, flowed sombre under an overcast sky, seemed to lead into the heart of an immense darkness.

Which last would be the version I should today adopt, as being, with its punctuation and all, the most tranquilly classic.

But I suppose that, in the end, we both of us got up one morning feeling unbridledly and unrepentantly Gallic—and so you have only one comma and a French dash for punctuation of the whole sentence and the relatively harsh 'seemed,' instead of the tender 'seeming.'

I remember that at that time, over the proofs of this story, I succeeded in persuading Conrad that he was really an Elizabethan writing almost-blank verse, as thus:

> The peroration was magnificent . . .
> It made me tingle with enthusiasm.
> This, the unbounded power of eloquence,
> Of words, of burning, noble words. There were
> No practical hints to interrupt the magic
> Current of Phrase, unless a kindly note
> At the foot of the page . . .

and so on over pages and pages.

I would go on reading page after page of blank verse like that from the writings of that poor astonished fellow. . . . Remember that I was young and unscrupulous then. . . . And he, blinking, half-ravished because he thought blank verse something noble, and half-alarmed because Mr. Shaw had told him that blank verse was the easiest of all things to write, would sit looking like an eagle to whom someone had announced that one of his wife's eggs had produced a phoenix with all its fabulous gifts—or perhaps as if I were a conjurer who should have produced from his tall hat a colony of turtle doves. For that inspired writer with his matchless flair for the significance and life and suitability of words, as if he were a Beethoven that should never hear his own symphonies, had hardly the remotest idea of how, in English, or even in French, they sounded or were accentuated. He never, for instance, could see that in French rhymed Alexandrines the muted *e*'s counted in the beat, and if I chose to read out, 'The offing was barred by a black bank of clouds,' he would accept it as if it were one of the mightiest of Marlowe's lines, or as he would equally have accepted, 'The offing was barréd || by a black bank of clouds' . . . accepting them with that naïve astonishment and joy that was one of his greatest charms, whether as great writer or as great man. For it should never be forgotten that an artist or great man remains great only as long as he can remain naïve and astonished and can examine with a vivid curiosity the minutest, as well as the most enormous, of the workings of nature or of humanity. As soon as he becomes *renfrogné,* conscious of his importance, listless in face of phenomena, grown up . . . the comedy is finished. Let him, as it were, take his seat in the House of Peers; the Commons will be below and beyond his forces.

The sea has two disadvantages as pabulum for the writer. Seen from the shore it cuts your horizon in half. If you write about human voyages upon it, your work will inevitably be set down as boys' books. That is the final insult that humanity addresses to Captain Marryat.

For Marryat, who was Conrad's first master, wrote even less about the sea and even more about the pursuits and endeavours of men. Conrad at times—and too often, really—anthropomorphized that lugubrious element; Marryat never did. For the author of *Midshipman Easy* the sea was a necessary nuisance that occasionally slopped over into being a menace. For Conrad, anxious to be polite to Anglo-Saxon,

Viking-born, week-end-cruising financiers, the sea became—yes, too often—an immense, all-embracing human-divine Being, menacing, capricious, smiling, august, inspired with blind rages, sinking into be-sunned tranquillities. The terrific storm in *Peter Simple* is hardly less of a storm than the storm of *Typhoon*—but it is much less human-divine.

Marryat, realizing that a world of men without women is in truth a world of only a half-horizon, got his heroes' young women as often into his books as he could. Conrad, sensing the same thing, left women, for a great part of his writing career, alto-gether out of his books and supplied their place with the epicene great waters, attributing to them all the passions and pretty ways of he-male rages and feminine coquetries.

But, as he left the hated sea further and further behind him, women and non-seafarers came more and more into his books—and political intrigues and the careers of republics entered more and more largely. *Nostromo,* an immense book, the first that he evolved after he had definitely left the sea far behind, is the first of his political romances—and the one he loved best. It retained, still, some of his early quality of gusto. To give it a frame, he must needs invent a whole human cosmogony—a whole republic, with a governing machine, a constitution, intrigues, commerce, industry, graft . . . and a gallery of women from Mrs. Gould downward.

And, as he went onward, women became of more and more importance in his political romances—and it was more and more the political romance that occupied his mind. *The Secret Agent* is the romance of international communism, with Mrs. Verloc as its *dea ex machina; The Arrow of Gold* is the romance of royalist machinations, with the Rita of his first love dominating its every sentence; *Under Western Eyes* is the romance of Russian-Swiss nihilism, over which floats continuously, as mists float above a city, the serene and beautiful spirit of Miss Haldin.

But indeed, the political motive is discernible enough even in his earlier, Malay-marine excursions. *Almayer* is an exposure of Dutch exploitations of the spice islands; *The Outpost of Progress,* a cynical and dreary exposé of the darker sides of imperialism; and *Heart of Darkness,* the most impassioned unveiling of the hidden springs of human hypocrisy, greed, bloodlust—and of course heroism!—that the pages of any book have ever recorded. Conrad was, at heart, an aristo-royalist apologist; the whole Left in politics was forever temperamentally suspect for him, and, at the bottom of his heart, all his writing wistfully tended towards the restoration of the Kingdom of Poland, with its irresponsible hierarchy of reckless and hypersophistically civilized nobility. He saw in nothing else the salvation of mankind. . . . But he was a poet even before he was a Polack *pan* . . . and the blood-plus-gold-and-rubber enrichments of the Dutch in Malaysia or of a vampire so foul as Leopold II—who must have been the most ignoble financier whose actions are recorded in the pages of all the histories of all the ages—those horrors were too much for even his royalist gorge.

In any case he was a great poet and a great novelist. I imagine that few men have had much more power to see vividly the opposing sides of human characters. The faculty that made him be able to prostrate himself in unbelievable politenesses before

Messrs. Gosse, Garnett, and Galsworthy, not to mention such relatively humble persons as his child's nurse and myself, let him, at other times, perceive and express the bitterest, the almost most sadistic, contempt for those three gentlemen—and, of course, myself—though he was, as a true Polack *pan,* almost always a miracle of patience with his child's faithful attendant.

And that two-sidedness let him be as relatively fair in his treatment of his temperamental political opponents as it is reasonable to expect of mortal man. *The Secret Agent* represents the anarchist-communists of London as being a pretty measly set of imbeciles, but it represents the *agent provocateur*—whom I knew well—as even more loathsome than the hideous Azev really was and the employer of that sad scoundrel of even more imbecile, if more sophisticated, than the shadows of Krapotkin, Stepniak, Volkhovsky, Bakunin, and the rest. And he had really made efforts to get behind the revolutionary mind. I supplied him with most of the material of that sort in the book, and it was instructive in the extreme to see him react to those accounts of revolutionary activities. . . . 'His omniscient friend,' he calls me in the Preface to the book. . . . He would shudder at the mere idea of coming into mental contact with revolutionary activities and then set himself seriously to work to examine into the altruistic motives that might lie hidden in the backs of the minds of those, to him, repulsive scoundrels. But he speaks truth when, in the same Preface he says, 'There had been moments during the writing of the book when I was an extreme revolutionist'—to such an extent did he try to read himself into their frames of mind. . . .

And then to relieve the strain he would contemplate
for an hour or so the moral and mental perfections
of the Scotland Yard Chief Inspector, and of the
Assistant Commissioner, and of the Home Secretary
—in actual life, Sir William Vernon Harcourt, that
brilliant and cynical last of England's Whig politicians. He would rest his poor mind on those perfected
embodiments of the quality of shipshapeness and
then, with a sigh, return to his occupations in the
underworld. . . . The result is one of the best—and
certainly the most significant—detective stories ever
written.

For that is the astonishing conclusion to which I
have come on re-reading, twenty years later, that
astonishing book. And do not imagine that in writing
those words I am trying to belittle my dead friend.
The best technical work that is being done in the
novel today is, perforce, being put into the romances
of mystery that pour from all the world's presses.
These at least *must* be well done, must progress from
paragraph to paragraph until the final effect is got
by the last word—must, in fact, embody all that
technique that poor Conrad laboriously evolved for
their benefit. Else no one would read!

An omniscient friend of my own was the other
day accounting to me for the temporary eclipse of
this great writer in the New York which, fifteen
years ago, lay prostrate before his feet. He said that
Conrad was dead because his books lacked the spirit
of mass action; the world had passed the day when
books devoted to individuals could hold a public
attention that saw the world in terms only of mass
action.

But seeing the world in those terms is only a phase like any other phase. Temporarily, the background has usurped the position of the figures of the play. The individual will return. The king shall enjoy his own again simply because we are all kings—if only over a kingdom of our own minds.

And, even at that, my friend was still thinking of Conrad only in terms of the writer about the sea—a writer of books in which childlike individuals battle with an obtuse adversary. For the best seaman has to be eternally unsophisticated; when, like Conrad, he is a hypercivilized being, whom the illusions of youth have tricked into following the tides, he will react into the hatred that was later Conrad's.

And indeed Conrad, if he was never class-conscious in the present sense of the word, became, later in life, mass- and universe-conscious enough to serve anybody's turn—almost infinitely obsessed by

the vision of an enormous town . . . of a monstrous town, more populous than some continents and in its man-made might as if indifferent to heaven's frowns and smiles. . . . There was room enough there for any passion, variety enough for any setting, darkness enough to bury millions of lives.

It was no longer the Port but the City that then engrossed him. And so in *Nostromo* you have the whole of a vast, imagined republic, where all humanity's passions, meannesses, and failures from ideals may run riot. In *Under Western Eyes* you have all Russia forever alive in the background of a mass movement—and in that book Conrad lets his Polish hatred for the Russian Czars make him almost kind, even to revolutionaries, who in the end must give Poland her freedom. And you have *The Secret Agent,* the immense thriller with its enveloping background of a darkness enough to bury millions of lives . . . and with the eternal mother-woman dominating the whole of it.

I suppose Conrad to be indeed suffering a commercial and fashionable eclipse. I hear that his bric-a-brac and souvenirs fetch almost nothing at auctions. I rang up a dozen booksellers the other day without being able to obtain copies of his works. His very publishers told me that they could not supply me with a complete set of his books—though they subsequently succeeded in doing so.

But he will return. Every great man suffers a thirty to sixty years' eclipse after his death—or a longer one if he is immensely great. (In 1663, Samuel Pepys was still talking of *Hamlet* as 'a barbarous and antick piece.') But I think that it will be rather on account of his land books than on account of his marine tapestries that Conrad will eventually re-emerge and be accounted great. It will be rather *Nostromo* than *Lord Jim*—though *The Nigger,* the only mass romance of the sea, must always be regarded as a work of a master. For his methods as a writer were inspired by an immense common sense. It is not mere fantastic overscrupulousness that makes a man devote three days to four sentences of the end of a story. It is sheer workmanlikeness, because your last paragraph is what will leave the taste in your reader's mouth and reveal the last secret of your tale. . . . And he had his incomparable naïveté—his unrivalled and passionate curiosity as to the minutest and the most huge of human manifestations. For if you wish to be a great writer, it is not sufficient to say, *Nihil humanum a me alienum puto,* you must be able to inscribe on the forefront of all your work, 'And the dwarf said, "Something human is dearer to me than all the wealth of the Indies."' That Conrad did.

D. H. LAWRENCE

In the year when my eyes first fell on words written by Norman Douglas, G. H. Tomlinson, Wyndham Lewis, Ezra Pound, and others, amongst whom was Stephen Reynolds, who died too young and is much too forgotten—upon a day I received a letter from a young schoolteacher in Nottingham. I can still see the handwriting—as if drawn with sepia rather than written in ink, on grey-blue note-paper. It said that the writer knew a young man who wrote, as she thought, admirably but was too shy to send his work to editors. Would I care to see some of his writing?

In that way I came to read the first words of a new author:

The small locomotive engine, Number 4, came clanking, stumbling down from Selston with seven full waggons. It appeared round the corner with loud threats of speed but the colt that it startled from among the gorse which still flickered indistinctly in the raw afternoon, outdistanced it in a canter. A woman walking up the railway line to Underwood, held her basket aside and watched the footplate of the engine advancing.

I was reading in the twilight in the long eighteenth-century room that was at once the office of the *English Review* and my drawing-room. My eyes were tired; I had been reading all day so I did not go any further with the story. It was called *Odour of Chrysanthemums*. I laid it in the basket for accepted manuscripts. My secretary looked up and said:

'You've got another genius?'

I answered: "It's a big one this time,' and went upstairs to dress. . . .

It was a Trench dinner at the Pall Mall Restaurant —a Dutch Treat presided over by Herbert Trench, the poet, and Dutch Treats being then new in London, Trench dinners were real social events. You sat in groups of five at little tables and the big hall of the restaurant was quite full.

I was with Mr. H. G. Wells, Mr.. Hilaire Belloc, Mr. Maurice Baring, and Mr. G. K. Chesterton. At other tables were other celebrities. In the middle of an astounding story about the Russian court, told by Mr. Baring, who had lately returned from being first secretary or something at our embassy in St. Petersburg, Mr. Belloc's magnificent organ remarked to an innocent novelist called Kinross, who at the next table was discussing the New Testament with Ladies Londonderry and Randolph Churchill, the reigning beauties of that end of a reign:

'Our Lord?' Mr. Belloc's voice pealed among the marble columns and palms. 'What do *you* know about Our Lord? Our Lord was a Gentleman.'

To turn the discussion I remarked to Mr. Wells that I had discovered another genius, D. H. Lawrence by name; and, to carry on the good work, Mr.

Wells exclaimed—to some one at Lady London-derry's table:

'Hurray, Fordie's discovered another genius! Called D. H. Lawrence!'

Before the evening was finished I had had two publishers asking me for the first refusal of D. H. Lawrence's first novel and, by that accident, Lawrence's name was already known in London before he even knew that any of his work had been submitted to an editor. . . . The lady who had sent the story to me chooses to be known as 'E. T.' and she had not even told Lawrence that she was sending the mss.

So next morning I sent Miss E. T. a letter, a little cautious in tenor, saying that I certainly liked the work she had sent me and asking her to ask her friend to call on me when he had the opportunity. I appear to have said that I thought Lawrence had great gifts, but that a literary career depended enormously on chance, and that if Lawrence had a good job in a school he had better stick to it for the present. It was probably a stupid thing to do and I have regretted it since for I was certain that that writer had great gifts and the sooner a writer who has great gifts takes his chance at writing, the better.

Miss E. T. in her lately published little book on the youth of Lawrence[1]—and a very charming and serviceable little book it is—seems to be under the impression that she sent me as a first installment only poems by Lawrence. Actually she first asked me if I would care to see anything—and then should it be

[1] *D. H. Lawrence, a Personal Record,* by E. T., London, Jonathan Cape.

poetry or prose. And I had replied asking her to send both, so that she had sent me three poems about a schoolmaster's life . . . and *Odour of Chrysanthemums*. I only mention this because I found the poems, afterwards, to be nice enough but not immensely striking. If I had read them first I should certainly have printed them—as indeed I did; but I think the impact of Lawrence's personality would have been much less vivid. . . . Let us examine, then, the first paragraph of *Odour of Chrysanthemums*.

The very title makes an impact on the mind. You get at once the knowledge that this is not, whatever else it may turn out, either a frivolous or even a gay, springtime story. Chrysanthemums are not only flowers of the autumn: they are the autumn itself. And the presumption is that the author is observant. The majority of people do not even know that chrysanthemums have an odour. I have had it flatly denied to me that they have, just as, as a boy, I used to be mortified by being told that I was affected when I said that my favorite scent was that of primroses, for most people cannot discern that primroses have a delicate and, as if muted, scent.

Titles as a rule do not matter much. Very good authors break down when it comes to the effort of choosing a title. But one like *Odour of Chrysanthemums* is at once a challenge and an indication. The author seems to say: Take it or leave it. You know at once that you are not going to read a comic story about someone's butler's omniscience. The man who sent you this has, then, character, the courage of his convictions, a power of observation. All these presumptions flit through your mind. At once you read:

'The small locomotive engine, Number 4, came clanking, stumbling down from Selston,' and at once you know that this fellow with the power of observation is going to write of whatever he writes about from the inside. The 'Number 4' shows that. He will be the sort of fellow who knows that for the sort of people who work about engines, engines have a sort of individuality. He had to give the engine the personality of a number. . . . 'With seven full waggons.' . . . The 'seven' is good. The ordinary careless writer would say 'some small waggons.' This man knows what he wants. He sees the scene of his story exactly. He has an authoritative mind.

'It appeared round the corner with loud threats of speed.' . . . Good writing; slightly, but not *too* arresting . . . 'But the colt that it startled from among the gorse . . . outdistanced it at a canter.' Good again. This fellow does not 'state.' He doesn't say: 'It was coming slowly,' or—what would have been a little better—'at seven miles an hour.' Because even 'seven miles an hour' means nothing definite for the untrained mind. It might mean something for a trainer of pedestrian racers. The imaginative writer writes for all humanity; he does not limit his desired readers to specialists. . . . But anyone knows that an engine that makes a great deal of noise and yet cannot overtake a colt at a canter must be a ludicrously ineffective machine. We know then that this fellow knows his job.

'The gorse still flickered indistinctly in the raw afternoon.' . . . Good too, distinctly good. This is the just-sufficient observation of Nature that gives you, in a single phrase, landscape, time of day, weather, season. It is a raw afternoon in autumn in a rather accented countryside. The engine would not come round a bend if there were not some obstacle to a straight course—a watercourse, a chain of hills. Hills, probably, because gorse grows on dry, broken-up waste country. They won't also be mountains or anything spectacular or the writer would have mentioned them. It is, then, just 'country.'

Your mind does all this for you without any ratiocination on your part. You are not, I mean, purposedly sleuthing. The engine and the trucks are there, with the white smoke blowing away over hummocks of gorse. Yet there has been practically none of the tiresome thing called descriptive nature, of which the English writer is as a rule so lugubriously lavish. . . . And then the woman comes in, carrying her basket. That indicates her status in life. She does not belong to the comfortable classes. Nor, since the engine is small, with trucks on a dud line, will the story be one of the Kipling-engineering type, with gleaming rails, and gadgets, and the smell of oil warmed by the bearings, and all the other tiresomenesses.

You are, then, for as long as the story lasts, to be in one of those untidy, unfinished landscapes where locomotives wander innocuously amongst women with baskets. That is to say, you are going to learn how what we used to call 'the other half'—though we might as well have said the other ninety-nine hundredths—lives. And if you are an editor and that is what you are after, you know that you have got what you want and you can pitch the story straight away into your wicker tray with the few accepted manuscripts and go on to some other occupation. . . . Because this man knows. He knows how to open a story with a sentence of the right cadence for holding the attention. He knows how to construct a paragraph. He knows the life he is writing about in a landscape just sufficiently constructed with a casual word here and there. You can trust him for the rest.

And it is to be remembered that, in the early decades of this century, we enormously wanted authentic projections of that type of life which hitherto had gone quite unvoiced. We had had Gissing, and to a certain degree Messrs. H. G. Wells and Arnold Bennett, and still more a writer called Mark Rutherford who by now, I should imagine, is quite forgotten. But they all wrote—with more or less seriousness—of the 'lower middle' classes. The completely different race of the artisan—and it was a race as sharply divided from the ruling or even the mere white-collar classes as was the Negro from the gentry of Virginia—the completely different class of the artisan, the industrialist, and the unskilled labourer was completely unvoiced and unknown. Central Africa and its tribes were better known and the tombs of the Pharaohs more explored than our own Potteries and Black Country.

It was therefore with a certain trepidation that I awaited the visit of Lawrence. If he was really the son of a working coal-miner, how exactly was I to approach him in conversation? Might he not, for instance, call me 'Sir'—and wouldn't it cause pain and confusion to stop him doing so? For myself I have always automatically regarded every human being as my equal—and myself, by corollary, as the equal of every other human being—except of course the King and my colonel on—not off—parade. But a working man was so unfamiliar as a proposition that I really did not know how to bring it off.

Indeed, E. T. in her account of the first lunch that I ever gave Lawrence and herself, relates that Ezra Pound—who has a genius for inappropriate interpolations—asked me how I should talk to a 'working man.' And she relates how she held her breath until, after a moment's hesitation, I answered that I should speak to him exactly as I spoke to anybody else.

Before that I had had some little time to wait for Lawrence's visit. I found him disturbing enough. It happened in this way:

It would appear that he was on his holidays and, as one can well believe, holidays on the seashore from a Croydon board-school were moments too precious to be interrupted even for a visit to a first editor. Indeed, as I heard afterwards, he had talked himself into such a conviction of immediate literary success that he could not believe in the existence of a literary career at all. He had, I mean, said so often that he was going to make immediately two thousand —pounds, not dollars—a year and had so often in schemes expended that two thousand a year in palaces with footmen that, when he came to himself and found that he had not so far printed a word, a literary career seemed part of a fairy tale such as no man had ever enjoyed. And there were no doubt shynesses. Obviously you cannot approach the utterly unknown without them. Yes, certainly there were shynesses.

It must have been on a Saturday because otherwise Lawrence would not have been free to leave his school and come up from Croydon, which was a suburb but not part—as poor Lawrence was to find to his cost—of London, and it cannot have been a Sunday because we were working. And I certainly must have been in the relaxed frame of mind that comes just before the end of the week. I was, I suppose, reading a manuscript or some proofs in a chair that looked towards the room door. My secretary, Miss Thomas, who afterwards won renown as the war secretary of Mr. Lloyd George, presumably heard someone knocking at the outer door, for I was dimly aware that she got up from her desk, went out, and returned, passing me and saying, Mr. Someone or other.

I was engrossed in my manuscript or proofs. Miss Thomas, imagining that she had been followed by the individual she had found at the outer door, sat down at her desk and became engrossed in her work. And deep peace reigned. The room was L-shaped, the upright of the L being long and low, the rest forming an alcove in which was the door. . . . And suddenly, leaning against the wall beside the doorway, there was, bewilderingly . . . a fox. A fox going to make a raid on the hen-roost before him. . . .

The impression that I had at my first sight of Lawrence is so strong with me at this minute that the mere remembrance fills me with a queer embarrassment. And indeed, only yesterday, reading again —or possibly reading for the first time, for I did not remember it—Lawrence's story called *The Fox*, I really jumped when I came to his description of the fox looking over its shoulder at the farm girl. Be-

cause it was evident that Lawrence identified himself
with the russet-haired human fox who was to carry
off the as-it-were hen-girl of the story.

And that emotion of my slightly tired, relaxed eyes
and senses was not so bad as a piece of sensitized
imagination. The house itself was old and reputed full
of ghosts, lending itself to confusions of tired eyes.
. . . My partner Marwood, sitting one evening near
the front windows of the room whilst I was looking
for something in the drawer of the desk, said suddenly:

'There's a woman in lavender-coloured eighteenth-
century dress looking over your shoulder into that
drawer.' And Marwood was the most matter-of-fact,
as it were himself eighteenth-century, Yorkshire
Squire that England of those days could have produced.

And I experienced then exactly the feeling of embarrassment that I was afterwards to feel when I
looked up from my deep thoughts and saw Lawrence, leaning, as if painting, beside the doorpost.
. . . It was not so bad an impression, founded as it
was on the peculiar, as if sunshot tawny hair and
moustache of the fellow and his deepset and luminous eyes. He had not, in those days, the beard that
afterwards obscured his chin—or I think he had not.
I think that on his holiday he had let his beard grow
and, it having been lately shaved off, the lower part
of his face was rather pallid and as if invisible,
whereas his forehead and cheeks were rather high-
coloured. So that I had had only the impression of
the fox-coloured hair and moustache and the deep,
wary, sardonic glance . . . as if he might be going
to devour me—or something that I possessed.

And that was really his attitude of mind. He had come, like the fox, with his overflood of energy—his abounding vitality of passionate determination that seemed always too big for his frail body—to get something—the hypnotic two thousand a year; from somewhere. And he stood looking down on the 'fairish, fat, about forty' man—so he described me in his letter home to E. T.—sprawling at his mercy, reading a manuscript before him. And he remarked in a curiously deep, rather musical chest-voice:

'This isn't my idea, Sir, of an editor's office.'

That only added to my confusion. I had not the least idea of who this fellow was—and at the same time I had the idea from his relatively familiar address that it was someone I ought to recognize. But I was at least spared—since I did not know it was Lawrence—the real pain that his 'Sir' would have caused me had I known. For I should have hated to be given what I will call a caste Sir by anybody who could write as Lawrence could. But I was able to take it as the sort of 'Sir' that one addresses to one's hierarchically superior social equals . . . as the junior master addresses the Head, or the Major the Colonel. And that was it, for when a little later I reproached him for using that form of address, he said:

'But you are, aren't you, everybody's blessed Uncle and Headmaster?'

For the moment, not knowing how to keep up the conversation with an unknown, I launched out into a defense of my room. I pointed out the beauty of its long, low, harmonious proportions; the agreeable light that fell from windows at both ends with trees beyond one half of them; the pleasant nature of the

Chippendale chairs and bureaus that had been in my family for several generations; the portrait of myself as a child by my grandfather, and his long drawings for stained glass. And I ended up by saying:

'Young man, I never enter this room, coming from out of doors, without a feeling of thankfulness and satisfaction such as I don't feel over many things in this world.' . . . All the while asking myself when I was going to pluck up my courage to say to this supervitalized creature from a world outside my own that I could not for the life of me remember who he was.

He continued to stand there, leaning still slightly against the doorpost with his head hanging a little as if he were looking for his exact thoughts. Then he raised his sardonic eyes to mine and said:

'That's all very well. But it doesn't look like a place in which one would make money.'

I said with the sort of pained gladness that one had to put on for that sort of speech:

'Oh, we don't make money here. We spend it.'

And he answered with deep seriousness:

'That's just it. The room may be all right for your private tastes . . . which aren't mine, though that does not matter. But it isn't one to inspire confidence in creditors. Or contributors.'

That fellow was really disturbing. It wasn't that his words were either jaunty or offensive. He uttered them as if they had been not so much assertions as gropings for truth. And a little, too, as if upon reflection I might agree with his idea and perhaps change my room or neighbourhood. And he added:

'So that, as a contributor, the first impression . . .'

And he answered my immediate question with:

'You are proposing to publish a story of mine. Called *Odour of Chrysanthemums*. So I might look at the matter from the point of view of a contributor.'

That cleared the matter up, but I don't know that it made Lawrence himself seem any less disturbing. . . .

I have had indeed the same experience lately whilst I have been re-reading him for the purpose of this article. Each time that I have opened one of his books, or merely resumed reading one of his novels, I have had a feeling of disturbance—not so much as if something odd was going to happen to me but as if I myself might be going to do something eccentric. Then when I have read for a couple of minutes I go on reading with interest—in a little the spirit of a boy beginning a new adventure story. . . . I will return to that side of the matter later.

Enthusiastic supporters of the more esoteric Lawrence will say that my perturbation is caused by my coming in contact with his as-it-were dryad nature. As if it were the sort of disturbing emotion caused in manufacturers or bankers by seeing, in a deep woodland, the God Pan—or Priapus—peeping round beside the trunk of an ancient oak. I daresay that may be something like it. At any rate if the God Pan did look at one round a trunk one might well feel as one felt when the something that was not merely eyesight peeped out at you from behind Lawrence's eyes.

For that was really what the sensation was like —as if something that was inside—inhabiting— Lawrence had the job of looking after him. It popped up, took a look at you through his pupils and, if it was satisfied, sank down and let you go on talking.

. . . Yes, it was really like that: as if, perhaps, a mother beast was looking after its young. For all I know it may have been that. Lawrence was extraordinarily—even to his detriment, I imagine—subservient to his mother, who would seem to have been a commonplace woman except for a jealousy that almost agonizedly transcended ordinary jealousies. I did not meet her but gathered as much from Lawrence's conversation about her. He talked about her and her opinions in a way that is unusual in young men out to make their fortunes.

On the other hand I did meet his father, from whom Lawrence seemed rather to shrink. He shrank from him, that is to say, in an official sort of way as if he had for so long been told to consider his father a disreputable person that he took it for granted that I or anyone else who came in contact with him might consider that Lawrence himself lost caste by having originated from any one of the sort. I think he was wrong. His father seemed by no means commonplace. He certainly drank . . . or no, he got drunk at times. But he exercised a good deal of influence over his mates in the mine and he was very ingenious with tools in his hands . . . and happy with them. That is in itself evidence of a creative gift such as in the next generation may become anything. It was probably not for nothing that the father of Jesus was a carpenter.

The darkest passage of his career and one that was as much as possible concealed was the fact that early in life he had conducted a dancing floor or saloon—or possibly a dancing floor in a saloon. Lawrence in mentioning the matter glanced at it so sideways that I had not the heart to try to find out from him what sort of an establishment it was. For what sort of dancing would there be in a modern, rather mushroom mining suburb of an old agricultural city of the Midlands in England? . . . I imagined it must have been something rather reckless and abandoned, resembling what took place in Poker Flat, Nevada.

In any case that early occupation of the father would seem to have been unknown to the mother at the time of the marriage and to have caused her infinite pain when at last the dark secret leaked out . . . pain that caused Lawrence, looking as it were from beside his mother's apron, to conceive almost a horror of his father . . . as if his father had struck her. For in the household the mother was regarded as a 'lady.' She had been the daughter of some sort of, I think impoverished, shopkeeper. . . . It astonished me at the time that it should be considered —and still more that it should be considered by Lawrence himself—that a shopkeeper was the superior of a miner, for it seemed to me that anyone who could do things with his hands was a producer and so akin to the artist, whereas the shopkeeper was relatively effeminate and parasitic. But at any rate in those days Lawrence considered himself rather shudderingly as the product of a martyred lady-saint and a savage lower-class father. As far as it was given to him to do so, he oriented his thoughts and his character along the lines that would be approved by his mother and those in similar circumstances. And he seemed to have, in consequence, an interest and an appetite in 'things' such as few young artists can have had. I remember his expressing a satisfaction that seemed to me to be incomprehensible over the fact that his mother's house—which seemed to me to be

like any other miner's cottage—had something—a
double passage or an alcove on the stairs, I could
not quite understand what, that none of the other
miners' cottages had. But it ceased to seem incomprehensible when I understood that that satisfaction
was not merely because that special appendage raised
him above the other miners' sons; it was that it was,
as it were, a proper homage that destiny paid to his
suffering, exiled-patrician mother. At any rate it had
given his mother infinite satisfaction as marking her
off from the other miners' wives. The house was at
the end of a row of cottages, giving on fields and,
what was an almost greater cause for satisfaction to
the children, its patch of garden was larger and more
private than that of any of the other cottages. And
they paid sixpence a week more rent for it. There
were always pansies and Michaelmas daisies and
wallflowers in the garden, according to the season.

The importance of these things in the childhood
of a man who afterwards became himself so important and so tortured, should not be underestimated.

The perturbation that his sudden appearance
caused me on that particular day lasted only a moment or two—and a similar perturbation and dying
down of the emotion attended my every meeting with
Lawrence, even if I met him twice on the same day
at fairly short intervals. For the young man that
succeeded to the fox appeared to be a rather keen,
North Country or Midland, normal, puritanish busi-
nessman. Of that type! . . . I mean that always, at
first, for a second or two, he seemed like the reckless
robber of henroosts with gleaming eyes and a mouth
watering for adventure and then, with the suddenness

of a switched-off light, he became the investigator
into the bases of the normal that he essentially was.

He told me later that what had passed through his
mind as he had stood looking down on me was that
there was nothing in particular to be shy about in
the placid-looking elderly gentleman with his effi-
cient-looking secretary. He had naturally been shy
enough coming up in the Croydon train. Yet they
sat there in a very unexciting, old-fashioned sort of
a room. . . . He had not yet come to regard Chippendale as 'antique.' . . . And there really had run
through his mind the idea that he might be able to
make something out of them.

For it must be remembered that, all his life
through, he considered that he had a 'mission.' As
to its exact nature in those early days he was more
than a little vague and I do not know that, in later
years, he had any settled program for his missionings.
But missionaries of a non-conformist revival type had
been normal if notable figures of the landscape of his
boyhood, and the idea of a man moving among and
affecting the mentalities of crowds was a part of his
mental paraphernalia. Moreover, it was in the tradition of the English standard writer. And he was tremendously up in the traditions of the standard writers. I have never known any young man of his age
who was so well read in all the dullnesses that spread
between Milton and George Eliot. In himself alone
he was the justification of the Education Act, the
passing of which, a decade or so before, had split all
England. He was, that is to say, the miner's son with
nothing but pennies to spend on his education . . .
and he moved amongst the high things of culture
with a tranquil assurance that no one trained like

myself in the famous middle-class schools of the country ever either exhibited or desired.

Well, I told him what he had done in writing *Odour of Chrysanthemums* and he listened without much emotion to what would have sounded like extravagant praise to almost anyone else. And I more or less predicted to him what he would do. Over that he was a little more restive. I suppose that, intent on exploring the lives of artisans, I was inclined to prescribe to him a course of workingman novels, the idea of which he found oppressive. He wanted to try his hand at something more romantic and with more polished marble and gold and titled people among its furnishings.

I obviously could not blame him for that. A young man brought up in his circumstances would be less than human if he was not determined to have for himself two thousand a year and footmen and the intimacy of lords and, particularly, ladies. And you cannot make good novelists out of young men who are less than human. They will not understand the mainsprings of humanity.

On the other hand, Lawrence had inherited or imbibed from his mother a liberal share of puritanism and those two forces fought an unceasing battle in him. His father no doubt fighting his mother. For, for all I know, two beings may have looked out of Lawrence's eyes—a father-spirit who hoped you would put a little devil into him and a mother-spirit that dreaded that you would lead him outside the chapel-walks and persuade him not to wear flannel next his skin. It was no doubt something like that. . . . But at that day, in my room, it was, I imagine, the mother-spirit that prevailed within him.

He wasn't at any rate going to take any material chances without weighing them very carefully. There he was in his teacher's job at Croydon, secure, making what he considered to be remarkably good money. Forty shillings a week. More than his father had ever earned and he was only twenty-one. And with sufficient hours of freedom during which he could write. He had to perform his mission: he had to write. So that there he was, to use a later phrase of his own, inside the cage. He would have to think twice before anyone persuaded him to get out.

For before that first interview had ended I had begun lightly to persuade him to get out. It was quite obvious to me that here was a young fellow who ought to write, who, indeed would write, so the sooner he got to it the better. One would have to find some way for him. I was never one to be afraid of taking on responsibilities.

He shied a bit at that, plunging away, as if he had been a startled colt, from a too attractive novelty. It wasn't that the two thousand a year and establishment and titled company were not as real to him as his life in the cage. He felt himself as sure of the one as of the other. He was going to have them when the time came as certainly as he was going to have his next week's and all the ensuing weeks' salary from the Croydon School Board. He was quite tranquil about *that*.

And, before he had seen my office, he had made up his mind that I was the person who was to effect that translation. But the office had given him a bad shock. It hadn't seemed the proper frame for a person with influence, wealth, and the acquaintance of the titled. His own acquaintance with the world had been very limited and he imagined an Office, to be reassuring, must resemble the office of the colliery company for which his father worked—the handsomest, brick and shining granite building in the valley, with counters and swing-doors and brass and the clink of coins unceasing on the air.

So it had occurred to him that, even if he did take command of that ship of mine, there might not be behind it enough money to make the transition from his safe schoolmastership very advisable. . . . That was Lawrence—a continual fight between the jovial pirate father and the cautious, disapproving, Nonconformist, pale mother, going on all the while in the very current of his thought. And the struggle went on within him to the end of his life, though towards the end he was inclined to give his father altogether best. That alone should be sufficient to give the lie to those lugubrious, Freudian-psychoanalytic souls who try to explain the Lawrence riddle by asserting that he was obsessed by a mother-complex. He wasn't. He was a little boy who had been sickly and who had had of necessity to depend on his mother for all the comfort and good things of his life whilst he was told that his father—who got drunk—by that deprived him of the new pair of shoes that he wanted for Sundays. . . . If you have, in addition to that, complexes of an esoteric aspect, you had better explain him along the lines of Amen-Ra, the Egyptian All-Father-Mother, who united in himself the male and the female properties so that he was at once his own father and mother and his own wife . . . and husband. And his own children who were the other hawk, bull, and cat deities of Egypt. And it is better to regard Lawrence's own preoccupation with sex and its manifestations with the same composure. As a mother-suppressed child in a Non-conformist household he was shut off from the contemplation of all natural processes to such an extent that, when he grew to have control of himself, he was full of perfectly natural curiosities and, since he happened to be a writer, it was in the writing of speculations that he took his fling. If he had been a banker or a manufacturer he would have found other derivatives. As a child I was inhibited from ham and cream by a careful mother who considered them too expensive. So, when I came to man's estate, I indulged in orgies of ham and cream until for years I could not bear the sight of them. Now again I rather like cream but can do without ham unless it is the very best Virginian, such as one comes across only once every four years or so. Lawrence had the misfortune to become conscious of life in London and in a class in London that by a sort of inverted puritanism insisted that a sort of nebulous glooming about sex was a moral duty and a sort of heroism. That did not help him much. What he would have been if those influences had not bulked so largely on the horizon of his youth it is difficult to say. And it does not very much matter. He was good enough as he was. He had a white flame of passion for truth.

I cannot say that I liked Lawrence much. He remained too disturbing even when I got to know him well. He had so much need of moral support to take the place of his mother's influence that he kept one —every one who at all came into contact with him —in a constant state of solicitude. He claimed moral support imperiously—and physical care too. I don't

mean that he whined. He just ordered you to consider that there he was in Croydon subject to the drag
of the minds of the school-children for hours of
every day in a fetid atmosphere. . . . And that is
the great curse and plague of the schoolmaster's life
. . . the continuous drag of the minds of the pupils
pulling you down . . . and then with the tired mind
to write masterpieces in the odd moments of silence.

And then came the scourge! He was pronounced
tubercular. I don't know how we knew that he had
been so pronounced. I don't think he ever mentioned
it to me; perhaps he did not to anyone. It was a subject that he was always shy of mentioning. But Galsworthy and Masterman and even the solid, stolid
Marwood—and of course several ladies—went about
for some time with worried faces because Lawrence
was writing masterpieces and teaching in a fetid
atmosphere. He had to be got out of it. He ought to
be allowed to resign his job and be given a pension
so that he could go on writing his masterpieces.
That was where Masterman, who was a Minister of
the Crown and supposed to be scheduled as the next
Liberal Prime Minister, came in. He was to use his
influence on the educational authorities to see that
Lawrence got a pension as having contracted tuber-
culosis in the service.

Alas, alas. Croydon was not within the Administra-
tive County of London. The London County
Council gave pensions to invalided schoolteachers.
But the Kent County Council did not. Not even the
Crown could coerce a county into doing what it did
not want to do. . . . In the end, I think he was
allotted a small lump sum. But one had had a good
deal of anxiety.

There had been no difficulty in finding a publisher for him. The odd, accidental, as if *avant la lettre* notoriety that he had gained at the Trench dinner made several publishers be anxious to compete for his suffrages. They even paid him good little sums for his first books. He didn't have then, if ever, any very serious difficulties. And the London of those days was a kind place to people who were reputed to be writing masterpieces. There were kind, very rich people who asked nothing better than to be nice to young men of gifts. So that in a very short time Lawrence was writing home exultantly that he had dined with two Royal Academicians, several *Times* reviewers, Cabinet Ministers, and Ladies of Title, galore, galore. I don't mean that the exultation was snobbish delight at mingling with the Great. No, it was delight at seeing himself by so far on the road . . . towards the two thousand a year. . . .

In the course of a good many Saturday afternoon or Sunday walks in the Gardens or Park, there came home to me a new side of Lawrence that was not father-mother derived—that was pure D. H. It was his passionate—as it were an almost super-sex-passionate—delight in the opening of flowers and leaves. He would see in the blackish grass of Kensington Gardens a disreputable, bedraggled specimen of a poor relation of the dandelion whose name I have forgotten. . . . Oh, yes, the coltsfoot—the most undistinguished of yellow ornaments of waste places and coal dumps. . . . And immediately Lawrence, who had been an earnest *jeune homme pauvre* with a fox-coloured poll, drawing wisdom from a distinguished, rather portly Editor, would become a half-mad, woodland creature, darting on that poor thing come there by accident, kneeling before it, feeling with his delicate, too white and beautiful fingers, the poor texture of its petals. And describing how, the harbinger of spring, it covered with its sheets of gold the slag-heaps and dumps of his native countryside. . . . With a really burning language!

And it was not the starved rapture of the Cockney poets to whom flowers were mysteries. He knew the name and the habits and the growths of every flower of the countrysides and of stoats and weasels and foxes and thrushes. Because of course Nottingham, for all its mining suburbs, was really in and of the country, and a great part of the time—the parts of his time when he had really lived—had been spent on the farms that surrounded his home. . . . That, of course, you can gather from his books. . . .

Above all from his books. The nature passages of the ordinary English novelists are intolerable—the Dartmoors and Exmoors and Woodlands and the bearded tits and comfreys and the rest. (I am not talking of naturalists.) But the nature passages of Lawrence run like fire through his books and are exciting—because of the life that comes into his writing even at moments when he is becoming rather tiresomely introspective. So that at times when you read him you have the sense that there really was to him a side that was supernatural . . . in tune with deep woodlands, which are queer places. I rather dislike writing just that because it sounds like the fashionable writing about Lawrence which gloomily identifies him with Pan—or Priapus or Pisces or phalluses—which you don't find in Nottinghamshire woodlands. . . .

Well. . . . He brought me his manuscripts—those of *The White Peacock* and *Sons and Lovers*. And he demanded, imperiously, immensely long sittings over them . . . insupportably long ones. And when I suggested breathing spaces for walks in the Park he would say that that wasn't what he had sacrificed his Croydon Saturday or Sunday for. And he held my nose down over this passage or that passage and ordered me to say *why* I suggested this emendation or that. And sometimes he would accept them and sometimes he wouldn't . . . but always with a good deal of natural sense and without *parti pris*. I mean that he did not stick obstinately to a form of words because it was his form of words, but he required to be convinced before he would make any alteration. He had learned a great deal from reading other writers—mostly French—but he had a natural sense of form that was very refreshing to come across—and that was perhaps his most singular characteristic. His father was obviously not a dancing teacher and minor craftsman for nothing.

And then one day he brought me half the ms. of *The Trespassers*—and that was the end. It was a *Trespassers* much—oh, but much!—more phallic than is the book as it stands and much more moral in the inverted-puritanic sense. That last was inevitable in that day, and Lawrence had come under the subterranean-fashionable influences that made for Free Love as a social and moral arcanum. So that the whole effect was the rather dreary one of a schoolboy larking among placket holes, dialoguing with a Wesleyan minister who has been converted to Ibsen. It gave the effect that if Lawrence had not met that sort of religion he might have been another . . . oh,

say, Congreve. As it was it had the making of a
thoroughly bad hybrid book and I told him so.

I never saw him again . . . to talk to. But he did,
in successive re-writings, change the book a good
deal . . . at least I suppose there were successive
re-writings. . . . And I suppose I hurt his feelings
a good deal. Anyhow I am glad I did not have to go
through his manuscripts any more. I don't—and I
didn't then—think that my influence was any good
to him. His gift for form, in his sort of long book,
was such that I could suggest very little to him and
the rest of his gift was outside my reach. And, as I
have said, he is quite good enough as he is—rich and
coloured and startling like a medieval manuscript.

The last time I saw him was during the War when,
of course, he was a pro-German and was supposed
to be a good deal persecuted. That is to say, Authority—in the shape of the Minister of Information—
was afraid that he was being persecuted and I was
sent down to see what could be done for him, Mrs.
Wells—who was as worried as anyone else about
him—kindly driving me the thirty or forty miles
down into Sussex where Lawrence had been lent the
house of Mrs. Meynell, the poetess. . . . But I was
not talking without the book when I said that I never
saw him again to talk to. The Gods saw otherwise.
For the moment we arrived at that pleasant place,
Mrs. Wells, who was very small, and Mrs. Lawrence,
who resembled the Germania above the Rhine at
Rüdesheim—fell into a discussion as to the merits
of the Belgians. And, as Mrs. Lawrence saw fit to
address, on the side, unfavourable remarks to the
uniform I was wearing, I thought it was better—
because I *was* there to make a report to Authority—

to retire to an outhouse and await the close of the discussion. So that the last image I have of Lawrence is his standing there, a little impotent, his hands hanging at his side, as if he were present at a dog fight in the beautiful, white-walled, shady, aesthetic room of Mrs. Meynell. He was smiling slightly, his head slightly bent. But his *panache,* his plume of hair with the sunlight always in it—and his red beard—were as disturbingly bright as ever.

THOMAS HARDY

THE first words of Thomas Hardy's that I ever read I read editorially and they were the title of a poem—'A Sunday Morning Tragedy.' They were in his clear, large handwriting that seemed like the cuttings of a chisel on hard stone. That I should have read him only so late—in 1907 or so—was because my youth was crushed between the upper and nether millstones of Somerset House and the vast Ionic building in Great Russell Street. As a child, that is to say, I was carefully shielded from the companionship of Common Little Boys. In consequence, such consciousness of the Higher Things as has been vouchsafed me awakened in the contemptuous companionship of the children of Doctor Garnett of the British Museum and the still more contemptuous society of the still younger Rossettis, whose father, my uncle by marriage, was another prop of the Empire in that he was Secretary to Her Majesty's Inland Revenue—pronounced Revennue. The one gang of my persecutors represented orthodox Anglicanism and Virtue; the other stood militantly for Established Rationalism, which at the time was a menacing affair. The result was that I never read Hardy, whom I understood to represent reasoned revolt against Established Anglicanism. I wanted a plague on both those houses. . . . Nevertheless I was extremely aware of a sort of astral presence of Thomas Hardy, as if he were planing, eagle-like in the empyrean, immensely afar from the sphere of our quarrels.

That was in the days before *Tess* whilst Mr. Hardy had an aura of being just as 'advanced' as the Quite Nice could allow themselves to go. It was a little daring that to a Church of England Ruling Class the English peasant should be represented as having a psychology at all. But once you had got over that there were considered to be lots of buttercups and chaffinches and country dances and hawfinches and bottle-tits, and little tits in his pages that could not shock the most delicate mind. . . . I suppose I wanted my mind to be shocked.

To normal, healthy youth, then, Mr. Hardy was already a Classic—and a Classic is a thing you do not read. I am not talking of *the* Classics. A good many of us would still read with enthusiasm both the *Bacchae* and the *Satyrikon* and most of what lay between. But when we read for entertainment we read Artemus Ward's *Among the Mormons* or *Sam Slick* or *Soldiers Three* or *Life on the Mississippi* . . . not *The Mayor of Casterbridge* . . . not even *Tess* when she came. We were aware that Deans and Archdeacons condemned that work as being immoral; but the Distinguished Unorthodox, the followers of Darwin, Huxley, and Ingersoll, proclaimed that to the pure it would prove a miracle of Uplift. That was enough for us. If we wanted smut we knew where to get it and it would have no uplift. So that Hardy as a writer became even more aloof and soli-

tary-soaring . . . a part, as it were, of Her Majesty's
Opposition and thus unreadable.

Besides, we could not but be aware that the book
concerned itself with the hanging of a nice young
woman. I don't know that I didn't even glance at the
last pages and read the episode of the black flag going
up over Salisbury Gaol. And I did not think—as I
don't now, just after reading the book for the first
time—that one ought to be harrowed by having to
read of nice young women being hanged.

At the same time I was keenly aware of a Mr.
Hardy who was a kind, small man, with a thin beard,
in the background of London tea parties . . . and
in the background of my mind. . . . I remember
very distinctly the tea party at which I was introduced to him by Mrs. Lynn Lynton with her para-
lyzing, pebble-blue eyes, behind gleaming spectacles.
Mrs. Lynn Lynton, also a novelist, was a Bad
Woman, my dear. One of the Shrieking Sisterhood!
And I could never have her glance bent on me from
behind those glasses without being terrified at the
fear that she might shriek . . . or be Bad. I think
it was Rhoda Broughton who first scandalized London by giving her heroine a Latchkey. But Mrs. Lynn
Lynton had done something as unspeakably wicked.
. . . And I was a terribly proper young man.

So, out of a sort of cloud of almost infantile
paralysis—I must have been eighteen to the day—I
found myself telling a very very kind, small, ageless,
soft-voiced gentleman with a beard, the name of my
first book, which had been published a week before.
And he put his head on one side and uttered, as if he
were listening to himself, the syllables: 'Ow . . .
Ow . . .'

I was petrified with horror . . . not because I thought he had gone mad or was being rude to me, but because he seemed to doom my book to irremediable failure. . . .

I do not believe I have ever mentioned the name of one of my own books in my own print . . . at least I hope I have been too much of a little gentleman ever to have done so. But I do not see how I can here avoid mentioning that my first book was called *The Brown Owl* and that it was only a fairy tale. . . . I will add that the publisher—for whom Mr. Edward Garnett was literary adviser—paid me ten pounds for it and that it sold many thousands more copies than any other book I ever wrote . . . and keeps on selling to this day.

And on that day I had not got over the queer feeling of having had a book published. . . . I hadn't wanted to have a book published. I hadn't tried to get it published. My grandfather had, as it were, ordered Mr. Garnett to get it published. . . . I can to this day hear my grandfather's voice saying to Mr. Garnett, who was sitting to him on a model's throne:

'Fordie has written a book, too. . . . Go and get your book, Fordie!' . . . and the manuscript at the end of Mr. Garnett's very thin wrist disappearing into his capacious pocket. . . . And my mother let me have ten shillings of the money paid by Mr. Garnett's employer. . . . And that had been all I had got out of authorship. . . . So that I thought authorship was on the whole a mug's game and concealed as well as I could from my young associates the fact that I was an Author. I should have told you that that was my attitude and should have believed

it. My ambition in those days was to be an Army
Officer!

And then suddenly, in Mrs. Lynn Lynton's dim,
wicked drawing-room, in face of this kind, bearded
gentleman, I was filled with consternation and grief.
Because it was plain that he considered that the
vowel sounds of the title of my book were ugly and
that, I supposed, would mean that the book could
not succeed. So I made the discovery that I—but
tremendously!—wished that the book should succeed
. . . even though I knew that if the book should
succeed it would for ever damn my chances as one
of Her Majesty's officers. . . .

And I could feel Mr. Hardy feeling the consternation and grief that had come up in me, because he
suddenly said in a voice that was certainly meant
to be consolatory:

'But of course you meant to be onomatopoeic.
Ow—ow—representing the lamenting voices of owls.
. . . Like the repeated double O's of the opening of
the Second Book of *The Aeneid* . . .'

And he repeated:

'COnticuer' Omnes intentiqu' Ora tenebant
Inde tOrO pater Aeneas sic Orsus ab altO'—

making me really hear the Oh . . . Oh's of those
lamenting lines. . . .

. . . Years and years afterwards, when I was
walking with him over the links at Aldeburgh, I re-
minded him that he had quoted those onomatopoe-
isms to me and he would not believe that he had ever
thought anything of the sort. Then he said:

'Oh, yes, of course. . . . And isn't it true? Because if you go on to the third line you get: "Infandum, Regina, iubes renOvare dOlOrem . . ." And then, "MyrmidOnum, DOlOpumv" aut duri miles. Ulixi . . .'

. . . But, on that distant day in Mrs. Lynton's drawing-room, I was struck as dumb as a stuck pig. I could not get out a word whilst he went on talking cheerfully. He told me some anecdotes of the brown owl and then remarked that it might perhaps have been better if, supposing I had wanted to represent in my title the cry of the brown owl, instead of two 'ow' sounds I could have found two 'oo's.' . . . And he reflected and tried over the sound of 'the brooding coots' and 'the muted lutes.' . . .

And then he said, as if miraculously to my easement:

'But of course you're right. . . . One shouldn't talk of one's books at tea parties. . . . Drop in at Max Gate when you are passing and we'll talk about it all in peace . . .'

Marvellously kind . . . and leaving me still with a new emotional qualm of horror. . . . Yes, I was horrified . . . because I had let that kind gentleman go away thinking that my book was about birds . . . whereas it was about Princesses and Princes and magicians and such twaddle. . . . I had written it to amuse my sister Juliet. . . . So I ran home and wrote him a long letter telling him that the book was not about birds and begging his pardon in several distinct ways. . . .

Then a storm burst on the British Museum. The young Garnetts went about with appalled, amused, incredulous, or delighted expressions, according as the particular young Garnett was a practicing Angli-

can, an Agnostic, or a Nihilist. . . . It began to be
whispered by them that Mrs. Hardy, a Dean's daughter, had taken a step. . . . She had been *agonized*
. . . she hadn't been able to *stand* it. . . . The reception of *Tess* had been too *horrible* . . . for a
Dean's daughter. . . . All the Deans in Christendom
had been driven to consternation about *Tess*. They
had all arisen and menaced Max Gate with their
croziers. (I know that Deans do not wear croziers.
But that was the effect the young Garnetts had produced.)

It came out at last. . . . Mrs. Hardy had been
calling on Doctor Garnett as the Dean of Letters of
the British Isles and Museum to beg, implore, command, threaten, anathematize her husband until he
should be persuaded or coerced into burning the
manuscript of his new novel—which was *Jude*. She
had written letters; she had called. She had wept; like
Niobe she had let down her blonde hair. . . . The
Agnostic and Nihilist young Garnetts rejoiced, the
Anglicans were distraught. Doctor Garnett had obdu-
rately refused. . . . I don't believe I cared one way
or the other. I didn't like the Church of England.
On the other hand I didn't want any lady or a multitude of Deans to be distressed. . . .

A long time after—six months, I dare say—I had
my answer from Mr. Hardy. It seemed to be part of
his immense kindness that, though he should have so
long delayed the answer, nevertheless he should have
answered. The tendency of ordinary men, if they
have not answered a letter for a long time, is to tear
it up and throw it into the waste-paper basket. I
imagined him to have waited until the tremendous
stir and racket over *Jude the Obscure* should have

died away, but never to have put out of his mind altogether the letters that his kindness told him he ought eventually to write.

Mr. Hardy told me again to drop in on him any time I might be in the neighbourhood of Dorchester. He told me not to be ashamed of writing fairy tales. Some of the greatest literature in the world was enshrined in that form. When I came to Dorchester he would perhaps be able to give me pointers out of his store of Wessex folklore. So I staged a walking-tour that should take me by Weymouth and Wooler and the Lyme Regis of Jane Austen and Charmouth . . . and of course Dorchester, for I could not bring myself to take the straight train down to that city. I had to obey his orders and 'drop in' casually whilst strolling about that country of chalk downs and the sea.

Alas, when I got to Max Gate, Mr. Hardy was away for the day. He had gone, I think, to witness a parade of the militia at Weymouth which I had just left. So, instead of listening to Mr. Hardy's Wessex folklore, I listened nervously whilst Mrs. Hardy in her Junonian blondeness of a Dean's daughter read me her own poems over a perfectly appointed tea-table in a room without roses peeping in at the windows but properly bechintzed.

I don't know whether it was really a militia parade that he had gone to Weymouth to witness any more than Mrs. Hardy was really a Dean's daughter. That was merely the Garnettian slant on the Hardy household. Those lively young people, whose father was really very intimate with the novelist, had projected such an image of that household that I had gone there expecting to find in a low inner room of a long white farmhouse with monthly roses peeping in at the window, the kind elderly gentleman who had held his head on one side and said: 'Ow . . . ow.' . . . And in another room the Dean's daughter would be burning the manuscript of *Jude the Obscure*.

It was all naturally nothing of the sort. Max Gate was not an old, long, thatched farmhouse; it was quite new, of brick, with, as it were, high shoulders. Not a single rose grew on it at that date. And the Dean's daughter was not a dean's daughter but an Archdeacon's Niece . . . the Archdeacon of London's niece. And she was not burning *Jude the Obscure*, but read me her own innocuous poems. And the kind bearded gentleman whose beardedness made him resemble any one of the elder statesmen of the day—Sir Charles Dilke, or Lord Salisbury, or the Prince of Wales of those days, or Mr. Henry James . . . that kind bearded gentleman was not there. . . .

And immediately on hearing that he was out, my mind had jumped to the conclusion that he was witnessing a review of the militia . . . I suppose because I knew that one of his stories was called *The Trumpet Major*. . . .

And then nothing more for years. *Jude the Obscure* came out amidst a terrific pother. But the pother took place in circles remote from my own . . . circles where they still fought bloodily about the Real Presence, the Virgin Birth, or whether the human race had in the beginning been blessed with prehensile tails . . . none of which seemed to be any affair of mine. . . . And the Literary Great of the country sat about each on their little hill . . . Mr. Meredith at Box Hill, Mr. Kipling at Burwash, Mr. Hardy at Max Gate, and the William Blacks and James Payns and Marion Crawfords and Lord Tennysons each on his little monticule. . . . Official Literature in short drowsed on on its profitable way and we, *les jeunes*, had other fish to fry.

For myself, I could not believe that that kind bearded gentleman could have written anything that need really have brought the blush to the cheek of the purest virgin in her white chamber. That I knew to be the real test of the Official Literature of the day. There must be some mistake. And if I could have convinced myself that *Jude the Obscure* was really terrible I should have read it. Once or twice I nearly did. But the impulse passed and with it Mr. Hardy himself passed regretfully from my mind . . . regretfully, because my one contact with him had left me with the impression of his great, benevolent, slightly muted charm. . . .

Then I heard that he had given up novel-writing for good . . . because of the pother over *Jude the Obscure*, and was going to take to poetry. I remember thinking that he might do something good, for in those days I held—and I don't know that I don't still hold—that the British novelist would almost invariably be better employed writing verse. The climate, the unmanageable language, the untidy minds, the dislike of definiteness, all seemed to make it desirable that they should employ the easier, the less scientific method. . . . Mr. Meredith was certainly a better poet than novelist; Thackeray might well have been; or Dickens; or Mr. Blackmore, author of *Lorna Doone*. . . . So it might very well be with Mr. Hardy. In my bones I felt him writing very English, fantastic, a little harsh, woodland idylls . . . a cross, perhaps, between Donne and Tibullus . . . so in my

mind I wished him well and didn't see how his wife
and the Archdeacons could get at him any more.

And then one day there burst on me, sitting on
the terrace of my cottage that overlooked the Rom-
ney Marsh and the Channel and the coast of France,
beneath the immense pale blue sky flecked with little
pink, dolphin-shaped clouds . . . there burst in, his
features white and rigid with fury, that Tory Yorkshire Squire, Arthur Marwood—usually pink-and-
white faced, stolid, expressionless, bulky—like a meal
sack. His voice shook as he held out a paper—I never
knew what it was—and exclaimed:

'The *Cornhill* has refused to print Thomas Hardy's
last poem!' And as a corollary: 'We must start that
Review at once to print it.'

The incident introduced me immediately and forcibly to Thomas Hardy as a poet. And I am glad the
introduction took that form . . . that, I mean, the
first words of Hardy to which I paid any serious
attention should have been in his lovely, rugged manuscript and should have been a poem called *A Sunday
Morning Tragedy*. It gave me at once if not the
measure of the very great man that England, in
Hardy, had produced, then the very strong sense of
what his exact excellence really was.

Till then I had felt strongly enough his personality
and the sense that he existed—gentle, modest, kind,
unassuming . . . extremely sensitive and easy to
hurt, even. He had seemed, for me, till that moment,
to float as I have said like a serene eagle, in heights
not meant for me and mine. . . . Very high, in a
blue heaven, on a Sunday morning, with, miles beneath, the scent of Russian leather hymn books and

gloves, of the beef roasting for dinner and cauliflower a-boil, and the rustle of starched petticoats running downstairs so as to be in time to walk very slowly to church, and the bells pealing from the steeples . . . all over the country of my birth . . . that perpetual irruption into the hodden Victorian week of a gilt-framed half-day when what spirituality there was—and all its adiposities of comfort—manifested themselves at their fullest and most tranquil all over the broad counties and the rolling shires.

It had always seemed to me, in short, that such a civilization—if it could be called a civilization—so interrupted, could not possibly produce a Great Man since it had so little to express that its expression could not possibly lead to greatness. . . . But there, in the enraged, pale face and shaking voice of my Yorkshire Tory friend, I had at once at least the forewarning that I was going to come on Greatness. A Yorkshire Tory of his intensity had to be continually expressing contempt for the stupidities of his Party over the innumerable small matters with which Parties occupy themselves. But this white flame of passion could only have been induced by a manifestation so stupid that it must be of the type that causes disaster not only to Parties but to Countries themselves.

And that was what it really was. . . . Marwood was not the man to pay any more lip service than George II to 'bainting and boetry,' but he had vision sufficient to see that a Toryism that permitted its principal Organ to refuse publication to its chief Brain was a Toryism that must soon die . . . and with it the spirit that had given greatness to the nation. It was about the end of what Toryism could

allow itself. . . . So there *must* be a Tory organ that
could publish Hardy.

Until that time we had regarded our proposed
Review mostly as a means for putting money into
the pockets of Conrad for whose career that York-
shireman who affected to despise literature was at
least as anxious as myself. And we had hitherto
hesitated in the uncertainty as to which would the
more contribute to Conrad's material prosperity—
to set up for him a sort of fund or to spend the
money on a *Review* which should give him less
money but greater public backing and support. The
censoring of *A Sunday Morning Tragedy* left no
doubts in Marwood's mind and I was ready to follow
him. I was not actively interested either in Toryism
or in saving the Nation, but if Marwood could get
that much extra fun out of our joint venture I was
going to be glad enough. In the meantime I knew
that my scale of things was going to be presented
with another great man.

So, in due course, that sheet of manuscript that
I can still see with a startling plainness came onto
my desk . . . and it did not take me two lines of
reading of harsh, unsinging, but as if chanting, words
that had been knocked out of old woodland rocks
. . . not two lines, not even one whole one, to see
that what I had foreseen had come true . . . and
that I had at my disposal a long tale of living reading.

To say that my eyes had never fallen till that day
upon a word of Thomas Hardy's might not be true
literally. I had vaguely at the back of my mind the
idea of the servant girl who got her letters to her
lover written for her by her mistress—which is the
tale called *On the Western Circuit,* and another story

of a man who met his own executioner somewhere on the tiresome cliffs of Wessex. So I must actually have looked into *Life's Little Ironies* or one or other of Mr. Hardy's books of short stories. But my active professional mind had not been occupied with the tales. It was completely taken up with what was then Literary Modernism.

Thus the stories had made almost no impress on me. They were good enough anecdotes put down with the gentlemanly amateurishness that distinguished my countrymen. . . . Yes, good anecdotes. . . . Indeed, I had then the impression that today's re-reading merely strengthens in me, that the rather tremendous situations the anecdotes set up were merely glanced at and not treated at all. There was about Hardy none of the tremendous passion that Conrad displayed for getting the last drop of interest out of a subject. He heard a good story, got it down anyhow and always rather listlessly—as if his heart was not much in his work—and let it go at that. This was particularly the case with *On the Western Circuit,* which is one of the worst instances of the throwing away of a subject that I have ever come across. Listen to it. . . .

A servant girl who has been seduced by a young barrister gets her kind young mistress to write him delicate and uncomplaining love letters . . . because she cannot write. Writing her love letters the kind young mistress falls in love with the barrister and the barrister falls in love with the writer of the letters . . . thinking of course that it is the servant girl who has written them. So he marries the girl who, anyhow, is going to have a baby. And on the wedding day the truth comes out between barrister and kind young mistress. . . . And the story ends there.

But for the merest tyro amongst professional novel writers the 'subject' could only begin there, given that the barrister was any kind of man at all. For even if you didn't—which you probably would—want to treat the subsequent relations of the barrister and the kind young mistress as an adulterous 'affair,' there would still remain the relations of the barrister and the illiterate servant girl whom he had married because he had taken her to be an epistolary poetess. . . . Goodness me! . . . Hardy might at least have taken the trouble to invent an accident in which the girl could have had her hand cut off or rendered nerveless. As it was he took a subject that every real novelist would itch and ache to handle and, having thus spoilt it for others, just dropped it as he might have dropped a bunch of withered flowers. It was rather wicked of him.

It was wicked of him in the sense that it was wicked to 'restore,' as in his youth he did, innumerable beautiful and ancient churches . . . against his conscience, just to make a living and in the barbarous fashion of the mid-Victorians. He used, he said, sometimes to writhe in his bed when he thought of what he had done to those beautiful monuments of antiquity. And if he didn't go as far as to admit to himself or anyone else that he had as cruelly mangled in his Wessex novels and tales an infinity of beautiful subjects, his novels and tales seemed to present almost no interest to him at all once he was done with them.

Indeed, one may be pretty certain that it was with a sigh of relief that he dropped from his shoulders the yoke of the prose writer, once *Jude the Obscure* was published and the outcry with which it was received by Mrs. Hardy and all the Archdeacons, Deans, and female columnists of two hemispheres, at its height. One may even imagine that he took, in his perverse, ironic way, a little pleasure in exaggerating the outrageousnesses of his hero and heroine because he wished to bring about an outcry that would give him an excuse to abandon novel-writing for ever. . . . *Jude* is at any rate so far and away his best book . . . is to such an extent inspired by the passionate mind of a great nature . . . that one can be pretty certain that in its working out he did employ some sort of conscious artistic knowledge. And it is interesting to speculate as to what he would have done in the way of novels if he had not abandoned the trade just at the moment when he seemed to have awakened to the fact that that avocation was really an art. For the difference between *Jude* and *Tess* is the difference between a mass of clay handled rather indifferently by a tiredly sentimental sculptor and another mass bitterly handled and struck and wrestled with by a creator until suddenly it comes alive. The other novels form indeed a long, more listless or less listless string of prentice works for that last near-masterpiece. *The Mayor of Casterbridge* isn't 'done' at all—if we compare it with the bubbling, boisterous *Grandeur et Décadence de César Birotteau* of another—but an immense, high-blood-pressured amateur. *The Woodlanders* is enlivened by the touches of rather impish adultery, the rendering of which always brought Mr. Hardy to life.

But in *Jude,* the passionate protest of the great writer's soul against, not the creed, but the practices of mid-Victorian Anglicanism—against the Russian leather of the hymn books, the starched petticoats, the sirloin and cauliflower and the cap-touchings beneath the pink clouds to the peals from the steeples —that passionate revolt of a being who was a woodland man shot through with the impishnesses of Pan, inspired him in those pages to a skill such as he only elsewhere displayed in his poems.

He was, in short, a great poet of a great nature. It is impossible not to be thrilled by any two or three pages of Hardian prose that you take up and into which you dip. I was, as it were, startled out of my life a month or so ago when, after not having looked at the Wessex novels for at least twenty years, I read the first three or four pages of *The Mayor of Caster-bridge*. Like Thackeray over his own work I struck my forehead and exclaimed: 'Why, this is genius!' Because the writing, if it isn't the writing of me and mine, if I may be excused the phrase, is the authentic writing, chiselled and firm, of a real writer. And the temperament, in the comment on bird or married couple, is the contemplative temperament of the tranquilly consummate poet. And the projection of the incidents seems to herald the unfolding of an immense tragedy.

But Hardy was not a novelist, never wanted to be a novelist, didn't care what he did in his novels so long as decently they brought him in enough money to maintain the niece of an Archdeacon in the style to which she was entitled. And once he could find a decent pretext for giving up labour of that sort he took it, and for the rest of his life was like a man who having for years been married and faithful to an uncongenial and domineering wife suddenly sees himself at liberty for the rest of time to sport in woodlands with . . . the muses! . . . It had not been for nothing that, at about the time when he was contemplating the writing of *Jude*, he shaved off his beard. It is always an ominous sign, that. .

I don't mean to say that he was not lamentably hurt by the world-wide, sadistically imbecile chorus of abuse that saluted *Jude*. He was to a singular degree naïve in the ways of the world. So that he really imagined that if he revealed, powerfully, over-whelmingly, the core of heartlessness that underlay the Russian leather of the Sunday morning hymn books, the Deans and Archdeacons would get down off their stalls and thrones and say to the first intelligent man who happened to be standing about: 'Please take my seat, Mr. So and So!' . . . Something like that. . . .

But it is to be remembered that, criticize as he might the temporal dispositions of the Anglican Church, he remained a Believer. Indeed, I think one of the most memorable occasions of my life occurred when before the fair-sized house-party at Mr. Clodd's at Aldeburgh, Thomas Hardy made the curiously shy avowal that he was a practicing and believing communicant of the Church of England. It fell, I believe on all the rest of the party, with a little shock of surprise.

The party itself has, I believe, been made famous by another writer. Mr. Clodd had invited some representative English people for a long week-end with the purpose of ascertaining to that extent the complexion of the religious belief of the country at the time. Mr. Clodd had been in the eighties a militant leader of the agnostic wave that swept over the world

after the publication of *The Origin of Species,* and
Mr. Hardy's shyness at making his confession arose
from his dislike of hurting the feelings of his old
friend. It was indeed a bad day for Mr. Clodd. Of
the nine people present, five of us announced ourselves as Roman Catholic at least in tradition and
turn of mind—all being writers of a certain position.
A very distinguished Professor of Greek at Oxford
professed belief in some form of spiritualism that
included somewhere a black velvet coffin. There was
another spiritualist or theosophist present, the only
agnostic besides Mr. Clodd being a relative of his.
The agnostic pendulum seemed indeed to have swung
back.

In such a body Mr. Hardy's confession might well
come as a shock since neither Catholics nor Spiritu-
alists—nor yet indeed Agnostics—are inclined to
regard the Church of England as anything but a social
Institution. . . . And Mr. Hardy's profession of belief impressed myself—and I dare say several of the
others—with a feeling that if the creed of that church
could in that day and hour hold the mind of a man
so indisputably great as the author of *The Dynasts,*
the church was as a spiritual organization worthy of
a respect that one had hitherto withheld from her
. . . just indeed as one may well feel today that if
Victorian England could produce a figure so authen-
tically great as that little, inwardly smiling, ineffably
modest poet, there is more to be said for Victorian
England than one is usually inclined to say.

He stood there indeed a singular and intriguing
mystery. He seemed to have dropped on that remote
seashore out of clouds of temporal glory such as

could have attended on few not themselves tempo-
rally royal in origin. As far as one could trust the
papers, behind the billowing skirts of Mrs. Hardy he
passed continually across the lawns of royal garden
parties; sat in the carriages of the vice-regal lodge at
Dublin; mounted the stairs of the Admiralty; vice-
presided at his own table over incredibly be-coro-
netted ranks of guests. . . .

And there he was—infinitely simple, extraordinarily
self-effacing; as if ineradicably a peasant, with a face
varnished and wrinkled by the weather as the exposed
roots of ancient oaks are gnarled amidst their moss
. . . and with amazing powers of perception in his
keen, limpid, liquid, poet-peasant's eyes . . . and as
instinct with the feeling of escape as a schoolboy who
had run out from his school ranks on some down and
was determined on naughtiness. . . . Much as I
have seen Henry James suddenly look naughty when,
temporarily escaping from the vigilance of his doctors, nephews, and housekeepers, he had determined
to have a glass of port. . . .

I imagined Mr. Hardy to have looked like that
when, shaving off his elder-statesman's beard and
waxing his moustache till it stuck out like that of
the sergeant major of a bantam regiment, he determined to abandon prose for poetry. . . . He was a
man obviously of free passions who had borne long
disciplining with a silent patience and had now
definitely retired from trade to take up his life's
hobby to the exclusion of all else.

Because first—and long before he had had any
prevision of becoming a novelist—he had yearned
with an almost green-sickness to be a poet. And he

had practiced poetry and studied prosody minutely
and with passion . . . for years. At a turning of the
ways such as must be occasioned by the contemplation of marriage with a young woman of position, he
had had to decide whether to earn his living as an
architect—by restoring churches—in a profession
in which he was already middling well-established.
In that way he would have been able to continue being a poet on the side. But at the instance of his
bride-to-be, he had launched out into the occupation
of the commercial novelist—an occupation of a
breathless labour that left him almost no time for
anything else.

That he cared almost nothing for novel-writing,
though he was almost oversensitive about the reception of his works of fiction, is amply proved by the
continual alterations he made in his stories to suit
the prudishnesses of editors and of old-maid readers.
No novelist of passion could have done that, whereas
he gave almost as much trouble to restoring his novels
to their original form after they had been mangled
for purposes of serialization as he gave to the original
writing. The restoration of *Jude* took years and left
him long prostrate with exhaustion.

Of his verse, on the other hand, he was fiercely
jealous. No one could have persuaded him to alter
a word either in the interests of fluidity of meter or
of the delicacies. The shocked *Cornhill* would have
published *A Sunday Morning Tragedy* if he would
have omitted some verses and changed others, and
would have published 'Who now remembers Almack's
balls?' if he would have altered a word or two—
though I can't imagine what words they could have

desired to see altered . . . unless they are perhaps
contained in the lines:

> Is Death the partner who doth moue
> Their wormy chaps and bare?

And I like to think that some of his lightness of
heart during that Aldeburgh week-end was caused by
the fact that he had at last at his disposal a periodical
that would publish whatever he wrote exactly as he
chose to write it. It was, as it were, another escape.
. . . And it was symbolic that at Aldeburgh he only
once mentioned his novels . . . that being to say
that until the publication of *Tess* he had made almost
no money in the United States by his books because
of the non-existence till that date of copyright for
foreign authors. . . . On the other hand he talked
—after sufficient pressing—by the hour about *The
Dynasts,* going over page after page minutely in a
nook on the beach, explaining why he had used here
heroics, here Alcaics or Sapphics or ballad forms or
forms invented by himself, explaining how such and
such an incident had been suggested to him . . . and
keenly delighting in his achievement. For you could
trust that mercurial, simple old peasant to know
what he had done and what a great thing that tragedy
is. . . .

For me, I have a passionate liking for passages in
literature which open up physical immensities of
landscape, and that pleasure I get supremely from
that work. One stands on a height and sees at infinite
distances tiny sailors hauling up boats, tiny hussars
dismounted, digging entrenchments, tiny tricolours

prancing from Paris to Rome. . . . I can get no greater pleasure from literature.

But indeed the whole of his poetic work forms such another immense panorama . . . of the great landscape of the human heart. It is a matter of observation of minutenesses rendered with an immense breadth and breath. You would imagine there is nothing human, hodden, and down to the ground that he had not noticed with his quick glances. They penetrated right in behind nearly all surfaces as if he had been an infallible sleuth of all human instances. I still remember my extreme amazement—as if of a Doctor Watson—when looking at a fisher boy who was patching an old boat, he told me that that boy whom he had never seen before was probably the stepson of a woman lately widowed—who got on well with him. . . . He had deduced it—and it was quite correct—from the boy's red canvas trousers which had been cut down and patched with blue cloth. . . . Think what an amazingly handy gift that was for a projector of panoramas of the human heart.

H. G. WELLS

Mr. H. G. Wells and I must have been enemies for more years than I care now to think of. And the situation is rendered the more piquant by the fact that one or the other of us must by now be the *doyen* of English novelists—though I prefer not to discover which of us it is. At any rate in the kingdom of letters Mr. Wells and I have been leaders of opposing forces for nearly the whole of this century.

I do not think that it is immodesty in a man to claim that he is a leader of forces when his military unit is indeed a unit. One may be allowed, I mean, to say that one is one's own leader . . . for it is getting on for a great number of years since I could say that I had in England even a comrade in arms, so complete has been the triumph in that country of Mr. Wells's forces. But there were good old days when the forces were more equal—and when I was hardly more than the camp-follower of a goodly Army. What we contended was that the world could be saved only by the Arts; Mr. Wells and his followers proclaimed that that trick could only be done by Science. What, secondly, we contended was that if you intended to practice the Arts you had better know something of the mental processes of how works of art are produced; the enemy forces proclaimed, with drums a-beat and banners waving, that to be an artist of any sort you had only to put some vine leaves in your hair, take pen or brush and paper or canvas and dip pen or brush in inkstand or paint pot, and Art would flow from your fingertips. The opposing doctrines were, in short, those of Inspiration and of Conscious Art.

Even at that date in England the forces were unequal. In America, writers at least have always taken some interest in the 'how' of their Art . . . beginning the practice with Poe and going on to the last neophyte emerging from the Short Story Class of, say, Northwestern University. But in England, disgrace has always attached itself to Conscious Artistry.

On the face of it you would say that the Man in the Street would be on our side. It would seem the merest common sense to say that if you are going to do something, you should first try to know something of how that thing is done. The watchmaker, the railway engineer, the potter, serve apprenticeships in how to make their wheels go round. Why not then the writer? But in England to take an interest in what used to be called technique was to stamp yourself at once as a dirty foreigner. A *very* unclean alien. Other writers were just low fellows whom you would not introduce to your wife.

And indeed the conscious artists in the England of those days were all either actually foreigners or returned, or not even returned, expatriates. In my day they consisted of three Americans and a Pole —Henry James, Stephen Crane, W. H. Hudson, and Joseph Conrad. Before their powerful appearance there had been a crowd of French- and Russian-inspired writers who centred round W. E. Henley and, to a lesser extent, Robert Louis Stevenson and, in the alternative, round the once famous *Yellow Book*. The *Yellow Book* itself had been inspired by one Paris-American, Henry James, and was admirably conducted by Henry Harland, the author of *The Cardinal's Snuff Box,* another Paris-American.

Around these foreign cohorts, taking for their slogan Mr. Kipling's

> There are five and forty ways
> Of inditing tribal lays
> And every single one of them is right,

raged the stout, lusty, God-fearing English novelists of position. They are nearly all forgotten. Of younger English writers of that day, two at least nibbled at the alien bait. They were Mr. Galsworthy and Mr. Wells. Both with a flirt of the tail glided serenely away into depths more illuminated.

The Mr. Wells that one knew of in those earliest days was the imaginative Scientist—Scientist professedly but imaginer above all things as far as we were concerned. In those days no one bothered his head about Science. It seemed to be an agreeable parlour game—like stamp-collecting. And I am bound to say that it still seems to me like that. One did very well without it in those days; one will do still better without it in the not-distant future when it will be dethroned.

One heard that a singular little man had visited Mr. Frank Harris in the *Saturday Review* office and had asked to have the reviewing of scientific works for that periodical confided to him. Mr. Harris had said, Hell, Damn, Blast, Bloody, why don't you write funny stories about Science? . . . I don't know which of his elaborate expletives he used, but he used some.

The products of that advice began to appear on the market—and I do not have to assure you that it did not take us long to recognize that here was Genius. Authentic, real Genius. And delightful at that. Genius is so often forbidding. . . . But it was delightful to think of all the inhabitants of London going about in the condition of the blue-behinded baboon. For one of Mr. Wells's stories was about an Anarchist—those were the days of Militant Anarchism—who visited a Scientist with the idea of stealing a phial of typhoid germs and dropping them into the reservoir of the Primrose Hill Waterworks, which then supplied most of London. And he stole by mistake a phial containing the bacillus of the coloration of the stern of the blue-behinded baboon. We were delighted. We imagined ourselves—and still more our not so dear friends—going about, nervously hitching ourselves, with our backs to cheval glasses.

And we welcomed Science—Mr. Wells's brand of Science—with acclamations. Fairy tales are a prime necessity of the world, and he and Science were going to provide us with a perfectly new brand. And he did. And all Great London lay prostrate at his feet.

Mr. Wells struck the Empire with all the impact of Mr. Kipling. He struck everybody. He delighted the bourgeois profane with his imagination, and we intelligentsia snorted with pleasure at the idea of a Genius whom we could read without intellectual effort. And with immense admiration for his 'technique.' One could ask no more. The other idols of

the intelligentsia of those days were a little forbidding
—Ibsen and Björnson and the Nordics generally, and
Hauptmann and Sudermann. Gloomy and forbidding.
So we devoured Mr. Wells.

He liked the process; nevertheless, inspired with
the gospel of Science, he snorted a little on the side
. . . not loudly, but with meaning. We, his snorts
said, we who delighted hilariously in his works were
poor idiots towards whom a dark shadow was swiftly
drifting. Science was going to devour us as the under-
ground working populations of one of his stories
crept out and at night devoured the butterfly beings
of the planet's surface. Good for Mr. Wells; good for
Science; good for everybody. Particularly good for us
intelligentsia because we began to see that Mr. Wells
too was a pessimist. We slapped each other on the
back hilariously. The note of the world of those days
was hilarity. It was good to think that our pet Genius
was going also to develop into an Intelligence.

So Mr. Wells went snooping about the world, emit-
ting from time to time a prophecy in the form of an
entertaining and magnificently machined gem of
fiction. And with extraordinary speed he assumed the
aspect of a Dean of Letters. He was going to put
writing on the social map. Pure writing, mind you.
Pure imagination backed by an impeccable technique.

And re-reading as I have just done the magnificent
volume called *The Country of the Blind* I see how
absolutely right we were in our appreciation. It con-
tains all Mr. Wells's short stories. It is a book that
is Literature and one that is also delight. It is a book
that prophesied so far ahead that it is still modern,
and one so instinct with the observations of human
nature that he has picked up in the course of his

snooping—so full that it is not of any date at all.
It has the quality of the Greek idyll of the two women
watching a procession, holding up their children and
treating themselves to ha'porths of perfume from
the slot machine in the temple of the Great God.

Snooping is really the word: it was not spying and
it was not looking consciously for copy. It was a sort
of catching things on the hop, in side glances. Whenever anything happened Mr. Wells was always there
or thereabout, turning up you did not quite know
how, looking on, snorting little reflections under his
breath.

One day he said to me, 'What do you say, Fordie,
to giving a novel the form of a sonata?' [1]

I jumped a little. I had never imagined Mr. Wells
as taking interest either in novel forms or in music.

'You know,' he went on, 'first subject: Hero. Second subject: Heroine. Because you must never introduce your hero and heroine in the first chapter. It's
uneconomical. . . . And then Working Out and Re-
capitulation.'

I see now that that was Mr. Wells taking his nibble
at the ideas and practices of Conscious Artistry . . .
for I understand that he has lately confessed that
he once investigated the subject and, finding it sterile,
had ceased to think about it. But the conversation
remains in my mind. At the time I had not the least
idea that Mr. Wells was snopping round Literary
Consciousness. I imagined him the serene Short Story
Writer, roaming wide plains in the search of human
instances. But serene and consummate in his particu-

---

[1] Mr. Wells has denied with extreme vehemence that
he ever said anything of the sort. The Reader must judge
between us!

lar gift. It struck me that he was guying me—or trifling with an idea as you trifle with a windlestraw before throwing it away. I had really no inkling that he was thinking of attempting the full-dress novel of straight modern life. One loved his longer books for the arbitrary conceits of *The First Men in the Moon, The Time Machine*—and above all *The Sea Lady*, which united to the conceits, inventions, quips, and brilliant images of the others a certain poetry and regret.

And then gradually one realized that more and more frequently there crept into Mr. Wells's work the note of exasperation at the futility of human life. . . . Or no, that is not perhaps the way to put it. I remember Henry James talking about Mr. Wells one day, wondering, as it were, what had got into him:

'You'd say . . . um-um,' he said, 'that he had everything. Everything that one can desire. His enviable . . . his really enviable gift; his enviable . . . but supremely enviable, popularity. His stately treasure house on the seashore. His troops . . . his positive hordes of flushed young things bursting new into life. . . . Tempered of course with what in places of liquid entertainment, if you'll pardon me the image, they call a "splash" of elder statesmen who have seen, pondered, accomplished. . . . Troops, then, of flushed neophytes relieved by the suavely Eminent. . . . Nevertheless, there is this pervading note . . . this burden . . . this undersong and overtone . . . of the creaking door. . . . Upon my soul this Fortunate Youth—for compared to myself, *moi qui vous parle*, he is immoderately richly endowed with the splendid gift of youth—might be

—making allowances for the differences of circumstances and, of course, cadences—your friend Conrad's monstrous master mariner, Marlow, who is always addressing to the moon his hyper-Slav complaints as to the lugubrious ends, inevitably attending on human endeavour.'

He drew a deep breath and began again rather quickly:

'You don't suppose . . . it has been whispered to me . . . you know swift madness *does* at times attend on the too fortunate, the too richly endowed, the too altogether and overwhelmingly splendid. You don't suppose then . . . I mean to you too has it been whispered? . . . that . . . well, in short . . .' And very fast indeed: 'That-he-is-thinking-of-taking-to-politics?'

I really jumped when I heard that suggestion. Then with immense fervour and earnestness I burst into indignant denials that anything so scandalous could be imagined about my friend. . . . Alas!

I have heard, I suppose, most—or at any rate many—of the great talkers of my time, and amongst men of letters I should give the palm to M. Anatole France, Mr. R. B. Cunninghame Graham, and Conrad. But a special niche should be reserved for H. G. He must be one of the greatest exponents of back-chat conversation there ever was.

In those far-off days it was a standing—an unfailing—delight to listen to Mr. Wells conducting a conversation. For that was what it was. The others, M. France, and the rest, talked, *ore rotundo*. Mr. Wells, with his little self-communing snorts and his bright, blue, beady glance darting all over the place, mono-

logued occasionally in a conversational tone until he
had led the discussion into the strategic position that
he had chosen—and then defended it, like a warrior
on a crag, warding off the darts aimed at him. He let,
that is to say, his hearers say a word or two and then
with extraordinary quickness suppressed them—either
with the quick Johnsonian flat negative of superior
knowledge or some quip that completely changed
the course of the discussion.

Outwardly Mr. Wells of those days always seemed
to me most to resemble one of those rather small
British generals who were so unlimitedly beloved by
their men—a Buller or a Bobs. Blond, rather stocky,
with a drooping cavalry moustache and with eyes
always darting about, I fancy he would have been
happy as a general, commanding bodies of men to
do things and they doing it . . . commanding them
in writing from a headquarters table and surrounded
by a deferential troop of staff-neophytes to carry his
orders.

But, in those days, when he was already in the saddle and had glimpses of all the worlds that he might
conquer, what struck one most was his tough, as it
were Cockney, gallantry of attack—upon anything.
. . . I am not being rude when I use the word that
describes persons born within sound of Bow Bells. I
am a Cockney myself and so is Mr. Charles Chaplin
and so was Keats. And if London is the great place
that it is and if during years we endured the late War
without any hope of winning it, and if, supposing
those things to interest you, the country governed by
London is the first to show signs of getting over the
present crisis, it is all because of the indomitable
courage of the little poets, the little generals with

their blue eyes and drooping cavalry moustaches, the little pawky-tongued shopkeepers, the little soldiers who have forever on their tongues the saying, 'What a hope!' and yet go on—and the quality of all of them of having no one and nothing in the world in awe, and never, never knowing when they are beaten.

All those attributes were possessed by the Mr. Wells of Spade House, on his grass terrace over the English channel of Sandgate. . . . And indeed later when he left off being primarily an imaginative writer and became a politician or something of the sort, and when he made his determined attempt to capture with the aid of his flushed neophytes one of the most formidable and dangerous political organizations in the British Isles—why then I really used to see him as another Mr. Chaplin of the days when that hero used to attack an enormous, a gigantic, black-bearded villain—flying from the top of the kitchen sink at the giant's neck, being thrown through the windows, plunging down the chimney to kick his foe in the rear, being thrown through the ceiling, flooring the giant with tiles from the roof. And so on for ever and ever. There was indeed a memorable meeting during that famous struggle when Mr. G. B. Shaw and the Sidney Webbs between them managed dialectically to wipe the floor with Mr. Wells. And it was all I could do, much as I deprecated Mr. Wells's desertion of Literature for Public Affairs, to prevent myself shouting: 'Oh, H. G. There's the lecturer's bottle behind you. Smash them on the head with it. For Heaven's sake!' . . . So much affection did H. G. inspire even in his enemies and so much did one dislike to see the Old Gang, as they were even then called—Mr. Shaw and the Sidney Webbs, now

Lord and Lady Something or Other—combine with grim coldness to get the better of that beloved general of young things and causes that were then also young.

I remember now the sunlight over Sandgate and the sea, and Mr. Wells and I descending the steep brae that goes down from the hutments of Shorncliffe Camp to the narrow High Street, whose outer row of houses was so close to the sea that in great westerly gales the Indiamen going ashore used to poke their bowsprits through the windows. I have seen them do it. For that was the landscape at once of my childhood's school and of Mr. Wells's *Sea Lady*. At the time of which I am thinking he had taken a furnished house on the beach whilst he waited for Voysey to build for him on the chalk slopes above what Mr. James later called his lordly treasure house. And in the days of which I am talking the rest of the personages of my young drama—Conrad, James, Crane, Hudson—dwelled in a half-circle at distances of from five to thirty-odd miles round Spade House. So it was not to be wondered at if we lived rather in each other's pockets and interested ourselves rather in each other's affairs.

And Mr. Wells really had for us the aspect of the Dean of our Profession. We regarded him, a little wistfully, as having innumerable things, appurtenances, gadgets, retainers, immense . . . but immense sales, and influence, and the gift of leadership. . . . And we all should never have any of those things nor ever bask in those public lights. So, in some mystic way, Mr. Wells might have put Literature on the map. . . . That was how it seemed. Alas, he was to become the Lost Leader!

That went in this way:

The day before we descended the slope into Sandgate High Street, intent on getting an appetite for dinner, Mr. Wells had been up to Town. And after we had proceeded silently for some minutes he exclaimed suddenly:

'You know, Fordie, there's something in those old Classics after all.'

On his way up to London he had bought at Sandling Junction a copy of More's *Utopia* in Dent's newly published Temple Edition, that was then putting cheaply before a very large public a number of books that they would never otherwise have read. He had read it in the train going up to Town, in his hotel bedroom, and on his homeward road. And that was his verdict.

I made the sort of silence that indicates the words: 'I told you so,' for the words are not good ones to utter, and we walked on meditating till suddenly he exclaimed:

'You know, if I had the education of this country in my hands I could make something of it yet.'

And we walked on in silence some more. I imagined that we were both thinking about Education, which for me seemed to have nothing to do with Instruction, and for him, as far as I could see, seemed to be nothing else. . . . That at any rate had been the lines that our arguments had taken. . . .

The Mr. Wells of that date affected with some ferocity to regard what I regarded as Education as bilge, useless and merely ornamental if not actually a detriment to the human intellect. And he affected the air of the educational rough, self-made diamond.

He said bedamn to the Classics—let bugs be your only study.

Actually, Mr. Wells was much the better educated, even in my own sense, of the two. He had been brought up, since his tenderest years, at one of those sixteenth-century, Edward VI grammar schools that are one of the most genuine glories of English education and of which the soundest possible grounding in the classics is the chief feature of the curriculum. On the other hand, going to one of the great public schools on whose playgrounds the battles of Waterloo were fought, I had had no education at all, except that, at the end of the birch rod, I had acquired a prodigious facility at writing Latin verse so that to this day I can write it faster than English prose.

And Mr. Wells, though he affected to have hated the Classics as useless flummery, must have been really pretty sound at them since his headmaster offered to take him as his assistant when the young man was approaching the school-leaving stage. Mr. Wells preferred to run away and, fortunately for the world, to become successively an assistant in the shop of Charles Baker at the north end of Tottenham Court Road, an usher in a North Kent private school at no distance from the one in which D. H. Lawrence afterwards taught the budding Kentish Man: a science student at South Kensington; a science instructor for correspondence classes; the writer at first of a manual of biology and then of *The Wonderful Visit, The Invisible Man,* and all the other glories of those years.

So we continued our walk in silence. I don't know what he imagined I was thinking about, but I certainly thought he was mentally outlining a scheme of scientific education for the youth of England—with perhaps a dash of the Classics to temper the wind of microscopic bugs and bacilli. I imagined, that is to say, that he was softening. For I had asked him shortly before at what date he considered civilization to have begun. And he had answered with a quick snort of scorn that civilization had begun when soft iron was discovered accessible enough and in sufficient quantity to make practicable the extensive manufacture of machines. . . . That of course finished the wiping out of the Classics. They had all been written before the discovery of soft iron. Therefore they had not contributed to civilization.

Now, I imagined, he was softening a little under the influence of the beloved statesman of Henry VIII. He may have been. But it was not about the evolution of a New Education that he was thinking on that walk. He was thinking about becoming the one and only Arbiter of the World.

The moment you looked back through the already long list of his stories that became clear. They were all about men who might have become arbiters of the world by means of one scientific gadget or another: The Invisible Man, the Man Who Could Work Miracles, the Man Who Could See in the Country of the Blind. They might have become the Arbiters of the World; but they did not because they had not sufficient imagination. They ended always in a sort of infuriated and dyspeptic frustration. Or, at best, in giving blue behinds to the population of London town.

But after reading More's *Utopia,* Mr. Wells saw that he, he only and no other, was actually the Man

Who Could See in a Country of the Blind. Life at once became clear to him and it was *Utopia* that had showed him the way. In our Nordic world, imaginative writing is a despised, an as if effeminate occupation, and the imaginative writer a something less than a He-man—and one whom you could not introduce to your wife. His chance of becoming an Influence is almost less than nothing; his chance of saying to the world 'Do this' and of seeing it done was even less. Yet that ought to be the destiny of the Remarkable Man. He should be, as it were, a General directing forces to the attack on Ignorance and Evil.

And the way to do it was to write Utopias—to prophesy what the world would be like when the forces of Ignorance and Evil should have been forever overthrown. By the quality of your writing and your quick, brilliant touches, you would make that imagined Future look so attractive that mankind would call on its statesmen and politicians to give them that sort of world and no other. . . . If you could do that you would indeed become the General Officer Commanding the Forces of the Universe. You would shout to the world: 'Humanity will Advance by the Right! Move to the Right in Fours! Form F–O–U–R–S! . . . RIGHT!' . . . And Humanity would do it.

So began Mr. Wells's period of Utopian Romances with their paraphernalia of Daimios and Japanese chivalry, called I think *Bushido*, and the rest of it. I am a little hazy about them because I did not read them. I was rather disgruntled and wished that Mr. Wells would not spend so much time over them. I wanted to know more about the gentlemen who threw each other onto red-hot cones or how, as in *Fear*—which is perhaps Mr. Wells's greatest piece of writing as writing—the candles went out without draughts or human agency.

Still, that appeared to be Mr. Wells's affair. If a gentleman prefers as a pastime writing Utopias to playing Badminton or demon poker it would seem to be within his rights. I continued to walk beside Mr. Wells on the slopes of the chalk-down behind Sandgate and continued to draw in instruction from his words and delight from his imaginative quips and conversational quirks. . . . And I may as well say that all the instruction I ever had—exception made of that in vegetable gardening—I had from the mouth of H. G., and if I ever have astonished people—and Mr. Wells himself once wrote a book of caricatures in which he portrayed me as a monster of omniscience—it is simply because I have a wonderful memory and Mr. Wells hasn't. I remember, I mean, all the things that Mr. Wells has forgotten that he told me. Whenever I have had occasion to say rude things about Science and to show that I knew at least something about it, the knowledge came from Mr. Wells's discourses—on the theory and practice of organic and inorganic chemistry, bacteriology, biology, physics, or the origin of species . . . all that stamp-collecting made vivid in the blue weather with the larks singing over Caesar's Camp. . . .

But most vividly, most unforgettably of all, there comes back to me an immense conversation beginning in the reptile house of the Zoological Gardens in London and going on for hours and hours in the damp shades of the Inner Circle of Regents Park . . . a conversation in which Mr. Wells related the

whole of his biography—as I have set it down here
and elsewhere . . . and in addition inducted me
into the deepest *fonds* of the theory of protective
coloring in birds. . . .

It was the beginning of the end.

For one day Mr. Wells said to me, 'Fordie, I'm
going to turn the Fabian Society inside out and then
throw it into the dustbin.'

My heart sank into my boots. There went through
my head words like

> Just for seventeen tons or so of silver he's
>   leaving us,
> Just for a ribbon that would stretch from here
>   to the moon and back to stick in his coat
> Gaining all the gifts of which fortune bereft
>   us . . .

and so on. The words are perhaps not quite right.
But the only anthology of English verse that I pos-
sess—that made by Mr. Walter de la Mare—does
not contain *The Lost Leader* or indeed any word of
Browning's. . . . And I exclaimed:

'Good God, no, H. G.!'

It would be as well, perhaps, to explain that the
Fabian Society was in those days about the most
unpleasant feature of English public life. As it were,
a Socialist Tammany Hall! It proposed to reform
society by means of statistics, and its publications
were so dull that no one not spurred on by a sort of
sadic lust to destroy his fellow men could possibly
have read them. Its members have since mostly
become peers, but I cannot for the life of me remember their names. There was one who as Cabinet Min-

ister was responsible for most of the calamities that have befallen the Jews in Palestine. . . . The Society, in short, got for a time its stranglehold on the British Government, not so long ago.

That they would was already manifest at the time —the long-distant time—of which I am talking. They loomed already, then, very large on the political horizon. Mr. G. B. Shaw, as I have said, was one of them and the Sidney Webbs were two. And what I dreaded was that Mr. Wells was contemplating taking hold of that Society, jettisoning the Webbs and Shaws and Hobsons and Radical Professors and Political Economists, and so wading bloodily amongst cracked crowns to the Arbitership of the Universe.

He assured me that that was not the case. Never would he think of becoming anything so detrimental as a politician. He was just going to upset the Society for a lark because it was so dull and pompous and because he wanted to introduce some imagination into its methods . . . and because he wanted to study the methods of politicians. Then he would pull out and write political romances with all the local color correct.

Alas! . . . The rest belongs to History. . . . That would be in 1908 or 1909.

A decade and a half or so afterwards I was sitting in the Closerie des Lilas and some French novelist or other was discanting on the disappearance of the Great Figure from the Earth. He was a violent anti-Plutarchian and declared that the war just ended had made all the leaders of men appear such feckless fools that never again would Society consent to be led by Great Men. And he turned on me furiously and asked me if I could name any one man who was known as an Influence to anything like a considerable portion of the surface of the globe.

I answered almost automatically, 'H. G.'—and no one present disagreed.

That was right enough. The Mr. Wells of those days looked very much like being the Arbiter of the World. In a universe bewildered after the War he had no one to stand up against him—no one who had any confidence in anything, and he was, still, all bright confidence. He was like a portent that flashed from the Kremlin to the White House—as he did only last year again but less prodigiously. He lectured potentates and proletariats who sat in rows all round the world like fishes waiting to be fed with good doctrines. You saw people reading him in all the trolley cars from the Boulevard Saint Michel to Main Street, Tokyo, and all the *dâk* bungalows and *posadas* from Bombay to Buenos Aires and back again to the open-air restaurants in Stockholm, where they offered you as you entered copies of the Tauchnitz edition of *New Worlds for Old* along with travelling rugs in which to wrap yourself. And white beneath the sun and pale beneath the moon and stars all round the world went the great flood of the world's papers, every one of them making front-page quotations from Mr. Wells's latest prophecy of war and his pronouncements on Religion, Love, Hygiene. . . .

Later of course his image was obscured by that of the then Prince of Wales, who prophesied the color of the pajamas youth would next be wearing and, later still, by that of the rider of the *Spirit of St. Louis*. But today still sees Moscow and Washington lending deferential attention to his *dicta,* and I

notice that still, under his spirited and indefatigable
direction, volumes of counsel as to the conducting
from the cradle to the grave of all our lives are being
published.

Mr. Wells, then, has had a life of many glories.
And fittingly . . . and of many experiences. He
was watching the world before Mass Production was
so much as an invented word and, during the late era
of Prosperity at Any Price, he saw his prophecies
come true. And indeed, mayn't he be said to have had
a certain hand in bringing about the era of hilarious
thoughtlessness? For I doubt if the world would have
so unquestionably accepted those irrational specious-
nesses if it hadn't been for Mr. Wells with his prophecies of the triumphs of Science and the Machine.
We accepted, I mean, millionwise production of
everything, universal sterilization, the asphyxiation
of tens of thousands, the razing from the earth of
whole cities, largely because Mr. Wells had prepared
our minds for those horrors. We accepted them as
inevitable because that immensely read writer had
told us that they were inevitable. Without that a shuddering and hypnotized world might have made a
greater effort to shake off these tentacles.

I know that because of one of those queer coinci-
dences that at times overcome one. It was on a day
during the late Armageddon when I had seen Mr.
Wells in a staff car whilst bands were playing troops
into the line—somewhere in France. That same night,
in a perfect, clear, still moonlight, I lay in a tent,
obsessed by insomnia, and suddenly heard an officer
say from another tent: 'Orderly, ask the Major if
he has finished with *Mr. Britling Sees It Through*'

. . . a work through which once again some of the poetry and genius of Mr. Wells really pierced. . . . And I will interpolate that, for myself, I had been reading, actually, *The Red Badge of Courage* by the light of a candle stuck onto a bully-beef case at my camp-bed head. And so great had been the influence of that work on me that, when at dawn I got out of bed and looked out of my tent flap to see if a detail for which I was responsible was preparing carts to go to the Schiffenberg and draw our Mills bombs . . . against and below hills and dark woods I saw sleepy men bending over fires of twigs, getting tea for that detail, it did not seem real to me. Because they were dressed in khaki. The hallucination of Crane's book had been so strong on me that I had expected to see them dressed in Federal blue.

But Mr. Wells can have his revenge. For when, during that same day for the first time I smelt the enemy's gas, I said to myself, 'H. G. prophesied this, years ago,' and I did not make half the effort that I might have made to get away, for I felt as if it had been wished on me. . . .

That is what I mean when I say that Mr. Wells had hypnotized the world into believing that almost any horrors of Science and the Machine are inevitable . . . and into accepting them supinely.

I hope Mr. Wells goes on being the eternally cheerful politician, the eternally benevolent adviser of humanity, the forever glorified snooper, the noble and ever-victorious Enemy General. And if not, then at least he can have the assurance of leaving behind him a body of sheer literature such as few others of us will have left . . . all those inspirations of the

Spade House days when the world was young and
hope on every bacteriologist's tongue. That should
be enough for one man's lot.

The lay reader may say: Here's a tremendous
pother of enmities, but what's it all about? . . . The
answer is this: If this civilization of ours is to be
saved it can only be saved by a change of heart in
the whole population of the globe. Neither improve-
ments in machines nor the jugglings of economists
can do it. To have a living civilization we must have
civilized hearts. I don't mean to say that it is a very
good chance. But it is the only one. And it is a
change that can only be brought about convinced
worlds by the artist—by the thinker who has evolved
living words that will convince . . . as, say, the
Parables of Good Samaritans. . . . And every real
artist in words who deserts the occupation of pure
imaginative writing to immerse himself in the Public
Affairs that have ruined our world, takes away a little
of our chance of coming alive through these lugubrious times. And when it is a very real artist with
a great hold on the people, it is by so much the
more a pity. . . .

GALSWORTHY

...ᴜsᴛ have asked myself a hundred times in my ... there had been no Turgenev what would have ... of Galsworthy? . . . Or, though that is the ... question has always put itself to me, it ... truer to the thought I want to express to ... at would Galsworthy have become?

...t have asked the same question about Henry Ja... or the influence of Turgenev on James must ha... b n enormous, but I did not know James be-for... had come across Turgenev, whereas I did kno... lsworthy whilst he was still himself and still ...t ishingly young. And I remember distinctly the ... that came over me when Galsworthy one morn... mentioned Turgenev for the first time at break... It was both the nature of the mention of the beau ful Russian genius and Galsworthy's emo-tion of the moment that alarmed me. I had known him for a long time as a charming man-about-town of a certain doggedness in political argument. Indeed, I don't know how long I hadn't known him; to find out exactly I should have to do more delving in thought into my own past than I care to do. But I knew that he was passing through a period of great emotional stress, and as I had a great affection for him I was concerned to find him expressing more emotion over an anecdote than I had ever known him to show.

The anecdote was this: Turgenev had a peasant girl for mistress. One day he was going to St. Petersburg and he asked the girl what he should bring her back from town. She begged him to bring her back some cakes of scented soap. He asked her why she wanted scented soap and she answered, 'So that it may be proper for you to kiss my hand as you do those of the great ladies, your friends.'

I never liked the anecdote much, myself. But Galsworthy, telling it in the sunlit breakfast room of my cottage at Winchelsea, found it so touching that he appeared to be illuminated, and really had tears in his eyes. I daresay the reflection of the sunlight from the tablecloth may have had something to do with the effect of illumination, but it comes back to me as if, still, I saw him in a sort of aura that emanated from his features. And from that day he was never quite the same. . . . The morning is also made memorable for me by the ghost of the odour of a very strong embrocation that hung about us both. He was, at the moment, suffering from severe sciatica, and I had spent the last half-hour of the night before and the first half-hour of that morning in rubbing him in his bed with that fluid which consisted of turpentine, mustard, and white of egg. And suddenly I had of him a conception of a sort of frailty, as if he needed protection from the hard truths of the world. It was a conception that remained to me till the very end . . . till the last time but one when I came upon him accidentally watching one of his own plays in New York, all alone and, seemingly, very perturbed. I don't know by what.

The disease from which he suffered was pity . . . or not so much pity as an insupportable anger at the sufferings of the weak or the impoverished in a harsh world. It was as if some portion of his mind had been flayed and bled at every touch. It entered into his spirit at about the date of which I am speaking and remained with him all his life. And, for me at least, it robbed his later work of interest, since the novelist must be pitiless at least when he is at work.

And it filled me with disappointment. I think I must have been the first person really to take Galsworthy seriously as a writer. For most other people who knew him then—except of course for the lady who subsequently became Mrs. Galsworthy—he was still an amiable, rather purposeless man-about-town, with a liking for racing, with some skill with the shotgun, a proper connoisseurship in cricket. But I had already recognized in him a certain queerness, a certain pixylike perversity . . . and a certain, slight, authentic gift. So that I had expected him, if he persevered, to provide for us another—a possibly sunnier kind, of Trollope, and I very much did not want him to become overserious or emotional.

And suddenly there was Turgenev—the most dangerous of all writers for his disciples—Turgenev and emotionalism appearing in the mentality of that sunny being with the touch of genius. . . .

I am always being hammered by my associates for saying that Galsworthy had a touch of genius as a novelist. And indeed I was hammered by Galsworthy himself for telling him that that was what he had. He was himself obstinately of the opinion that if ever a writer was constructed it was he. And in the process of getting himself made he submitted to an incredible

amount of buffetings by advisers. It used to seem
almost a miracle that he could find his way about his
own works whilst he was writing them, so frequently
was he counselled by one person and another to
change all the salient passages of his books. Certainly the Galsworthy who emerged from all that
was someone immensely changed, hardened, and,
except for his plays in which his native gift was more
allowed to have its way, he was dulled. . . . To that
I shall return. Let me for the moment try to finish
getting in my original Galsworthy.

During the earlier years of our acquaintance I had
gathered the impression from Conrad, who knew
him as a pleasant idler long before I did, that his
rather slight figure and blond head contained a frame
and a brain of iron. Conrad, with characteristic
generosity when speaking of a dear friend, used to
declare that Galsworthy held the mile record at
Oxford. At times it would even be the world record.
But it was certainly the Oxford one. And, on my
first meeting with him—though not my first sight,
for I had seen him at a club—he had elected, rather
than to ride in my dog-cart, to trot beside me the two
miles from Sandling Junction to the Pent. He said
he needed exercise, but as the road was uphill it had
seemed a stiffish way to take it. So I had accepted
Conrad's account of his friend's exploits without
demur and, as it wasn't the kind of thing that Eng-
lishmen would talk about, there was in my mind
no question of his being a mile record-holder at the time
I rubbed him in Winchelsea.

Actually he had rather distinguished himself at
Harrow at cricket and on the cinder track. If I had
known that, I should have considered his first literary

efforts more seriously. Because for a man to go through the terrific grind of preparing himself when comparatively mature for the effort of taking a mile record would be the worst training imaginable for a literary life, whereas for an adolescent to distinguish himself at Harrow would merely mean that he was a stocky fellow.

These slight shades of English ruling-class life at that date are difficult to convey, but they are worth dwelling upon. To excel in those days in anything— even in private—was regarded as extremely danger- ous. To excel to the point of anything like publicity would be to write yourself down a bounder, and if you incurred the slightest suspicion of that it was all over with you. It was nice to have a Blue—for cricket or rowing. It would even help you at the bar after- wards if you wanted to be a practising barrister . . . But then in the boat there were eight of you and on the cricket team eleven, so you did not stand out. And I am certain that, just as my friend Marwood, who was one of the finest mathematicians of his day —just as he purposely made a slip in his final exami- nation at Cambridge so as to be second and not Senior Wrangler—so Galsworthy, if there had been any danger of making a record at Oxford, would have stumbled before reaching the tape.

Later, indeed, I happened to ask him some ques- tion about running—it was at the time of the first Olympic Games in Athens—and said innocently:

'You hold the mile record at Oxford, don't you?'

He really jumped a couple of feet away from me —we were walking in the Park—and exclaimed:

'Good gracious, no! Oh goodness gracious, no! I did a little running at Harrow. But at Oxford I never did anything but loaf about the High . . .' As a matter of fact, he declared, the very little running he had done at the school on the hill had injured his heart so he could not have done anything in that line at Oxford. And, as a matter of fact, too, he had, he said, not done anything in any line at all. He had just scrambled through his examination for the bar. That was all.

He had duly eaten his dinners at the Middle Temple and, like every other gentleman's son of those days, had been called to the bar. That is to say that if one was at all 'born,' one had, till about then, gone either to the bar or into the Army. Or if one were born and a very younger son one went into the Church. But at the time Galsworthy was called to the bar, the Army was already showing signs of becoming a rather serious affair, and with the fall in the value of agricultural tithes, the Church had become a not very lucrative profession. So he had donned wig and gown for a ceremonial attendance on the Courts, as being the proper thing for a gentleman's son who had no ambitions and intended to loaf through life. He had, I understood, appeared once or twice in cases, representing, as a junior counsel, the important firm of which his father was the chief partner, and, during the voyage on the *Torrens,* of which ship Conrad was the chief mate, he had rather desultorily studied naval law.

And there he was, an athlete with a mildly damaged heart, a barrister with no desire for briefs, the perfect man-about-town . . . and for me a very incomprehensible figure. Conrad said that he was as hard as iron under a soft exterior and tenacious as a bulldog in spite of a carefully feigned pococurantism. On and off I saw a good deal of him, but his talk was mostly of the Eton and Harrow cricket match, the sires and dams of race-horses, very desultorily of tariff reform, the woes of Ireland, the behaviour of the Boers. Occasionally he would talk a little about some concert or other, his sister, Mrs. Reynolds, being melomane, and occasionally he would talk about pictures, his sister, Mrs. Sauter, being married to an artist. When it was a question of books, I did the talking and he would listen with an interest that I took to be merely polite.

We both at that time inhabited an august, sedate hilltop in the royal borough of Kensington called Campden Hill, he on the one side and I on the other of a concreted open space given up to tennis courts —it was really the cover of a waterworks reservoir. And on days when I was not expecting Conrad, who was in lodgings not far off, I would breakfast with Jack in his sunlit, converted stable.

At any rate that is how it comes back to me—the doors and windows always open, the sunlight streaming in on the hissing silver teakettle, the bubbling silver entrée dishes, the red tiles of the floor, the bright rugs, the bright screens. And we would talk until it was time for me to go back along the waterworks wall and take up the interminable job of writing, in my dining-room, patchwork passages into *Romance,* when Conrad was not writing *Nostromo* up in my study. And Galsworthy would be going to ride in the Park. . . .

And then, suddenly, they all went . . . Pop! As if someone had cut the key string of a net, they all unravelled and disappeared—those tranquillities.

It began with that Turgenev anecdote. I had been right to be alarmed. I had by then known for some time that Galsworthy occasionally wrote a short story, rather desultorily as young ladies paint landscapes in water-colours. Then one day with a rather ironic, dubious expression, Conrad told me that 'poor Jack' wanted me to read some of his stuff . . . and I rather liked some of it. Even at that he seemed too shy to talk about his writing, so I had made a few remarks as to *progression d'effet*, the *mot juste*, and the like. And I had imagined that he had dropped his writing. But immediately after the Turgenev anecdote I opened inadvertently a letter addressed to him in care of myself. It was the morning after he had gone back to Town. Then I knew immediately after the reading of merely three amazing words and the signature that poor Jack had his troubles of the heart.

It gives the measure of the passion that I have for not knowing anything about the private lives of my friends—particularly if they are writers—that, as I have somewhere related, I should have gone to extremes of trouble over the forwarding of that letter. I desperately did not want Galsworthy to know that I knew. It seemed to me that that must inevitably take the bloom off the pleasure that I had in our gentle and unexciting conversations. I knew then at once that the emotion he had shown over the Turgenev anecdote was a sign that he was suffering a great deal over his hidden affair of the heart. I knew from the signature that it was one that could not run smoothly. If he had been an ordinary layman I should have stuck the letter up, inscribed it 'Opened by mistake,' and forwarded it to its owner. But Galsworthy was by now more than an ordinary stockbroker or politician. He had come alive. And I took a great deal of trouble to get that letter to him without any indications of its having been opened.[1]

Galsworthy gave no signs of thinking that the letter had been tampered with, and for a little time it looked as if everything was as it always had been. We breakfasted and talked about the weather and the crops; we went together to concerts that his sister, Mrs. Reynolds, was organizing; we discussed the alterations that his sister, Mrs. Sauter, suggested in the story he was writing . . . which was, I think, then the *Villa Rubein,* a book for which I had and still have a great affection. Then gradually the change came.

He began to talk of Turgenev as the emancipator of the serfs in Russia; about the reform of the poor laws; about the reform of the incidence of the income tax on the poorer classes. And above all, of course, about the reform of the marriage laws, and perhaps still more about the re-estimation of marriage as an institution. He uttered one day the sentiment that where there is no love, there is no duty.

Then one evening he knocked on my door in a really pitiable state of distress. I was giving a rather large dinner, one of the motives of which was to introduce Galsworthy himself to the more formidable critics and men of letters of the London day. His

[1] I told this story of the letter recently, as a case of conscience, in one of my books, suppressing of course Galsworthy's name. Now, however, that his official biographer has told the whole story of the fortunate love affair of the author of *The Man of Property,* there seems to be no reason for further concealment.

book was then near publication and Conrad and I had conspired to do that amount of log-rolling. And suddenly there was Galsworthy at seven-thirty saying that he could not come to that dinner. He said that if I knew what was happening I should not want him to come to dinner; that all my guests would think the same. Mysterious things were happening to him; he would probably never again be invited to dinner by anyone. I should know all about it tomorow; then I should see how right he was.

It was no use saying that if he had been hammered on the stock exchange or neglected to pay his racing debts it would make no difference to my desire to have him at that dinner. He said: No, no! It would be unthinkable. It would be an offence to myself such as he would never pardon if it had been offered to him. . . . It was the first time I had come up against his immense, his formidable, obstinacy.

He wrote to me next day to say that he had that afternoon been served with papers as co-respondent in a divorce case. Of course my guests would have hated meeting him! And he wanted to know if it would make any difference in our friendship.

Times of course have changed, but I think that even then the ordinary man would have taken the matter less tragically. Galsworthy, however, insisted on considering that his social career and more particularly that of his future wife was at an end, and that for the rest of their lives they would be cut off at least from the public society of decent people. He was, of course, quite wrong. Even at that date London society took the view that, for a decent man and woman, passing through the divorce courts was a sufficient ordeal to atone for most irregularities.

Once they were through, they had taken their punishment and decent society does not approve of two punishments being exacted for one misdemeanour. . . . But at the time it was no good putting that view to Galsworthy. He was in many ways singularly old-fashioned and strait-laced.

But more than anything he was sensitive to the sorrow of other people. He was that even before he had thus got, as it were, religion, and the long excruciation of waiting years for the opportunity of happiness had made him sensitive beyond belief. The anticipation of possible future grief for his wife rendered him at the time almost out of his normal mind, and the emotion was rendered all the stronger by the thought of the suffering that, for years before that, she had had to endure . . . with, as it were, Soames Forsyte. I really thought that, at about the time when he had just received those divorce papers, he might have gone mad. . . . And that note of agonized suffering at the thought of oppression or cruelty became at once the main note of his character and of his public activities. It led him, in his novels, into exaggerations of slight strainings of the humanitarian note which distinguished every page of his writings of that date and, as we shall see, it influenced the very framework of his novels themselves. And his very exaggerations tended to negate the truths of the morals that he meant to enforce.

So you had the once-famous controversy of the rabbit. . . . At the end of the description of a battue in *The Country House*, having rendered, with all the spirit of Tolstoi after his conversion, the massacre of game that had taken place, in order to get the full drama out of the stupidity and cruelty that obviously

distinguish those barbaric slaughters of harmless beings, he found it desirable to emphasize the note and
to describe how 'one poor little rabbit' crept out into
the open to die. Now, two sentences of the description of the slaughter of deer in the *St. Julien L'Hospi-
talier* of Flaubert, utterly dispassionate and without
comment as they are, might well suffice to put you
off the shooting of all game whatever . . . certainly
off the massacre of driven game. But wounded rabbits do not ever die in the open . . . of choice.
Even domestic animals, if you let them alone while
they are dying, will creep under a bush if a bush is
to be found . . . or else under a low piece of furniture. . . . And we ourselves seldom like to die under
the sky, preferring to turn our faces to some wall.

So someone noted this exaggeration of poor Jack's.
And controversy broke out, in the sporting journals,
in men's clubs, in bar parlors, in country-houses. The
more scientific readers of the journals wrote to say
that, wherever rabbits die, they never die in their
burrows. Their companions would force them out to
die where they could. Hardened rabbit-hunters for
the pot, warren-breeders, gamekeepers, wrote or declared in inn corners that that was all nonsense.
Again and again when digging out rabbits they had
found dead ones among the living. The scientists
declared that this only occurred when the dying
rabbit was too large and heavy to be forced out of
his lair. The living rabbits would then, in order to
avoid living with the putrefying body, have to abandon that home and dig a new one. . . . But one and
all declared that Galsworthy did not know what he
was talking about. So the book lost a good deal of
influence with its readers. It would be unfair to say

that it had been written with the sole object of stopping the practice of shooting driven game. But that had been one of its purposes. And he gave the upholders of game-preserving and intensive shooting the chance to say the damaging thing.

For Galsworthy knew perfectly well what he was talking about. But his Tolstoian reaction against his former life had made him forget what, in his subconsciousness, he must have known to be the truth. At any rate, before his regeneration, he had spent nearly all his autumns shooting driven grouse, pheasants, and partridges. Many of his earlier letters contain expressions of exhilaration at the thought that the game season was opening again. But his revulsion from the life of the man-about-town was at that date very thorough, and the emotion of shuddering at every one of his former habits penetrated to every fibre of his being. He was determined, if he could, to bring about a change of heart in human society.

There was at this time raging in literary and artistic society in London much such a clash of views as lately distinguished New York. Reformers of all types declared that no work of art could be real art if it were not also a work of propaganda for the Left. And nearly all serious English novelists were finally driven to take that view. The novel became a vehicle for every kind of 'ism'; a small but noisy minority backed Imperialism and bank-holiday patriotism, but the serious novel as a whole interested itself almost solely in sociological questions.

As against that, as I have already adumbrated, a still smaller but sufficiently formidable band of foreign writers had at the time settled mostly in the

South of England. The most important of them were
the writers I have here treated of, and the other body
of writers for the once immensely famous *Yellow
Book*. That organ had been founded by Henry Harland, the author of *The Cardinal's Snuffbox,* an
American who had come to London by way of Paris,
and its supporters were all either foreigners or had
had foreign, mostly Parisian, trainings. It was the day
when England, and America too, rustled all over its
literary quarters with the names of Flaubert, Maupassant, and, above all, Turgenev. That camp proclaimed that a work of art must be a passionless
rendering of life as it appears to the artist. It must
be coloured by no exaggerations, whether they tend
to exalt either the Right or Left in politics. The public function of the work of art in short was, after it
had given pleasure, to present such an epitome of life
that the reader could get from it sufficient knowledge
to let him decide how to model both his private and
his public lives. Thus Flaubert wrote that if France
had read his *Education Sentimentale,* she would have
been spared the disasters of the Franco-Prussian War.
He meant, not that France would have learned from
him how to choose a better rifle than the *chassepot,*
but that if France had learned from that book how
to question her accepted ideas she would have had
a set of citizens capable of studying public questions
with realism. Then she could have taken earlier precautions against the Prussians. . . . The business,
then, of the artist was to study the works of his
predecessors . . . the works that had given pleasure.
In that way he would learn how to give pleasure in
his turn. And, rendering the life of his day as he saw
it and without preconceptions, his world would at

least be enlightened as to the conditions in which it lived. It might even, then, improve itself.

Those at any rate were the two schools of opposed literary thought that divided the world when Galsworthy came on the artistic scene. In addition, as I have already adumbrated, the Conrad-James-Crane school, to which I belonged, believed that you could learn nothing technically from Turgenev. There are, that is to say, certain writers—Shakespeare is among them—who have not really 'methods' . . . who write, as it were, solely from their temperaments. Such writers are exceedingly dangerous to the learner. He can learn nothing technically from them and he is extremely likely to fall into an imitation of their mannerisms and into trying to assume their temperaments. Galsworthy says in a letter that Mr. Marrot prints[1] that he did not consider himself a born writer, but one who had made himself by the labours of the eleven years that preceded the writing of his *Man of Property*. At that I have already hinted. He said it again and again at many different stages of his life. He repeated it even in the draft of the speech in thanks for the receipt of the Nobel Prize, which death prevented his delivering. And if he said it at that moment of his apotheosis he must have believed it to be true. It was not true, of course.

It might have been true to say that he was not a born novelist and, from my particular angle, it might be true to say that he never was a novelist at all. But writing is not all novel-writing, and there were departments of the art of projecting things on paper in

[1] *Life and Letters of John Galsworthy*, by H. V. Marrot. The author kindly lent me advance sheets of the work when I had reached this stage of this article.

which he really excelled and was conscious that he excelled. It is true that a writer must be born a writer. But it is true, too, that a born writer can be made over . . . to his detriment; and I do not think that any real writer can have ever been so made over as the unfortunate young Galsworthy. I must have written him reams and reams of letters about his early work. Mr. Marrot prints one that takes up some four whole small-print pages of his book. And sometimes Galsworthy took my advice and sometimes he stood out against it with the grim obstinacy that was his chief characteristic. For myself I should have found such a letter intolerable if it had been addressed to me, but Galsworthy was always ready for more . . . and ready for more from almost anybody who would address advice to him. His chief advisers in those early days were Conrad, Mr. Edward Garnett, who was adviser to Fisher Unwin, the publisher; and his sisters, Mrs. Sauter and Mrs. Reynolds . . . and the lady who was to become Mrs. Galsworthy, and myself. And I think I can say that it was the last-mentioned two who had the earliest and most complete belief that he had genius.

I do not believe that any of the others, at any rate at that time, had at all that feeling. The sisters had towards him a nervous maternal attitude such as was natural in sisters with a brother who wanted to do anything as wayward as 'write.' For, if he would be merely normal, he would be assured of a perfectly comfortable position as a man-about-town and a member of the best clubs. Conrad never really liked Galsworthy's writing. He had for him, I should say, a real personal affection and appeared radiantly pleased when Jack came to visit him. But, I suppose just because of that personal affection, he was not ready to accord to that pleasant boy any share of talent. It did not seem that anyone so pleasant could have the sort of grim persistence that Conrad considered to be indispensable for a writer. He wrote him of course letters full of an appreciation of his work that he expressed in terms of superlatives. But at the same time in private he always spoke of 'poor Jack' with sighs; and as Mr. Marrot brings out, he wrote to his own private correspondents letters expressing no sort of opinion at all of Galsworthy's gifts. As against that he gave himself a very great deal of trouble to place Galsworthy's work.

And later, when Jack was beginning to succeed, Conrad's indignation at the younger man's dogged humanitarianism went beyond bounds. He used to say that, as a writer, Galsworthy took a sadic pleasure in rendering the cruelties that the world inflicted on the weak and the unfortunate . . . and that he would be upset if those wrongs were righted because then he would have so much the less to write about. That of course was not true.

But as I have said, Galsworthy had about him a pixylike quality that rendered him very difficult to understand. I don't mean to say that I understood him altogether. There were about him too many irreconcilabilities; there was the impressive surface softness and a subcutaneous quality, as if of corundum. His benevolences were unparalleled; no man can ever have given a greater share of his income or a greater proportion of his time and worried thought to the unfortunate of every type. This appears sufficiently in Mr. Marrot's book, but if Mr. Marrot had a great deal exaggerated that note he would still have been well within the bounds of the truth. I know this because of the constant stream of miserable people which came almost straight from Galsworthy's doorstep in Addison Road to the offices of the *English Review*. Nearly all of them Galsworthy would have already relieved. Or rather he would have relieved all of them. But occasionally he would telephone to me to say that if So and So should come to me he did not consider him to be a proper person to receive relief from the fund that at that time I administered for the help of literary men in distress. . . . And it is to be remembered that the cases that I knew of were merely those of writers . . . there must have been more than as many more again who were laymen that he helped. Mr. Marrot says that Galsworthy lived on half his income, devoting the rest of it to public charities or causes; but more than half the sum that he set aside for his own use must in addition have gone to private cases. For those private charities were to him his life.

I think that, even more than his writing or his public honours, they were his life. . . . But suddenly there would come out an incomprehensible touch of hardness, as if some unfortunate had incurred his displeasure, or as if some public cause had all of a sudden appeared to have undesirable aspects. These things would be irreconcilable. He would at one time declare that the very fact that a man was no good was the reason that he should be helped, untiringly. Because it is poor, weak things that must be helped. Men with backbone can always in the end help themselves. And then, suddenly, of the most dreadful case of totally undeserved misfortune that I have ever come across he said, shutting his jaw tight, that the fellow was no good and had better not be helped any more . . . and that after he had been helping the man for a long time.

Of course it is given to no man to be consistent. But in Galsworthy it was something more than inconsistency: it was two distinct psychologies working side by side in the same being. That was why I have said that he seemed to be like a pixy . . . as if he were one of those good, serene, and beautiful immortals that had not human souls and yet occupied themselves with human affairs.

It was something of that quality that I felt myself to discern in his earliest work. Conrad, in writing compliments to Galsworthy, said about one of his stories that enthusiastic as he was, my admiration was much the greater. And my emotion was much more of a keen delight in a natural phenomenon— as if a new bird had suddenly sung—than of pleasure in a technical, literary achievement. It was the pixy-like quality of his temperament that had called it forth. It was a quality that I hadn't found anywhere else in the world . . . and that I do not think you will still find anywhere else.

And that, in the end, is the justification of the artist in words—that he should be an express something that has never yet been, or been expressed. To me it became apparent gradually that Galsworthy was probably never meant to be a novelist. Or it would be more just to say that thoughts of the world of injustice pressed too strongly on him to let him continue to be a novelist. That was why, at Winchelsea, I was alarmed at his rendering of the Turgenev anecdote. . . . I can assure you that I felt a genuine pleasure and impatience at the thought of coming across a person with the aspects for me of an authentic genius . . . and if I perceived a threat to the prospect of the fruits of that genius growing eventually ripe beneath the sun, I was proportionately dismayed. And I thought I perceived that threat. I foresaw for a moment his preoccupation with the unhappiness of lovers and the helpless poor . . . and that preoccupation leading him to become not a dispassionate artist but an impassioned, an aching, reformer.

The premonition was too true. *Villa Rubein* was a novel of a sunlit quality. But its successor, *The Island Pharisees,* was already a satire, and *The Man of Property,* which came next, was an attempt to cast discredit on the marriage laws of the day. And after that, in his novels, he was the reformer almost to the end.

And unfortunately his temporal success as novelist obscured his much greater artistic achievement with the drama. His novels suffered from his dogged determination to find ironic antitheses. His one 'effect' as a novelist was to present a group of conventionally virtuous, kindly people sitting about and saying the nicest things about all sorts of persons. . . . A divorced woman is thrown over their garden hedge and breaks her collar bone, and all the kindly people run away and do not so much as offer her a cup of tea. And that goes on forever, the situation being always forced to bring in that or some similar effect. Mr. Marrot quotes a really amazing correspondence between Mr. Garnett and Galsworthy about the end of *The Man of Property*. It raged for months. Galsworthy was determined that his Bosinney—who was the last person in the world to do it—should commit suicide in order, really, to prove that the propertied middle classes were very cruel people . . . with of course the aim of shaming those classes into becoming really kinder. Mr. Garnett, all reformer as he too was, is shocked at the idea that Bosinney—who, I repeat, was the last person in the world to commit suicide—should be forced to take his own life so as to show the effects of the cruelty of the middle classes. What Bosinney would have done—and what the situation demands—would have been to run away with Irene and live in inconspicuous bliss in Capri ever after. But no, says Galsworthy, that would not prove that the middle classes are always cruel and victorious over the unfortunate. . . . And the argument seems to go on forever, each party maintaining exactly the same ground. In the end poor Bosinney has to be run over by a bus, the reader being left uncertain whether it is the result of an accident or a suicide . . . and there seeming to be no moral lesson at all.

But the same dogged determination to present antitheses which produced an effect of monotony in the later novels was exactly suited to the theatre. There effects are of necessity more fugitive and need to be harsher—more cruel. And the keen pleasure that, at the play, the mind feels at appreciating how, unerringly, Galsworthy picks up every crumb of interest and squeezes the last drop of drama out of a situation . . . that pleasure is the greatest humanity can get from a work of art. It is the greatest because pleasures, shared as they are in the playhouse, are contagious and can be unbounded. And it is one of the most legitimate of man's pleasures.

When you came away from the first performance of *The Silver Box* you knew that something new had come into the world . . . a new temperament, a new point of view, a new and extraordinarily dramatic technique. And the conviction was strengthened by each new play. For myself I preferred *Joy* to all the others because it was more a matter of dramatic discussion than of situations, and because it had some of the lightness that had distinguished the *Villa Rubein* of our youths. But the characteristic of building up antitheses which, monotonous as it becomes in the novel, is always legitimate and exciting in the swifter moving play, that characteristic distinguished as much his handling of situation as of staged controversy. And finally that conviction came to be shared by the large, unthinking public, the plays began to run for periods of years in both London and New York, and Galsworthy moved from triumph to deserved triumph. No other modern dramatist had anything approaching Galsworthy's loftiness of mind, his compassion, his poetry, his occasional sunlight or the instinctive knowledge of what you can do on the stage. And by himself he lifted the modern stage to a plane to which until his time it had seemed impossible that it could attain.

And so he made towards supreme honours a tranquil course that suggested that of a white-sailed ship progressing inevitably across a halcyon sea. You would have said that he had every blessing that kings and peoples and Providence had to bestow. Having refused a knighthood he was awarded the highest honour that the King had at his disposal—that of the Order of Merit. He presided in Paris at the dinner of the international P.E.N. Club, which is the highest honour that the members of his craft could find for him; and, in the end, the Nobel Prize Committee honoured itself by selecting him for one of its laureates. It seemed, all this, appropriate and inevitable, for, in honouring him, the world honoured one of its noblest philanthropists.

The last time I saw him was in Paris when he gave his presidential address to his beloved P.E.N. And singularly, as he emerged above the shadow of all those hard French writers, there re-emerged at any rate for me the sense of his frailty . . . of his being something that must be shielded from the harder earnestnesses of the world. I don't know that he was conscious on that last public triumph of the really bad nature of the hard men who surrounded him. The world had moved onward since the days when he had read Maupassant and Turgenev for what he could learn of them. Both those writers were what he called dissolvents and the Paris *littérateurs* now wanted above all constructive writing and would have agreed with him if he had said—as he did in one of the last letters that he wrote—that Tolstoi was a greater writer than Turgenev.

But, there, he said nothing of the sort. He seemed to float, above all those potential assassins, like a white swan above a gloomy mere, radiating bright sunlight . . . and with his gentle, modest French words he made statements that ran hissing through Paris as if he had drawn a whip across all those listening faces.

For the French writer of today, Maupassant is the Nihilist Enemy—an enemy almost as hated as the late M. Anatole France.

And Turgenev is an alien ugly duckling who once

disgusted the paving stones of Paris with his foreign footsteps. Nothing indeed so infuriates the French of today as to say that Turgenev was really a French writer. . . . And there, enthroned and smiling, poor Galsworthy told that audience that shivered like tigers in a circus cage that, if he had trained himself to have any art, and if that training had landed him where he was, that art had been that of French writers.

A sort of buzzing of pleasurable anticipation went all round that ferocious assembly. The author of *Fort Comme La Paix* looked at the author of *Nuits En-soleillées* and thought: 'Aha, my friend, this is going to be a bitter moment for you. When I consider the *dédicace* of the ignoble volume that this barbarian chieftain presented yesterday to me . . . when I consider the fulsome, but nevertheless deserved, praise that he wrote on that fly-leaf, I don't have to doubt whom he is going to claim as his Master. . . .' And the author of *Nuits Ensoleillées* looked back at the author of the other classic and thought exactly the same thing—with the necessary change in the identity of the author. And every French author present looked at every other French author and thought thoughts similar. And when the applause subsided poor Jack went on:

Yes, he repeated, all the art he had had he had had of the French. If he stood where he was, if he was honoured as he was, it was because all his life long he had studied the works, he had been guided by the examples of . . . Guy de Maupassant and of him who though a foreigner by birth was yet more French in heart than any Frenchman—Ivan Tur-genev!

I have never seen an audience so confounded. If an invisible force had snatched large, juicy joints of meat from the very jaws of a hundred Bengal tigers the effect would have been the same. They simply could not believe their ears. . . . As for me, I was so overwhelmed with confusion that I ran out of that place and plunged, my cheeks still crimson, into the salon of the author of *Vasco,* who was preparing to give a tea-party at the end of the Île St. Louis. And the news had got there before me. It was in the salon of every author of the Île, of the Rue Guynemer, of the Rues Madame, Jacob, Tombe Issoire, and Notre-Dame des Champs, before the triumphant Galsworthy had finished his next sentence. . . . For that was the real triumph of his radiant personality, that not one of the fierce beasts quivering under his lash so much as raised a protest. No other man in the world could have brought that off!

TURGENEV

THE BEAUTIFUL GENIUS

Henry James once said—to me, and to the curious being to whom I have referred as being his *âme damnée:*

'Ah, he was the real . . . but a thousand times the only—the only real, beautiful genius!' He added: 'One qualifies it with "Russian" for immediateness of identification by the unknowing. But for you, for me, for us . . . for all of us who are ever so little in as you might say the know of literary values, he must be always just that, *tout court* . . . the beautiful, beautiful genius.'

He was talking of Ivan Serguéivitch Turgenev.

For me, my life is glorified as by nothing else, by being able to state that I once offered that white-haired, white-bearded, and surely beautiful colossus . . . a chair. He was immense of stature in spite of the fact that his legs—though I don't remember the fact—are said to have been disproportionately short. But that gave him the aspect, when he was seated—because his trunk was naturally proportionately-disproportionately long—of something awesomely fabulous in bulk. I only remember once else in my life being similarly awed by a sense of incredible size in a created being—and that was when, in Paris, a young prize-fighter offered me as a present an Irish wolfhound that measured exactly twelve feet from muzzle to tail. . . .

When one is suddenly introduced to such immensenesses one—or at least *I* do—gulps in one's breath in awe and, for the moment, believes that one is being visited by some supernatural manifestation. Thus when I saw that wolfhound I felt some touch of the fear of the death that visits one when one sees Gods . . . as if in the grey beast, with outlines rendered dim by its length of hair, in a rather dim Paris salon that it seemed completely to fill from side to side, I were confronted with a dog specially built for the needs of the Irish Gods of a day when that was a land solely of Kings and Heroes.

But it was no doubt symptomatic that, in spite of the fact that, short though his legs may have been, I can't have reached much above his knee, I did not feel any awe at all in the presence of the beautiful genius. I had certainly the feeling that he must have come from among the roosalki and strange apparitions that swung from tree to tree or loomed in the deep shadows of Russian forests and could only be dismissed by making the sign of the cross in the elaborate Russian fashion. But I was conscious simply of a singular, compassionate smile that still seems to me to look up out of the pages of his books when —as I constantly do, and always with a sense of amazement—I re-read them. I felt instinctively that I was in presence of a being that could not but compassionately regard anything that was very young, small, and helpless. The year was 1881. He, sixty-three.

But I certainly can't have been awed, for I brought out in a high, squeaky voice and with complete composure, the words:

'Won't you and your friend be seated, Mr. Ralston?'

Mr. Ralston, Turgenev's first translator, almost the only English friend of any intellectual closeness that he had—and the only foreigner who ever visited him at Spasskoye—was another man exactly as tall and as white-headed and white-bearded as Turgenev himself. But, though he was an intimate friend of my family's—in which capacity he had brought Turgenev to call—and though for night after night he had told me the fairy tales of Krylof—which is how I came to know of the roosalki with the green hair who swing from tree to tree and the other beings who come back to me as *domvostvoi* and manifest themselves by making the wooden sides and beams of sheds creak all round you.—Oh, and of course the Cat of the House who swallowed the wedding procession and the funeral procession and the sun and the moon and the stars. And the dreadful lamb that shewed its teeth just beside your face and said horrible things—but in spite of my having sat on Mr. Ralston's knees night after night, drinking in those breathlessnesses, Ralston himself comes back to me as being the merest pale shadow beside the shining figure of the author of *A Sportsman's Sketches*. It was perhaps a merely physical fact because Ralston's hair, white as it was, had a bluish quality in the shadows, whereas Turgenev's had that tawnyish glow that you see in the foam of tidal estuaries. Or it may have been because the shadow of his approaching suicide—for one of the most preposterous reasons of misery and shyness after a fantastic *cause célèbre* that I have ever heard of—was already upon Ralston.

At any rate, there I was all alone in my grandfather's studio in the great house once inhabited by Thackeray's Colonel Newcome—who I dare say might physically have resembled either Ralston or Turgenev. And I come back to myself as being a very small boy in a blue pinafore, with long pale golden curls—as befitted a pre-Raphaelite infant—standing on tiptoe to look in at the newly hatched doves in my grandmother's dove cage. It had, as it were, a private compartment for the children. And suddenly I was aware of being walled in and towered over by those two giants—who looked down on the pink panting morsels in the cage-box . . . with even more curiosity and enthusiasm than I myself was shewing.

So I asked them to be seated.

I don't pretend that Turgenev discussed literary technique or the nature of things with me sitting on his knee. . . . The only thing that comes back to me is that he talked about the doves and then about grouse and that I called him to myself a bird man.

Indeed it does not really come back to *me* that I asked him to be seated. I know it because he told my mother and my mother frequently afterwards told me, imitating Turgenev's imitation of my squeaky voice. For my mother—who along with her sister and Mrs. Stillman was one of the belles of the then pre-Raphaelite day—he fell with the heaviness with which, till his dying day, he fell for any charming young woman in or near her early thirties. He was then, as I have said, sixty-three and my mother not quite thirty. . . . I remember her, later, standing in the space between the front and back studios that were lit with branch candlesticks against a Spanish leather gilt wall covering, with her back against the upright of the door, extremely blond, talking with animation to Liszt, Bret Harte . . . and the author of the *House of Gentlefolk* . . . And I remember her, too, with her eyes red with tears as she read and re-read that book of the beautiful genius. . . . She knew it as *Lisa,* in poor Ralston's translation. . . .

So that from my earliest age I was aware that that book was the most beautiful book ever written, and I was, as it were, transfused with a sort of rapturous admiration for that Master that has never left me. So that today, after fifty years, his image is as much as ever a thing of light to me—as it were of the light of candles in branched silver sticks shining against a golden surface that had embossed on it grapes and vine-leaves with their twisted tendrils. . . . And I am sure that if ever I—and how many others!—committed ourselves to little good and kindly actions or courses of life it was because we in our youths fell under the influence of that beautiful and lambent spirit. . . . His work had that effect on the world. . . . Do not forget that one single book of his brought about in three days a revolution such as cost the United States years of fighting and an infinite outpouring of gold and the lives of poor men . . . and such as only yesterday—and still today—is a pretext for international convulsions that for years to come will endanger our whole civilization. One single book!

For me, when I read in that book *The Singers,* or *Tchertop-Hanov and Nedopyushkin,* or that most beautiful of all pieces of writing, *Byelshin Prairie,* I am conscious, as I have said, always of Turgenev's face looking up out of the pages—but also of a singular odour, sharp and rather pinching to the nostrils. It is that of smelling-salts. The phenomenon had always puzzled me until only the other day the explanation came to me when reading one of the innumerable, not too sympathetic Russian biographies of Turgenev. I was conscious, that is to say, when I had sat on the knee of my Bird Man and he had told me something about the grouse that he had come to England to shoot, that he had seemed to have about him that particular odour. I had always thought that that had been an illusion of my olfactory nerves. It seemed incredible that so male a giant should carry about with him a specific so feminine. Or I would put it down to the fact that so inveterate a sportsman who at an advanced age came all the way to England to shoot grouse must have been wearing Harris tweeds, which are impregnated with the queer musty odour of the peet reek of the cottages in which the fabric is woven. . . . But yesterday I had my explanation. It would appear that Madame Pauline Viardot had, in the first place, prohibited for him the use of cigars, to which he was much attached . . . and then that of snuff-taking, which he had adopted as a substitute. So to titillate his poor nose he had taken to sniffing smelling-salts. . . . And it was typical of him that, unlike me or you or the milkman, even when the rolling seas divided him from that sister of the divine Malibran, he did not indulge surreptitiously in tobacco but carried about with him his smelling-bottle and, when the longing for nicotine came over him, took, rather sadly, a long whiff. . . . Perhaps, even, the singular aroma may have served to keep off from him the attentions of the predatory charmers to whom his susceptible heart fell always so easily a victim.

I find faintly adumbrated in the same volume an anecdote that my mother used to relate with much more spirit in, I dare say, some approximation to the words Turgenev must have used when telling her the story. It was told amongst other items of affectionate making fun of poor Ralston at Spasskoye. It appeared that Ralston's singular physical approximation to Turgenev had caused amazement, and even concern, to the Master's serfs. They saw something supernatural about the whole affair, for it is to be remembered that they had never seen a foreigner, so remote were Turgenev's ancestral acres from the tides of outside humanity. So they imagined that this singular and fantastic double of their Master must have been introduced, incomprehensible language and all, with some sinister and even malign purpose. They were aware that as serfs they were extremely unsatisfactory, for Turgenev was utterly incapable of controlling anything but bird dogs, and his very house serfs when driving him in his landau on urgent errands would interrupt the journey in order to play cards on the box-seat—Turgenev being too shy to remonstrate with them. And even after the Emancipation—which he had brought about—they erected barriers across his only access to his only spring of drinking water. But now, they considered, the day of reckoning had come. The Master had imported a sorcerer to deal with them.

They saw the mysterious being enter all their huts, paper and pencil in hand, making copious notes. Actually, having his translation of the *Sportsman's Sketches* in mind Ralston was set on getting the Russian for every utensil and household article that their houses contained. Turgenev said that it was really extraordinary to see him run about, in and out of houses and barns and stable yards, his white paper, hair, and beard all fluttering together—searching for things he had not already observed. . . .

So, when he had gone, the peasants packed all their belongings on their poor carts and, sending a deputation into the Master's house, waited in a long file in the dusty road. The deputation wanted to know at what hour they were to start for England. . . . They had come to the conclusion that the Master was going to send them all into exile in that country . . . and to fill their places with a more obedient population. . . .

There remains one little puzzle of that distant day which I have never been able to solve. Turgenev spoke of grouse. Moreover his latest and most voluminous Russian biographer says that in 1881 Turgenev went to England to shoot grouse in Cambridgeshire. . . . But you cannot shoot grouse in Cambridgeshire for the same reason that you cannot catch snakes in Ireland. Nor could he have been in my grandfather's studio in months when you shoot grouse on the moors because we cannot have been in London during those months. We cannot have because by the Medo-Persian laws of those days you had at that season to be out of London. If your circumstances did not permit you to be out of Town, you had your windows boarded up, lived in your back premises, and only took strolls after dusk. . . . You had, during those months, to be shooting grouse on the moors, taking the waters at Baden-Baden. Or you had to confess that you were a nobody . . . which wasn't to be thought of!

So Turgenev had to be in England after partridge. . . . And indeed when someone—I don't think it can have been James—reproached him for not having appreciated Browning in Scotland eight years before, he excused himself by saying that when Browning had come over to see him from a neighbouring estate he himself had been so *éreinté* by the fatigue of following grouse over the moors that he could not have appreciated Shakespeare himself. . . . Not even Pushkin! And he had then declared that never in his life would he go to the grouse butts again . . . and then he had been only fifty-three, whereas, when he spoke to me of grouse he was already sixty-three and almost completely crippled for days on end, with gout. . . .

And the irritating thing is that the letter that he wrote my mother, thanking her for sending him some of the special preparation of colchicum that my grandfather used for *his* gout—that letter that my mother treasured till her last moments is, as you would expect, dated only '*jeudi le cinq*' . . . I suppose I could find out the exact date by consulting a calendar for 1881 and discovering in what month Thursday fell on a fifth. . . . But I don't suppose that Turgenev was ever accurate in his days of the month . . . and, if the truth must be told, I prefer not really to have the puzzle solved. Whilst it exists I can give myself the pleasure of thinking from time to time, at some length, of the beautiful genius—and of remembering that in his letter he talks of '*le charmant et intelligent petit*' who had asked him to be seated.

It is not wonderful that he should have made so profound an impression on that child of eight. Indeed of all the numbers of celebrated and great men that it was my rather mournful privilege at that date to see he most vividly comes back to me. As the home of a painter of French birth and tradition, the so-called Grandfather of the English pre-Raphaelites, the father-in-law of the redoubtable champion of the Music of the then Future who was reputed to be one of the best *raconteurs* in London, my grandfather's studio became on Thursdays a salon to which it was almost obligatory for any distinguished foreign celebrity to come during his visits to that metropolis in the seventies and eighties. So that the programme of my childish contacts has the aspect of something fabulous in the way of tuft-hunting . . . Why, I remember . . .

But that perhaps can wait indefinitely. . . . For the point is that nearly all those other figures are dim enough . . . the pre-Raphaelite poets and painters, and Wagner and the Zukunftsmusikers, and the French critics, and the German and American illustrious. Only Turgenev stands before me at this minute with a vividness that obscures the objects before my eyes . . . Turgenev, and perhaps Liszt. But the note of Liszt was not of quite the same innocent lustre. He had a greater self-consciousness, and that gave him in my eyes a touch of what I should today call the *cabotin*. He stood still or advanced slowly, with his dark brown face beneath its great carpet of white hair . . . he stood still or advanced slowly through salvos of applause, always making slight, hushing movements with his right hand, his enigmatic lips forming his famous Jesuit smile, and moving as if they wanted you to believe that they said that all this praise should be given not to him but to the Deity who had given him his gifts. What he expected that to mean to the four-wheel cabmen who, as I once saw, when Liszt was descending the steps from Saint James's Hall after a concert, climbed up the lamp-posts of Piccadilly and, waving their top-hats demanded three cheers for the Habby Liszt . . . what he thought it or he meant to them, there is no knowing.

But about Turgenev at that date there was no mistake. Standing . . . or rather, reclining on one elbow on a divan, he was a Deity all of himself. He had at that moment reached the height of his illustrious, world-wide fame . . . and, for the first time in many years, he was feeling physically fit. He was quite complacent on the subject of his health in the letters he wrote to Mme. Viardot; he had no fear of cholera in London; he had for the first time in his life succeeded in pushing aside the fear of death . . . and, although he complained that in Cambridgeshire he had missed a number of partridges, yet he could boast that he had hit a great many. So he seemed to radiate happiness and, leaning on his elbow, resembled one of those riverine deities who, in Italy, with torrents of hair and beards, recline in marble above the sources of streams, and let their waters render fertile the smiling valleys before them.

I prefer so to consider him. And always, except in the act of reading one or other of his lugubrious Russian biographers, my image of him swings back to that picture. His Russian biographers prefer, for as it were political reasons, to show always the reverse of that medal. They have to present him as a miserable expatriate from Russia, bound to the girdle of a tyrannous French harpy, groaning for ever that he was not in Russia, detesting his French literary colleagues, detesting France where he was forced to live . . . and groaning, groaning, groaning.

Turgenev of course groaned . . . in a groaning world which was in the backwash of the Byronic-Romantic movement. Everybody in fact groaned, particularly in their letters. Reading the correspondence of the middle two thirds of the nineteenth century is like sitting on a broken column by some grave beneath a weeping willow. Carlyle groaned, Flaubert howled groans, Georges Sand groaned, Sainte Beuve was perpetually depressed. Tolstoi, Maupassant, Dostoievsky, Queen Victoria, Schopenhauer, Bielinski. . . . But every one that Turgenev knew or ever heard of . . . they all lamented their miserable lots; the injustices to which they were subject; the unpicturesque figures that they imagined themselves to cut; the world, and they with it, that was going to the dogs!

Nevertheless, Georges Sand's apartment in Paris roared and rocked with the laughter of Flaubert, Turgenev, the Goncourts, Zola, Daudet, and Pauline Viardot when the depressed Sainte Beuve on a Sun-

day would turn himself into a whitened sepulchre in
the attempt with his lips to pick a wedding ring off a
pyramid of flour. One Paris restaurant after another
asked the five Hissed Authors—Flaubert, Daudet,
Turgenev, Goncourt, and Zola and now and then
the youthful James—to take their weekly dinners
elsewhere because their Gargantuan laughter and
Titanic howls of derision at the style of their contemporaries disturbed the other diners. Yasnya Pol-
yana—or whatever Tolstoi's lugubrious abode comes
out when it is correctly transliterated—that hermit-
age then rocked to its foundations with scandalous
mirth when Turgenev, aged sixty and declaring himself crippled with the gout, danced the *cancan* vis-à-
vis to a girl of twelve. . . . Tolstoi notes in his
diary: 'Turgenev; *cancan* . . . Oh *shame!*'

Similarly in *her* diary, the German Empress Victoria—*Die Englaenderin*—makes after the private
first night of an operetta that Turgenev had written
for the music of Mme. Viardot and for performance
by himself and the Viardot children, the note that the
operetta was charming but Turgenev himself not
quite *dignified*. . . . And Turgenev himself, lying on
the floor, in the costume of a Turkish Sultan, and
crawled over by adorable odalisques, was aware that
there was passing over the great lady's face that
singular English expression that we put on when we
ask, 'Isn't he being rather a Bounder, my dear?' But
Turgenev just says, 'Bedamn to that!' . . . And the
Empress sends down two or three times every week
to the Turgenev-Viardot villa to ask them to give
another performance soon or that Turgenev should
write another operetta for her at once. . . . And
didn't someone once hear Bielinski, or it may have

been Bakunin or Herzen or any other of those cheerful 'true Russians,' say to Turgenev after they had
talked from eight in the morning till past three in the
afternoon: 'You, Turgenev, are an incredible mate-
rialist. Here we have not yet finished discussing the
nature of the Deity and you are already talking about
lunch.'? . . . But the more usual true-Russian's
complaint of Turgenev was that after he had been
sitting with one of them for not more than half a day
he would begin to exhibit signs of uneasiness and
would say that Mme. Viardot's daughter or Mme.
Viardot's daughter's baby might be ill and he might
be wanted to run to the doctor's or the chemist. . . .
The true-Russians would declare that shewed how
cravenly Turgenev subjected himself to the yoke of
Pauline Viardot. But, knowing Turgenev and knowing what true-Russian conversation was then like,
one might be pardoned for imagining that what Turgenev really wanted was either his lunch or an inter-
val of blissful silence.

It is a good thing that no one ever did know what
was the exact relationship between Turgenev and the
great Pauline and that for the world at large and
Russia in particular it must remain in Turgenev's
own enigmatic phrase an 'unofficial marriage.' That
he was absolutely chained to the lady's apron strings
is obviously not true, or even that he was in the technical sense of the word today an unhappy expatriate.
His contacts with Russia—the as it were strings of
interests that went from him to her—were innumerable and for ever undissolved. His interest in her fate
was as constant as his interest in his own estate . . .
and that was really unceasing if the results were
never very satisfactory. He once told one member of

my family—I forget which, either my father or my
grandfather, that they must not think him merely
frivolous if at his age he came as far as England
merely to shoot partridges. Actually he could have
shot partridges anywhere—except perhaps round
Paris where the *chasse* was very expensive. But he
came to England to study on the spot the English
management of great estates and agricultural methods, which he declared to be by far the best in the
world. The immediate results of the emancipation of
the serfs in Russia had been an almost boundless
confusion, and the only pattern of which he could
conceive as being a fitting or even a possible solution
for the Russian situation was something like that
practised on the semi-feudal, semi-libertarian, great
estates in the English Dukeries and their purlieus.
Today that seems like irony; but for a liberal thinker
of that epoch it was something very like common
sense. . . . And it is to be remembered that Turgenev had practical reasons, apart from his own
necessities, for trying to evolve some sort of possible
working scheme for the Russian agricultural system.
During the earliest eighties, whilst Alexander II was
planning his constitution for Russia, the German
Ambassador in Petersburg wrote several times to the
Empress Victoria—who passed it on to Turgenev—
that it was a settled thing that Turgenev was to be
the first Russian Prime Minister. And with all his
real modesty there was no reason why Turgenev
should not take that piece of diplomatic gossip with
some seriousness . . . at any rate to the extent of
considering with some practical attention the question of what was the best constitution for his country's great landed estates, then in the possession of an

extraordinarily unpractical, frivolous, and absolute aristocracy. He had at least unrivalled reasons for knowing how difficult the task was; for within his heart all possible benevolence, he had only succeeded in making of Spasskoye one of the worst managed estates that even Holy Russia could show. . . . At any rate he never went back from England without carrying with him in baggage and brain some specimen of agricultural machinery or some detail of the estate-management of the Dukes of Norfolk or Northumberland. . . . I remember—I must have been told it by my mother—poor Ralston's agitation at not being able to find the manufacturers of some miraculous new plough of which Turgenev had heard in Russia and which he imagined might go far to solve the agricultural difficulties of his country.

In any case, if thinking of the interests and problems of one's native land suffice to prevent one's being an expatriate, Turgenev was none . . . and it is interesting to think of what would have happened to Russia if the Court Party had not let Alexander II be assassinated, if he had promulgated his Constitution, and if Turgenev had indeed occupied a high place in his first Constitutional ministry. That, as I have said, would not have been so astonishing. It is to be remembered that Alexander ordered the emancipation of the serfs three days after he had finished reading the *Sportsman's Sketches* and that twice at least the Empress had ordered the censor to refrain from interfering with Turgenev's books.

It is of course as impossible to know anything real about a sovereign as to know anything real about a novelist, both being so surrounded. But the figure— the sort of composite photograph—that passes for that Tsar would seem to have been intelligent, mild, well-meaning, and better acquainted—if mostly in a disciplinary manner—than are most sovereigns with the intelligentsia of his realm. He got to know them mostly by their getting themselves imprisoned at the dictates of the Censor—even Turgenev was imprisoned for a month for writing an article about the death of Gogol! When they were released or pardoned, he would send for them, lecture them, and relegate them to their estates for a period of repentance. . . . So that he might have got on well with Turgenev as a minister . . . and then our world of today would have been a different, and probably a preferable, affair.

I don't mean to say that Turgenev would have been a Heaven-sent statesman. One knows nothing about him. One knows less about him even than about Shakespeare. He moves surrounded by the cloud of his characters as a monarch by his courtiers; and, once more like a monarch, surrounded by crowds of admirers and detractors who all viewed him in the light of their own images, preconceptions, and desires. The result has been a cloud of witness all going to prove that Turgenev would have been a better Russian if he had never been out of Russia— with the implication that, in that case, he would have suffered less from the gout, not fallen under the influence of Pauline Viardot, and would, according to the political predilections of the particular writer, have been a better Terrorist, Slavophil, or Tsarist. Certainly you can prove all those things, and out of Turgenev's own mouth and writings.

That is because he was the supreme creative writer. And, no doubt unconsciously enough, society

exacts of its creative writers that they shall have no
personality. . . . The one thing that we *know* about
Turgenev was that he loved partridge-shooting—and
that on occasion he was ashamed of loving partridge-
shooting, or at any rate that he found it necessary to
excuse his passion. . . . Thus we don't even know
that. So that actually we know less about Turgenev,
who lived, as I have said, in a perfect cloud of witness, than about Shakespeare—who may, or may not,
have lived in as much of a cloud. For we do know
that Shakespeare, when he retired to Stratford on
Avon, sued out his coat armour, neglected to correct
the proofs of his plays, and left, as a gentleman
should, his second-best bed to his wife. . . . As an
English gentleman, with coat armour complete. Because your second-best bed was the one in which you
slept with your wife, the best being the one you
reserved for your guests. . . . So we know that
Shakespeare was a gentleman—with the habits and
tastes of a gentleman.

And certainly we know that Turgenev wasn't. He
was certainly noble. . . . But a gentleman does not
write operettas and lie on the floor, acting in them,
under the eyes of Empresses . . . at any rate after
he has become a gentleman. . . . For Shakespeare
may very well have played Bottom, say, under the
eyes of the Virgin Queen. . . . And indeed, as Mat-
thew Arnold so penetratingly observed, gentlemen do
not abide our question . . . Noblemen do, and say,
'Bedamn to you!'

So that we do not really even know that Turgenev
loved partridge-shooting . . . Certainly in all his
pages there is not a word about the noble bird suddenly turning a somersault in the air and falling to

the earth a mass of crumpled feathers . . . or not so
far as I can remember or have discovered. . . . Nor
indeed do I remember that in all his pages there is
any reference to . . . the bringing down of the game
in the other great *chasse!*

For I had been about to extend my hazarding of
conjectures into the real nature of the beautiful
genius by saying that one could be pretty certain, at
least, that he loved the chase of the Pretty Ladies.
. . . But did he even love that? . . . One may well
doubt it. You may add to the image of the riverine
deity that he certainly had the air of tranquillity of
the man of many 'successes.' . . . And there exist
innumerable of his passionate love letters to innumerable ladies. . . . But one feels when reading
them, the conviction that they are too well expressed.
. . . Of course he was a writer and could express
himself. . . . But a really violent sexual passion is
usually incoherent.

So perhaps one must confine oneself to one certainty . . . that he was not a journalist. . . . By
that I do not mean to utter an insult to my confrères
of the periodical press: I mean merely to say that a
journalist of genius is of a genius different in species
and especially in production from that of the creative
writer who desires to leave to posterity an enduring
image of his world and day. The journalists go to
things to look at them and use their genius in *report-
age*. The great imaginative writer lives . . . and
then renders his impressions of what life has done to
him. He lives, that is to say, in, if possible, a fine
unconsciousness . . . but certainly in an unconsciousness. He will not go to New York or the
Ukraine or Cambridgeshire in order to see what there

is to see, with the intention of writing about it. He will go to Spasskoye to set his estate in order, to Cambridgeshire to shoot grouse, to Bougival to continue his rather desultory courtship of Mme. Viardot, or to the limits of the Ukraine in momentarily passionate pursuit of some intelligent actress or some peasant girl of a pure heart. . . . Then, protesting that he will never write another word—and passionately believing that he will never write another word —he sits down and writes a masterpiece . . . not about the last passion or the latest trip to Spasskoye, but about the last but six, or the last but twenty. . . . Or about one that took place twenty years before he was born.

That is why the creative artist is almost always an expatriate and almost always writes about the past. He *must,* in order to get perspective, retire in both space and time from the model upon which he is at work. . . . Still more, he must retire in passion . . . in order to gain equilibrium.

Turgenev carried the rendering of the human soul one stage further than any writer who preceded or has followed him simply because he had supremely the gift of identifying himself with—of absolutely feeling—the passions of the characters with whom he found himself. . . . And then he had the gift of retiring and looking at his passion—the passion that he had made his . . . the gift of looking at it with calmed eyes. It was not insincerity that made him say to the French *jeune fille bien élevée* that her convent and home influences had made her the most exquisite flower of tranquillity and purity and refinement and devotion . . . and of course, that as a corollary, the Russian *jeune fille* was by comparison gross, awkward, ignorant, and sensual. That was his passionate belief in the presence of the daughters of his Pauline . . . who certainly were not his own daughters. . . . And yet it was equally his passionate belief, three weeks after in Spasskoye, that the Russian young girl was limpidly pure, pious, devoted, resigned—was all that he had projected in his Lisa —whilst, in contradistinction to her the *jeunes filles bien élevées* of Bougival were artificial products, *fades,* hypercivilized, full of queer knowledges that they had picked up behind the convent walls . . . sophisticated, in short. . . . No, he was not insincere. It was perhaps his extreme misfortune . . . but it was certainly his supreme and beautiful gift— that he had the seeing eye to such an extent that he could see that two opposing truths were equally true.

It was a misfortune for his biographers and for those who believe that biographies can ever illuminate anything. For the biographer and the consumer of biographies, looking only for what they seek, find what they want and play all the gamut of their sympathies or hatreds. But Turgenev was by turns and all at once, Slavophil and Westerner, Tsarist and Nihilist, Germanophile and Francophobe, Francophile and Hun-hater, insupportably homesick for Spasskoye and the Nevsky Prospekt and wracked with nostalgia for the Seine bank at Bougival and the rue de Rivoli. All proper men are that to some degree—certainly all proper novelists. But Turgenev carried his vicarious passions further than did anyone of whom one has ever heard. He would meet during a railway journey some sort of strong-passioned veterinary surgeon or some sort of decayed country gentleman. . . . And for the space of the journey he would be them. . . . And so we have Bazarov—whom he loved—and the Hamlet of the Tschigri district . . . whom perhaps he loved too.

It is because of that faculty that he made the one step forward. Flaubert—whom he also loved and who perhaps was the only man whom he really and permanently loved since they were both mighty hunters before the Lord of one thing or another—Flaubert, then, evolved the maxim that the creative artist as Creator must be indifferently impartial between all his characters. That Turgenev was by nature . . . because of his own very selflessness. Like Flaubert he hated the manifestations and effects of cruelty produced by want of imagination. . . . But he could get back from even that passion and perceive that unimaginative cruelty is in itself a quality . . . a necessary ingredient of a movemented world. To noble natures like those of Flaubert and Turgenev the mankind that surround them is insupportable . . . if only for its want of intelligence. That is why the great poet is invariably an expatriate, if not invariably in climate, then at least in the regions of the mind. If he cannot get away from his fellows he must shut himself up from them. But if he is to be great he must also be continually making his visits to his own particular Spasskoye. He must live always both in and out of his time, his ancestral home, and the hearts of his countrymen.

So having lived he must render. And so having lived the supremely great artist who was Turgenev so rendered that not merely—as was the case with Shakespeare—did he transfuse himself into all his characters, so that Iago was Shakespeare and Cordelia Shakespeare and Bottom Shakespeare and Hamlet.

. . . Not only then are Lavretsky and Bazarov and Lisa and the Tschigri Hamlet and the Lear of the Steppes all Turgenev but—and that is the forward step—they are all us.

That is the supreme art and that the supreme service that art can render to humanity . . . because, to carry a good enough saying the one step further we have got to go if our civilization is not to disappear, *tout savoir* is not only *tout pardonner* it has got to be *tout aimer*.

The humane Tsar lying down on a couch . . . I don't know why I imagine him lying down . . . perhaps because humane people when they want to enjoy themselves over a good read in a book always lie down . . . the humane Tsar, then, lying down with the *Sportsman's Sketches* held up to his eyes began to read what Turgenev had observed when shooting partridges over dogs . . . with the ineffable scapegrace serf Yermolaî at his heels. . . . And suddenly the Tsar was going through the endless forests and over the endless moors. He had the smell of the pines and heather in his nostrils, the sunbaked Russian earth beneath his feet . . . Yermolaî did not have the second gun as ready as he should; Yermolaî had not even loaded the second gun; Yermolaî, the serf, had lagged behind; serf Yermolaî had disappeared altogether; he had found a wild bees' nest in a hollow tree; he was luxuriously supping honey ignoring the beestings. . . . And suddenly the Tsar himself was Yermolaî. . . . He was a serf who might be thrashed, loaded with chains, banished to a hopeless district a thousand miles away, put to working in the salt mines. . . . The Tsar was supping the heather-scented brown honey in the hot sun. . . . He saw his Owner approaching. His Owner was fortunately a softy. Still it was disagreeable to have the Owner cold to him. . . . And quickly the Tsar sent his eyes over the country, through the trees in search of a hut. If he saw a hut he would remember the story of its idiotic owners. He would tell the idiotic story to the Owner and in listening to it the Owner would become engrossed in the despairing ruin of those idiotic creatures and would forget to be displeased and the Tsar would have two undeserved pork chops and the remains of a bottle of champagne that night in the wood-lodge.

And so the Tsar would become a wood-cutter in danger of being banished for cutting the wrong trees, and a small landowner being ruined by his own ignorance and the shiftlessness of his serfs . . . and a house-serf dressed as a footman with plush breeches to whom his Owner was saying with freezing politeness; 'Brother, I regret it. But you have again forgotten to chill the Beaujolais. You must prepare yourself to receive fifty lashes . . .' And the Tsar would be Turgenev shuddering over the Owner's magnificently appointed table whilst outside the footman was receiving the fifty lashes. . . . And Alexander II would become the old, fat old maid, knitting whilst her companion read Pushkin to her, and crying over romantic passages and refusing to sell Anna Nicolaevna to Mr. Schubin, the neighbouring noble landowner who had fallen incomprehensibly in love with Anna Nicolaevna. . . . And the Autocrat of All the Russias would find himself being the serf-girl Anna Nicolaevna, banished into the dreadful Kursk district because the incomparable noble land-

owner Mr. Schubin had fallen in love with her. . . .
And the great bearded autocrat with the hairy chest
would be twisting his fingers in his apron and crying
. . . crying . . . crying. . . . And saying, 'Is it possible that God and the Tsar permit such things to be?'

And so, on the third day, the Tsar stretches out his
hand for his pen . . . and just those things would
never be any more. . . . There would be other bad
things, but not just those because the world had
crept half a hair's breadth nearer to civilization . . .

. . . You may imagine how Turgenev's eyes stood
out of his head on the day when he met Mrs. Harriet
Beecher Stowe . . . who for her part had never been
below the Mason and Dixon line . . . and who was
introduced to him as being the heroine that had
made the chains to fall from the limbs of the slaves
of a continent. . . . He said that she seemed to him
to be a modest and sensible person. . . . Perhaps
the reader will think out for himself all that that
amazing meeting signified.

He will observe—perhaps with relief—that contrary to the habit of writers of my complexion I
have here said nothing about the 'technique' of my
subject. It can't be done. No one can say anything
valid about the technique of Turgenev. It consisted
probably in nothing but politeness . . . in consideration for his readers. He must have observed that the
true-Russians of his day, living amongst lonely vast-
nesses, were all perfect geysers of narration and
moral deductions. They were incredible, overwhelm-
ing, desolating. From the lowest peasant up to Tolstoi
everyone, at a moment's opportunity, would burst
into undamable spoutings of stories accompanied by

insupportable indulgences in the way of moralizings
. . . and self-analyses. It was the very genius of the
people. . . . He must have waited on a thousand
aching days for his lunch, and then have removed
himself from Russia with the oath never to make
anyone else go hungry whilst he told a tale; never
to draw morals; never to analyse his own or anyone
else's psychology. So you have his incomparable
projections of his world put before you with an un-
approached economy of words . . . and, because
his temperament was very beautiful, with great
beauty.

No, of Turgenev's technique one can say with
assurance no more than one can say with certainty
of his personality or of his relations with Madame
Viardot. The most you can say is that he was that
fabulous monster, a natural genius; when you have
said his name and those of Bach and Cézanne—and
one other that you can suit yourself about—you have
exhausted the catalogue, since the Crucifixion. As
with Hudson, as stylist, the dear God made Turgenev's words to come, as He made the grass grow.
It is there and there is no more to say about it.

For myself I prefer my own undepressed version
of the beautiful genius's personality . . . the giant,
indulging in night-long verbal pillow fights at Croisset, with the gigantic Flaubert . . . Flaubert's pa-
tient niece told me that when Turgenev came to
Croisset Flaubert always surrendered his own bed
to Turgenev and had one made up for himself in
the attic. . . . But fortunately they never went to
bed, preferring to talk all night about the assonances
in Prosper Mérimée. Fortunately, because Turgenev's
feet would have stuck far out over the end of Flau-

bert's bed and her uncle would never have slept on the shakedown under the tiles.

Talking all night with Flaubert then; next morning taking a walk with a true-Russian visitor and telling him that Goncourt was a bore, and Zola ill-mannered at table, and all French writers hard materialists and little Henry James too soft and the Terrorists heroes and the Tsarists fiends . . . or the Tsarists God-given if ineffectual statesmen and the Terrorists the spawn of the Devil; and taking a day's rest missing hundreds of partridges but killing hundreds too, and spending the night copying out Pauline Viardot's music for his operettas whilst sitting by the bedside of her sick grandchild who certainly wasn't his. And going to a tea-fight in some studio—and wallowing in adoration and adoration and adoration. And groaning that Life had no purpose and writing less. And telling some child about grouse to the acrid accompaniment of the odour of smelling-salts. And calming Ralston, in hysterics because the new steam plough was undiscoverable. And swearing to a pretty lady that he would never write another line . . . never . . . never . . . never. . . . And writing, some-where, anyhow, on any old piece of furniture with the dregs at the bottom of any old ink-pot . . . any old thing . . . *Fathers and Children* or *The Lear of the Steppes* or *The Death of Tchertop Hanov*.[1]

[1] I have hitherto, ungratefully, omitted to pay my tribute to Mrs. Constance Garnett's matchless translation of the works of the beautiful genius. The true-Russians say that Turgenev wrote very badly in Russian. He may have, but in Mrs. Garnett's achievement you have a monument in the sort of beautiful writing that deserves, if anything can, to outlast Time. For it, I at least shall never have sufficiently expressed my gratitude, for with-out it I could hardly have known Turgenev.

DREISER

WHEN I converse with Mr. Dreiser, he converts me, according to the temporary set of the tide of his passions, into a simulacrum of something that for the moment he abhors. I become for him a Nazi Jew-baiter; a perfidious Briton; an American financier; the proprietor of brothels in Paris; an unpractical poet; a mere unit floating in and indistinguishable from eleven hundred million similar units; a Jewish proprietor of chain-goods stores; a hereditary aristo-crat; an incapable and reactionary small farmer; a contemptible member of the official American Com-munist Party; a Washington hanger-on. . . . At all these simulacra of myself for hours and hours Mr. Dreiser hurls gigantic trains of polyphonic, linked insults. . . .

I have the sensation that I am walking in the dark along a railway line whilst Mr. Dreiser hurls at me immense handfuls of Pullman cars that go hurtling away over my head, invisible, resonant, innocuous. . . . There is a war time psycho-mnemonic reason for this image which I will later explain. . . . In the meantime, at odd moments, I say in a still, small, yet penetrating treble:

'Don't be so angry, Dreiser . . . *I* don't care.' Because, whatever simulacrum of myself he may be in the mood to rid the earth of, it is certain not to be the *persona* of the mood I am in for the moment.

Immediately silence falls. Then Mr. Dreiser says quickly and with almost feminine solicitude:

'What? What? . . . No, I'm not angry. . . . You mustn't mind me. . . . I'm emphatic by nature. . . . It doesn't mean anything. . . . All the same there *are* sixteen and a half million Knights of Columbus like you in this country. . . . That's a problem, isn't it? . . . You'll admit that it's a problem. We've got to get rid of all you lecherous and insupportable swine. . . . To Hell with you all. You're turning this country into the Pope's stamping ground. . . . You're . . .'

I am for the moment, say, in the mood to be a French Royalist. I advance along the rails that are darkly gleaming in the light of the star-shells over Albert behind me. I advance cautiously but with valour, in my mind whiffling before me a light rapier with which immediately or sooner or later I shall destroy the Titan who, couched in the dark valley behind Martinpuich, is hurling all those too elevated railway trains over my head. . . . It is in fact exactly the mood of the last duty I performed in 1916 before I lost my memory. The railway trains then overhead were our own naval howitzer shells which made exactly the noise of weary trains. . . . That mood always falls upon me when I confront the bellicosities of this giant of wrath and war who on occasion, with the swiftness of light, will become a prodigy of almost feminine solicitude . . . and then will go on all over again. Until he is exhausted.

It is with me conversational technique. I represent,

as the reader will by this time no doubt have observed, the novelists who believe that there is a way
of doing things as opposed to the novelists of genius.
These last set vine-leaves in their hairs, grasp pens
as large as weavers' beams, and with enormous
strokes pen polyphonic rhapsodies, accusing us meanwhile of carving ingenious patterns with tooth picks
on peachstones . . . or of being poets. . . . For
when Mr. Dreiser wishes finally to indicate that I am
a sort of fusionless village imbecile he says:

'You're a poet. . . . That's what you are. A
regular poet.'

Naturally I retort:

'It's you who are the poet,' and so get under way.

He, at the end of his voice's tether, sits himself
down at his long, Esherick-made table and lays out
the cards for a Miss Milligan. . . . In a voice so
low as to be irritatingly half-inaudible I take up
the discussion where he has left it. . . . I don't
know if I am as large as Mr. Dreiser. If he has the
advantage in height I take it out in girth; or, if I
am a little taller, he is larger-boned. At any rate we
are both big and tempestuous. But when it comes to
voice in argument his is that of several town bulls,
mine is as small and persistent as that of the cricket
in a stone wall. I have too the advantage that my
accent is unusual for Mr. Dreiser. . . .

I say . . . half-whispering:

'Obviously the first duty of Christendom . . . if
we can be called Christendom any more . . .'

Mr. Dreiser says:

'What? . . . What's that? I can't hear you . . .'

I repeat, only a quarter-whispering:

'The first duty of Christendom is to succour and comfort the brothers and collateral descendants of Our Lord . . .'

A look of horrified bewilderment comes over Mr. Dreiser's face. He slams the ten of diamonds on the nine of hearts when it should have been clubs. He is speechless in his incredulity

I continue:

'I suppose our comity of nations . . .'

And I go on and on, digressing, speaking almost inaudibly, starting one hare and chasing another . . . I continue to suppose we are a comity of nations in the Western Hemisphere; that we can call that comity Christendom. . . . Well, but even Mahometans still reserve special honours for the descendants of their Prophet; the Chinese for those of Konfutsze. . . . Occasionally Mr. Dreiser dashes out, like a bull at a picador. But he is exhausted by having shouted at me for four hours and I avoid his charge by making another digression of subject.

As a rule he gets the last blow in and when I talk I am usually wondering how he will do it. . . . The last time it went like this. It was past two in the morning after a Christmas dinner. He stood up violently; cast his cards all over the long table and exclaimed:

'You hell of a fellow. You're keeping the whole house up with your mumbling. . . . You'd go on . . . till the conversion of the Jews.'

There is of course no answer to that. You can't keep whole households up and it is not really proper to oppose anyone who can suddenly drag in for your confusion a line from the finest poem in the English language.

So we stagger off to our couches.

From all which it will be perceived that as the poet says:

> I've a friend across the sea; I love him and he
>   likes me.
> I'll murder you with savage looks if you don't
>   admire his books.

And I will, too.

I first came in contact with Dreiser in, I think, late 1914 . . . and the event, as all the major events of an existence are apt to be, was for me rather symbolical. I was Battalion Orderly Officer in Cardiff Castle at the time and part of that humble job being the disposal of hundreds of character sheets, a task taking hours and calling for no attention, I sent my bâtman from the guardroom into the castle to fetch me a book that the *Outlook* of London had asked me to review as a farewell to their public.

I had for years been writing for that journal a weekly article about anything that came into my head . . . mostly about books, but quite frequently about any passing event that amused me. And it was a symptom of the naïveté not merely of myself but of the ordinary public school Englishman of my day that I should be shocked by the howls about German atrocities that were going up from the more lively and excitable press. I wrote therefore a pained editorial in the *Outlook* suggesting that it would be a good thing if the Press in commenting on the proceedings of the Enemy Country should do so in terms of the 'gallant Enemy' as had been the case in the

Napoleonic Wars and the Middle Ages. I disliked thinking that civilization should in these matters have receded six or seven hundred years. War, I thought . . . and a good many of my compatriots then thought too . . . should be conducted along the lines of some sort of polite Queensberry rules before a well-conducted audience such as you see every fourth of July in the grandstands at Lords for the Eton and Harrow match that closes the London season.

And it was symptomatic of the rather languidly Tory audience of the *Outlook* of those days that my article evoked no protest from my readers, save for one letter written by a very old lady who said that, if I wanted the Enemy forces to win I was at liberty to do so, but that it was rude to say so in public. . . . Nevertheless it had become obvious to me that for my sort of philosophy the times were quite out of joint, and I signified to the editor that I should probably do his paper harm and I would prefer to give up writing for a London audience. He asked me to go on writing for him, but I was rather out of tune with writing at all in those days, and finally he sent me the *Titan,* asking me to review it for him as a farewell pledge of friendship.

If you could turn up that review you would be—I hope kindly—amazed at the unsophisticated pain of the little, young, naïf, correct soldier man who, standing on his feet before a guardroom window, had written it, almost in tears. . . . Because, whatever you may say for or against it, the *Titan* is a milestone on the long road of our civilization.

Reading again today that cool projection of the career of Mr. Yerkes who was later to cause no end of a storm in the tea-cup of London transport finance

I am amazed to find that it is really not such hot stuff after all. I don't see why, things being as they are, he shouldn't collar the tramway system of his adopted city. Everybody does—or tries to. I don't see why he shouldn't be promiscuous. Everybody is today—or is said to try to be. Obviously his earlier speculation with the city funds of Philadelphia was questionable. . . . But that had occurred in the *Financier,* an earlier book of the unfinished triptych. . . . And Cowperwood had paid for his being insufficiently dishonest to get away with it by spending some months in Clink where, amongst his meditations he had learned sophistication.

No, the *Titan* does not shock me today. It is just a rendering of normal life a few years ago when life was simpler and less corrupt. Reading it now I find myself unconsciously regretting that Cowperwood didn't bring off his final trolley coup and have a more agreeable time with women. If you sell your soul to the devil, I mean, you ought to see that you get a good price.

But, back in the second decade of this century while the Big Words were still alive, the *Titan* very naturally made one's gorge rise. The Big Words . . . Loyalty, Heroism, Chivalry, Conscience, Self-Sacrifice, Probity, Patriotism, Soldierly Piety, Democracy even, and even Charity which some translate as Love . . . those big words and the golden naïvetés that they stood for were probably in that year going stronger than they ever before had gone . . . certainly in officers' messes and guardrooms and no doubt outside, for all I know. The War had given them an extraordinary life with which to give their last kick. We were going—all volunteers at that date

—to damn well *make* the world fit for Heroes and Democrats and Patriots! . . . Christendom, that was what it was going to be. . . . And absolutely safe for the Taxpayer too. Because for us the lowest and most repulsive of all vices was malversation of public funds. . . . That really was so. . . . Well, there was probably a time when you too thought like that. . . . Unless you are very young!

Anyhow there I stood before the guardroom window, looking out on the battalion prisoners crouched at the feet of the high elms munching hunks of bread . . . and wrote with my fountain pen, about the *Titan* and the life that it revealed, what was really an unconscious keening for a world that was to pass away.

As in the case of Thomas Hardy I am pretty sure that the *Titan* was not the first book of Dreiser's that I had read. I know I had even then in the back of my head some idea of *Sister Carrie* as an agreeable fairy tale of an entirely cheerful kind. . . . A sort of glowing, goldenish spot, as for me it remains. I must have read it in one of the first years of the century when, after it had been murdered in New York by Mrs. Frank Doubleday, the London reviewers received it with spring torrents of praise. It must have struck me with pleasure as the story of a nice, pretty little, industrious and careful girl having a real good time . . . but real, you understand. That meant that Dreiser, at least in the girl's story, must have employed a pretty good technique. Otherwise my mind would have rejected the book altogether . . . as being false. The Hurstwood side of the story simply did not remain in my mind. I daresay the idea of an unemployed man, sinking amidst desperate expedients lower and lower, was in the early years of this century, so unfamiliar to me that it did not seem real. . . . Alas, alas! . . . Or perhaps the very nature of the catastrophe of that unfortunate individual seemed rather what the French call *voulu* . . . Arbitrary. I can't have believed that a smart man would have grabbed a handful of banknotes just because he found his employer's safe open. It must have seemed to me that the writer had not employed in inventing his catastrophe as much of the iron determination to make it not merely plausible but an act of the blind force called Destiny that is behind all human tragedy . . . as much as in those days I exacted of the novelist.

At any rate, for many many years I went about with, in my mind, the idea of *Sister Carrie* as a gold-enish spot in the weariness of the world. . . . And I don't know that now, when I have re-read the book a couple of times, I don't feel much the same . . . and I shall probably this afternoon take another read in it just for my own pleasure. There can no higher compliment be paid by one novelist to another. At any rate when ten or a dozen years ago I had my first eccentric meeting with Mr. Dreiser and when Mr. Dreiser said hurriedly that he had read all my books and liked them very much and I had replied just as hurriedly that I had read all his and liked them very much too, I was not lying as hard as he . . . for if I said that I liked *Sister Carrie* very much it was the exactly right phrase. And by that time enough water of horrors had flowed under the bridges of the world to make me regard the *Titan* as merely a record of normal life. As for the *Financier*, when I had read it in, say, 1919 it had struck me as another pleasant fairy tale in which a mildly amoral and not unpleasant character had found his sufficiently agreeable happy ending with promise of wedding bells complete. . . . And at that date, as far as I knew, *Sister Carrie,* the *Financier* and the *Titan* were all the books that Dreiser had written. . . . I had forgotten *Jennie Gerhardt* which I had not liked . . . and which I went on and go on not liking. I can't help it if, as I suspect, it is Mr. Dreiser's ewe lamb. At any rate it is the only one of his books which I ever heard Mr. Dreiser mention—several times and as if with regretful affection. . . . But indeed it is the only one of his books which I ever heard Mr. Dreiser mention.

I am not, at any rate for the moment, criticizing Dreiser—the spirit, the method, the impulse, the whatever it is that has hurled his books at us. And of course I am not criticizing the Mr. Dreiser who hurls those railway trains of imprecations over my head whenever he meets me. I am merely stating likes and dislikes—which is a very difficult thing. Let us be explicit. . . . There is Stendhal for whose methods I have the very greatest admiration. He is perhaps the writer type as conscious artist and his French is impeccable, flawless, like Toledo steel . . . Toledo, Sp. . . . . But I don't like him and except for the *Rouge et le Noir* I can't read him . . . not the *Chartreuse de Parme,* not his writings on Love. But poor dear old Flaubert, who was another shouting Berserker, I like and can read all the time, though today he is much out of fashion in the country of the Lilies.

So I like and can read Dreiser except for Jennie Gerhardt—and she depresses me.

I hear you say:

'How is this? . . . This man is denying his gods.'

But it is not so. . . . It is only that this man is like other men who after half a century, or a quarter, or a decade or à lustre or a year or a month or a week of sedulous bus-driving takes a busman's holiday . . . according to his necessities. I don't know why busmen in especial should be taken as given to resting their minds by riding on other drivers' buses, but so it is said to be. When they have had a hard week they spend their day off being driven in blissful idleness from Putney to the Strand or from Washington Square to Grant's Monument and back. They say they feel like gentlemen!

So during fifty years or so of sedulous bus-driving . . . or no, it is rather more like the occupation of the ringmaster. When you are a conscious writer you watch your subjects, your characters, your words, in particular, as you put them down . . . as if they were lions, wolves or plaguy little cats performing on the sawdust of the ring. And 'Crack!' goes your long whip and they skip into their places and Columbine goes slick through the paper hoop and lands beyond on the white horse's back like a gull on the wave-crest. . . . And at the end of fifty years or so—if you are any good—you can make the beastly little things called words do what you want even when your back is turned or your eyes closed. . . .

Only . . . at times, you know, it is wearisome, that job. You get so that you want to write like a drunken Irish carter galloping a waggonload of split infinitives down a blind alley on a Glasgow Saturday night. And then, afraid of yourself; afraid that if you go on in that mood you'll really get yourself into trouble with the critical Police and lose your job and see your children starve and your name dishonoured, you throw your inkstand, like St. Dunstan, at the wall and say—or at least I do—'Damn it all. Let's go and ride with Dreiser and see how he gets his old bus along.'

Did I ever tell the story of Mrs. Elliot of Old Elvit, Durham? She had gone to see a man hanged, up by the Castle, and had had a seat in the front row; coming home in the crowd an old gentleman in front of her had dropped dead in a fit; just as she was entering her door a coal-lorry ran away beside her and ran over two children who had been playing in the street. So she fell into her room; pulled off her bonnet by the strings; collapsed into a chair and exclaimed:

'Losh, mahn, will this day be *nowt* but pleesure!'

That's what riding with Dreiser is like . . . for me.

And I guess—and I am not using the word *vulgariter,* I am really hazarding the conjecture—that that's what reading Dreiser is for everyone and that is why, for his country and for the world outside Dreiser is a Doctor Johnson, or a Flaubert-plus-Balzac, or a Wagner or a Tolstoi or a Michelangelo or . . . I can't think of any others for the moment, but there are two or three more. . . . Men who outpass nationality as now and then peaks from the sea bottom transcend their fellows and emerge beneath the skies. . . . I am not of course appraising.

Dreiser may be as great as Michelangelo, or Tolstoi or Wagner, or less great or more. When you are beside a mountain you can't see its relative importance . . . but you can judge the nature of its stone. And Dreiser had the gift of universality. . . . If you like to call it American-ness you can—in the sense that a sort of uniform spirit has overrun the Western world so that they are eating nearly as many and nearly as filthily indigestible canned products in Paris and London today as they are in Chicago. In that sense Dreiser is even hyper-American, for London devoured his products with avidity thirty years before there was any Dreiser-consumption at all anywhere between Terre Haute and Sandy Hook. . . . And that was not merely generosity in the London critics. . . . It was because the London critic saw himself as he would like to be if he could be it without being discovered—in the figures of Cowperwood or Sister Carrie or the Genius. . . . As later the American *homme moyen sensuel* saw, but for the grace of God, himself in the hero of the *American Tragedy*.

To me it is magnificently symbolical that Dreiser should have been born in Terre Haute since that town has the aspect of being the very navel of the country. And it is French in name and Papist in origin and very largely German-speaking . . . or Irish or Swedish or any old language but English. And in Terre Haute two queer, nationalist-internationalist spiritual adventures happened to me before ever I knew that Mr. Dreiser had there been born . . . typically enough in a German, Catholic, lower middle class family. In, that is to say, a stratum of society that developed itself in the early decades of the nineteenth century between those of the least wealthy tradesmen and the cream of the mechanics —the children, let us say, of upper servants, sewing-machine drummers, non-articled lawyers' clerks. It was a very definite new stratum that arrived all over the world at about the date of Mr. Dreiser's birth and that under the stimulus of a compulsory education very superior to that paid for by the upper and middle classes was beginning to see the expediency at once of getting rid of the Big Words for which they had no especial use and of getting a grasp on all sorts of reins of power. . . . For it was not for nothing that there arrived almost simultaneously not only, in America, Mr. Dreiser and, in England, Mr. Wells and the late Arnold Bennett . . . but amongst Teutons, Latins, and Orientals, Mr. Hitler, Mr. Mussolini, and Kemel Pasha and Sun Yat Sen, all of them set on reducing the whole world to a sort of common denominator and all born to that stratum of society. . . .

Most of all it symbolizes for me the eclipse of the proud, real Middle-Class, Anglo-Saxon domination of the world . . . an image that came to me in Terre Haute itself . . . I was sitting, that is to say, some years ago, at two in the morning, with the window open and door ajar in the guest house of the convent of the Holy Child near that city. I was playing soli-taire—which is also one of the occupations of Mr. Dreiser—because the intolerably efficient central heating of that hospitable spot made it impossible to sleep. The door pushed itself open before the form of the local policeman. He said:

'Ye're English, ain't yez? . . . I've come to tell

ye I hate yez because of the sorrows of the Dark Rosaleen.'

His father had been born in County Sligo, but he himself had never been outside Hoozier land.

. . . And next morning, waiting for an automobile to take me away, I was looking listlessly at the programme and accounts of a local Americanization Society. A thrill went slowly through me. I had observed that all the Americanizers had names like Eltsheimer, Nielsen, Lobkowitz, Guertli, Wellenhausen . . . and those they were working to Americanize were called Drake, Hopkinson, Marsh, Masters. . . . And I heard myself say *Fuit Albion et magna gloria Victoriae.*

I am not making a song and dance about that. It is merely one of those coincidental phenomena that are apt to assume too great proportions for the observer far from his usual Paris, London or New York and in Indiana it is not so astonishing as all that. But if it is a small fact it is none the less a fact and when a day or so later I heard that Mr. Dreiser had been born in that place it gave me a mental shock that crystallized a great many images for me. I don't know why, but somewhere in the corner of the mind where inaccuracies are stored, I had hitherto thought that Mr. Dreiser was a born Philadelphian who had passed most of his years editing a newspaper in Baltimore. It was before the period when he had had the opportunity to use me as a mental punching ball for five hour periods and I had found him to be usually gently and almost wistfully speculative, inclined rather to listen to me than to indulge in tirades. . . . Indeed on the occasion of my first meeting with

the author of the *Titan* we had for a period of three
or four hours talked of nothing but words and styles
and Mr. Dreiser had been so completely in agree-
ment with me that I had taken him to be a larger
and gentler Conrad. He had disliked assonances
quite as much as I did . . . and the writing of
Mérimée, Balzac, and of all other writers whom it is
proper to contemn. . . . And we had agreed completely as to the main stream in the history of the
novel . . . as to its passing from Lope da Vega and
the Spanish picaresques, by way of Defoe and Rich-
ardson, to Diderot, Stendhal and Flaubert and so to
Conrad and James and the writers of the then just
awakening Middle West. . . . Indeed Mr. Dreiser,
even on the surface, seemed to know quite as much of
the technique of writing as I did . . . and I gave
him mental credit for knowing a little more. So that,
in that perverse corner of my mind I had summed
him up as any other Anglo-Saxon *generosus, filius
generosi* who had got his learning at one or other of
the older universities of Penn's state and had pursued
his studies of Latin civilization and letters in the
otiose editorial chair of one of the more august
Baltimore instructors of the public. I *knew,* you
understand, that that could not be the fact. . . . But
one's instincts nourished by inflections of the voice
and mildnesses of the mind are so much stronger
than mere knowledge. . . . Indeed, I don't know
that to this day I don't go on somewhere at the back
of my mind believing that Mr. Dreiser is a gentle,
highly cultured being, of an immense erudition and
a wistful desire to penetrate always deeper into the
interstices of pure learning . . . that that is what

you would find him to be if you scratched beneath the surface.

But on the Chicago day, after I had left Terre Haute, when someone brutally and with official print, in *Who's Who* or something of the sort, convinced me that Mr. Dreiser had been born in Terre Haute in such and such a *milieu* and such and such circumstances, it was as if an immense new pattern of the world revealed itself to me. And I am glad that the revelation came in that way—after I had satisfied myself by personal observation that Mr. Dreiser was something quite different. Had I, I mèan, been convinced before I met him that Mr. Dreiser was some sort of literary hobo I might well have taken on myself some such attitude as that of Mrs. Frank Doubleday and have gone on with averted nostrils calling for musk whenever his printed page swam before my eyes. . . . As it was, when I came upon some of his words that are no words, queer grammatical solecisms and the other harsh oddnesses that at times affected me as if someone were thrusting a sharp needle upwards through the seat of the chair I was occupying, I thought according to my mood that they must be due to indifferent proof-reading, haste, or the ignorance of English compositors setting up Middle Western expressions—or merely to the fact that Dreiser knew what he was about and was trying after effects hitherto unessayed. And I had had the extraordinary readableness of his books to confirm me in that last view. You have to remember that the English literary scene with which I was till then most familiar is one of a uniform sedateness that resembles the surface of a duck pond completely

covered by a North American water weed whose
name I cannot for the moment remember—something like Ina Canadensis. So that when anything
really exciting came along the English critic was apt
to be far more enthusiastic than his transatlantic
confrère . . . that is why so many of the really
American writers from Whitman and Crane to Ezra
Pound and Dreiser received their accolades in London whilst their home critics and public and publishers and their female relatives were still delicately
fainting at the thought of them. And by reversing
the orientation you see explained why a number of
British authors who cut no ice in their own countries
find their niches between Sandy Hook and the Golden
Gate.

And then . . . nothing was ever more true than
that *mal d'autrui n'est que songe.* To Mrs. Frank
Doubleday and the typesetters of Messrs. Harpers
and to Colonel Harvey and all the rest of those who
blocked Dreiser's career, Dreiser was an immense
big black wolf who would make the world unfit for
their delicate susceptibilities, corrupt their young
children, block their ambassadorial careers at the
court of Saint James's where Cowperwood's final
female companion was *persona grata.* . . . There
were in short, for them, a hundred reasons—But a
hundred thousand!—why the writings of Dreiser
should be a pain in the neck . . . and an immense
one that they all sensed without putting it to themselves in words. . . . They felt in their bones that
Dreiser was not merely a big bad wolf but a masto-
don-symptom of an ice-age, an immense, slow-mov-
ing convulsion of a continent that when it should
have passed would leave neither them nor their houses

nor their names, their accents, their syntaxes, their baby-talk nor their world any more observable beneath the indifferent skies that spread from Maine to the meridian and the Occident.

To the English critic all these pains were not even dreams. They were unaware that they had any Terre Haute, any Middle West; they were certain that they had no Dreiser to disturb the Ina Canadensis. And it *is* fun, when you spend your life aping sedulously the language of the front page of the *Times Literary Supplement* so as eventually to ensure your own appearance in that House of Lords of Reviewers. . . . And mind you, that is not an easy job. It calls for years and years of real good behaviour. . . . Damn it all, it *is* fun to see that poor old language, that vehicle for conveying moderated thoughts, having the guts kicked out of it, like a deflated football, over all the fields of the boundless Middle West. . . . Don't believe that it was only Taine who felt an irresistible urge to shout at afternoon teas in Oxford drawing-rooms the word of Cambronne. . . . So the poor tired London critic had his hours in the realm of transatlantic, underworld faëry and expressed in his journals his gratitude in a foam of praise.

Dreiser obviously is untidy . . . but he has to be untidy in order to be big. He wants you to read immense wads of pages; you could not do it if they were my peach-stone carvings. I know that he cherishes wistfully the idea that one day in a great good time and a great good place he will go through all his books, smoothing out excrescences, restoring neologisms like 'objectional' to their original form of 'objectionable,' introducing *charpente* into his frameworks and giving to all his novels *progressions d'effet* framed in words of an impeccable justness. Because Mr. Dreiser knows all about all those things. An immense, omnivorous reader with one of the most tenacious memories that the world can ever have seen, he knows as much about literary technique as about brokerage operations. . . .

There was a German philosopher called, I think, Weininger whose landlady's daughter would not let him seduce her. So he wrote an immense—I believe that it is in Germany a standard—book to prove that all women were rachitic nitwits. In the course of that work he had to prove that no woman had ever possessed genius. So he said that genius was made up of immense memory; no women ever had good memories; therefore no woman could ever be a genius. . . .

I think that, in his discovery that genius and vast memory were commensurable, that blind hen, as the Germans say, had found a pea. The writer of vast memory has an ease of production and in consequence a sureness that can never be aspired to by a writer who must document himself as he goes along. He can produce his instances without delay and, most important of all, he never has to force his subject around so as to bring in a second-rate instance. The difference between a supremely unreadable writer like Zola and a completely readable one like Dreiser is simply that if Zola had to write about a ride on a railway locomotive's tender or a night in a brothel Zola had to get it all out of a book. Dreiser has only to call on his undimmed memories and the episode will be there in all freshness and valour.

If you want an image of him at his writing you

have to imagine him like a compositor before the
formes of his mind. He stands at a considerable
height, back on his heels, passes his fingers through
the forelocks of his silver hair, pauses for an instant
and then like lightning his hands dart in and out
over the types. He has instance A, a reporter at a
lynching; instance X, a farmer seeking his lost
Phoebe; instance L, a man realizing that though he
is free by the death of his wife, his hands must fall
powerless at his side, for the only freedom for him
is that of death. . . . And so on through instances
", #, $, %, & Z . . . each instance a memory out
of years back or yesterday, of points here and there
and anywhere on the span of a continent or so.
And each memory becomes as it were a letter, a
colour, an illumination and so, with immense speed,
the pages build themselves up and become books. Of
course he will make slips.

In the revolution of the resounding ages Dreiser
stands for the emergence of the Teuton-Slav over
the surface of a world till yesterday given over
to Latin and then Anglo-Saxon cultural domi-
nance. . . .

It is that aspect of world change that he voices as
Defoe voiced London of the Plague, Lope da Vega,
Spain, and Petronius Arbiter, Rome . . . or Homer,
the Age of Bronze . . . I am again not making ap-
praisals. When you read him the North American
Republic has lost its Anglo-Saxon, Victorian aspect
to such an extent that you might say it has become
an appanage of the German one. . . . Or still more,
that it is undergoing an evolution that is part of a
world-convulsion. For, as I have already adumbrated
the same is true of almost every unit of the Western

world and of many Oriental congeries. We are all of
us going finally away from handicrafts towards a
life characterized above all things by an eschewing
of all sedulousnesses. We all wear shop clothes because the solitary tailor cross-legged on his bench
is a distasteful image to our mass-production minds;
we all—in whatever nation—use words in which
Bowery suffixes of Oriental origin are tacked onto
Hellenic, Teutonic, or Latin roots. . . . And with
that wordological time-saving we have leisure to
lounge from cafeteria to movie in long afternoons of
untroubled bliss . . . I read this morning in my
Paris paper that the French premier had *knockouté*
with non-Aryan thoroughness of rejoinder a Basque-
Celtiberian lower middle class deputy who posed as
the champion of the son of St. Louis, and I am
going to lunch on *cornid bif* canned in Madagascar
because, here in Paris, we are in the middle of a very
unspectacular revolution and the butchers are all
asleep beside their chopping blocks.

It is because he renders for us this world of
fantastic incertitude that Dreiser's work is of such
importance. . . . The note above all being that of
incertitude.

. . . And, most important of all, neither Mr.
Dreiser the private gentleman, nor Dreiser, the personality that emerges from his books, has any settled
panacea for world improvement or even for world
enlightenment. They have between them one settled
passion—but neither has any more pattern than has
a chart of the Milky Way. They will, passionately,
like you and me, see one aspect of life one day and
another the next—and if either of them is in the
mood for curing the ills of the world he may passion-

ately at one moment proclaim some panacea and very shortly after may declare with almost equal passion that the very ill itself will in the end save humanity. That is today inevitable for any man who is a thinker as opposed to the protagonists of one Interest or another . . . If it were my business to cure the ills of France this morning I should be sure—but absolutely certain that the only thing that could do the trick would be the restoration of the Monarchy. But I should go to sleep, probably, with a last thought to the effect that very likely Mr. Blum will do a lot of good.

For it is characteristic of a confused world dominated by a hybrid social stratum that of necessity never had any use for the Big Words . . . that along with the disappearance of Continence, Probity, and the belief in revealed religion, Truth should have developed the bewildering faculty of the chameleon and have taken on like Janus, two faces. . . . There is no longer any one Faith, no longer any one Cause, no longer any one anything for the reasoning man. So the novelist—the authentic and valid novelist whose duty it is to record his world in crystallized form so that it may be of advantage to posterity— the novelist seeing both sides of Truth can do no more than take one side at one moment and the other immediately afterwards. . . .

But you might as well add the corollary that no poet or novelist can stay in one road for long . . . and if, like Mr. Dreiser, he is a very passionate poet and filled with red blood, his course, viewed from the air, will appear a bewildering zig-zag; he will have his reactionary half-miles, dash passionately forward for some furlongs, progress horizontally, and finally ascend to the empyrean exclaiming, 'A curse on all your houses!' And at that Dreiser and Mr. Dreiser so rarely synchronize! . . .

Mrs. Dudley in her admirable book on Dreiser and his times—which is even more about the times than about Dreiser—recounts how Dreiser once declared that from now on Science should be his only guide to the problems of the dreary empty spaces that surround humanity. But before the pronouncement could appear in print he was already writing that Science was all blah and scientists pompous misleaders of the body politic. . . . And indeed, one day here in Paris, I had been reading one of Dreiser's wistful tributes to Latin-derived civilization and arts. But going out to have tea with Mr. Dreiser I found him cursing the French and all their Latin-derived and petrified characteristics . . . and cutting short his stay and taking the next boat to Germanic Gotham. . . .

And the one passionate belief, doctrine, rule of life, and morality that unites both gentleman and writer is this . . . that humanity has a right to happiness. . . . It is astonishing how the idea of happiness pervades his printed work and his conversation. It pervades them wistfully . . . 'I don't know whether this man was happy or not,' he will write . . . and it pervades them with a passion of rebellion, of hope or despair. There are times when you will see Dreiser—and imagine that you see Mr. Dreiser—shake fists at Heaven, Hell, Purgatory, the Earth, the Sea, Morality, Ethics, Laws, and Local Regulations and swear:

'By God, men *shall* be happy in spite of all your foul, unspeakable practices. . . .' In which, if you come to think of it, he unites the doctrines of Nietzsche and Christ.

Yet the last thing I heard him say, to remember, was as it were out of the blue, because we had been talking of a way of cooking bananas and he was just getting into his car:

'Ah, you think you will one day reach a stage when everything will be all right . . . a long period of quiet happiness. . . .' But—and he shook his heavy head mournfully: 'You never will. Never. Never. One never does.'

It was queer to hear him echoing in that *obiter dicta* the last words—'Never the time and the place and the loved one all together' of the octogenarian optimo-pessimist of the Victorians. . . . But I daresay, if you could pursue the train of thought, you might find a good many parallels between Browning and Dreiser.

At the same time I wouldn't mind betting, if not my hat then at least my second-best shoes, that, in this time of cherries—Oh, connaissez vous le temps *des cérises!*—with the gay sunlight pouring all across the Western Hemisphere, recumbent somewhere in California or Westchester County, Dreiser is declaring—with emphasis—that this is a gay old world with infinite, great, good places in which, for periods extending into eternities, one may have the best of all good times. . . . And I'm sure I don't know whether I do or don't agree with him.

SWINBURNE

I HAVE been passing, I think the most disagreeable
six weeks—of a sort of boding—that I can remember
since I was in the line in the late war . . . because
always at the back of my mind, since I was a very
small boy, must have remained the belief that we—
our civilization—had a Senior Service of which as it
were Algernon Charles Swinburne was Admiral of
the Blue.

In H. M.'s Army, that is to say, we have to give
the *pas* to those who go down to the sea in warships:
on public occasions we must call them just that—the
Senior Service. And when I was taking a parade
of several hundred Returned Expeditionary Force
scoundrels, all regulars who pretended to have the
worst drills, the most suffering feet, the most collaps-
ible spines that the world of heroes has ever seen, I
used, whilst the perspiring sergeants strove in vain
to get them into some sort of a line, to saunter up
and down in front of their ranks, dragging my cane
behind my back. From time to time I would direct
on them a sideways glance and exclaim, 'Thank God
we have got a navy!' They would groan at that insult
and pretend they were groaning over the pain of their
deep wounds which should keep them in barracks for

at least a year or till the duration of hostilities. . . .

You have already perceived the parallel. . . . For for years when one has been considering English literary prose—that affair of limping scoundrels of used words that return to one for service—one has groaned over the straggling array and has said, Thank God, we have got our Poets.

Our Poets are our Senior Service. By hundreds of thousands of years verse and rhythm poetry preceded the much more difficult service of the *prosateurs;* and Prose is judged by much more severe standards and is a much, much wearier job. So for years and years one went about that obscure and laborious industry. Because, of course, English is not a language for prose as is Latin or Chinese or even French. It is a feminine sort of thing full of unmanageable conditionals—like Greek or Japanese. So it is a weary pursuit, and those of us who for our sins seriously follow it know that we are a sort of chain-gang to whom no water-boy shall ever bring cooling fluids.

It has been our lifelong consolation to think that somewhere in the world there have been those happy beings, our poets, hitching up their slacks, dancing eternal hornpipes, taking unending poetic licences in honey-flowering meads. . . . Well, *you* know!

We didn't of course read them. Why should we? Who in fact does want to read Poetry . . . and who were we to presume to differ from other proper men? . . . But from time to time fragments of their verse would come flying towards us on the breeze. We would get somehow inaccurately by heart.

From too much love of living and life and death
    (sic) set free. . . .

Or:

> I that have love and no more, give you but love
>   of you, sweet
> He that has more let him give; he that has wings
>   let him soar

And we would marvel a little at the apparent ease of the poetic process and be glad that in this weary world someone was having so good a time and obtaining such high honours from pursuits so enviably otiose. And so we would return our noses over our raddled papers and whilst wearily chasing assonances out of our lines and racking our brains for words that would convey someone's chin with exactitude . . . or someone else's deer park—we would breathe fervently the words:

> Admiral Swinburne's . . . or latterly [Commodore
>   Sir John Masefield, P. L., Historiographer
>   Royal, 's] on his Quarter Deck,
> All's well with the world . . .

Because of course with our heavy and teasing preoccupations *we* could not be expected to do much for civilization. The Verse Poets must save it.

So, comfortably, we imagined the great gallions of the Poetry of Tennyson P. L., and Morris (William) and Austin (Alfred, P. L.) and Bridges (Robert, P. L.) running down the easting on the halcyon tides and Mankind, by a magic process, getting daily better and better and better. . . .

Then, six weeks or so ago I decided that, having come nearly to the end of this series of projections of the minds of my distinguished *prosateur* contemporaries, I ought to turn my attention to the mysterious realm of the Verse Poets. I obtained therefore the *Complete Works of Swinburne* and sat down to read. . . . To bathe in solar glory, to be enraptured by unbridled Hellenic eloquence, to lose myself, perhaps for ever, in the glamorous haze of a solar myth. . . . Only yesterday Swinburne meant all that to me. . . .

My first personal contact with the beautiful translator of pieces from Villon and Aeschylus and the Vidame de Paris occurred in 1879 . . . two years before I sat, as I have related, on the knee of Turgenev and saw Liszt descend the steps of Saint James's Hall under a rain of the applauding top-hats of four-wheel cabmen.

I was in the beautiful warm, glowing, great kitchen of my grandfather, watching the immense cook dish up the *pièce de résistance* for a dinner for twelve that was going on over our heads—and, I don't have to tell you, plaguing that red-hot functionary for bits of pie-crust sprinkled with brown sugar.

The cook was adjuring me to hold my tongue in words the remembrance of which at this day still makes my blood curdle. I was momentarily happy because my uniform of the infant pre-Raphaelite genius was hidden by a French smock in blue gaberdine. Later I should have to go up into the dining-room for dessert and to receive bits of *marrons glacés* and méringue from the forks of poets, painters, and poet-painters. My smock would before then be taken off and I should appear in the blushing, stammering horror of green velveteen corduroy, with gold buttons, one scarlet stocking, and one green and long platinum blond curls. . . .

But for the moment I was safe in that warm sanctuary amongst my grandfather's servants whose lightest private word would take the copper off the bottom of a Chinese clipper. . . . Nevertheless, upstairs or before, as it were, the public their demeanours were of a tart righteousness that, with their white aprons, white cuffs over the sleeves, white caps with large black streamers, always suggested to me that they were pillars of salt. . . .

And suddenly out of that warm drowsiness of piecrust—for the cook had had to give me pie-crust to keep me quiet—I was aware that Charlotte, the housemaid, was saying to a four-wheel cabman:

'*My* master's sitting at the head of his table entertaining his guests. . . .'

She was at her very saltiest and most pillarlike and she was addressing a four-wheel cabman who, as if by magic, had appeared within that warm circle of light and, with a sort of hieroglyphic stiffness, in a voice so hoarse as to be almost inaudible, kept addressing to Charlotte the mystic words:

'I've got your master very drunk in my keb.'

A four-wheel cabman was a very awful being to the young of that day. He wore, and apparently never removed, even in bed, a dingy top-hat, a red worsted choker, a top-coat adorned with an immense number of shoulder-capes; there were always straws attached to the bottoms of his trousers and he carried always pushed out at the end of a laterally extended arm, a hollywood whip . . . so that he appeared to be in an attitude of propitiating an Egyptian deity by the offer of that implement. . . . One half of the youth of London then used to spend their days riding on the back springs of four-wheelers, the other half adjuring the cabman, from the sidewalks, to 'whip behind!'

So that dusky monster continued to say that he had got Charlotte's master very drunk in is keb and, until the crucial moment, Charlotte continued to say that her master was sitting at the ed of is table.

At last she brought out composedly the words:

'That's Mr. Swinburne. Help me carry him upstairs and put him in the bath.'

And that was done.

It appeared to me to be quite all in the normal day's journey. My grandfather, the most benevolent of human beings, distressed at the predicament that overcame most of the pre-Raphaelite poets as a rule twice a week in those days, and rather than that they should spend cold damp nights in the stone jug, had hit on the device of having his own address inscribed on a tape label which was attached to the *revers* of the top-coats of the poets, so that on most evenings of the week a poet was conducted downstairs to the area and from there carried upstairs to the bath. . . . It might be Mr. Swinburne, it might be B. V., who wrote *The City of Dreadful Night* . . . it might be . . . oh, any one of half a dozen who have left respected names.

Nor are you to imagine that that indicated that the poets were what used to be called Bohemians . . . or that it was exclusively poets or artists who availed themselves of that kindly assistance. If I cut my catalogue of names so summarily it is that you may not be pained at coming across figures that were the glories of your youth and the moral props of your vigorous middle years . . . all being carried limply between Charlotte and a hoarse cab-driver, across the kitchen and up three weary flights of stairs to the bath on the second floor. . . . There was of course, in that vast house a separate staircase for the servants . . . indeed there were two—one for the men, the other for the maids. The stratagem of putting the poets and moralists in the bath was intended at once to protect them from bruising themselves in falling off a bed and to prevent them from getting out and making themselves nuisances to my grandfather . . . at the head of his table. Charlotte would dose them with dreadfully strong coffee and hold smelling-salts to their noses until, being able to get out of the bath unaided, they could descend the stairs and mingle with the other guests in the great studios. There, the vigilant Charlotte would see that they got nothing but toast and water to drink—that brownish fluid being utterly non-intoxicant and yet having the appearance of strong brandy and water so that the patients need not feel themselves humiliated. . . . And the pleading voices of poets and others that I can remember whispering: 'Just a drop . . . Charlotte, just a tiny drop of unsweetened . . . Charlotte, just listen!' . . . And Charlotte as unhearing as an Egyptian monolith! . . . Indeed she was as swarthy as a gipsy and as straight as Cleopatra's Needle, with the black vengeful eyes of Atropos and the expression of Rhadamanthus. . . . If you could read her Memoirs. . . . But I should not wonder if you have not and are not going to. For I do not know how many of my details of the lives of the great of the early eighties do not come to me from listening, unobserved, to Charlotte's conversations with my

mother in the great linen room of the Fitzroy Square
house. . . . Long, quiet monologues about Mr.
Swinburne and Mrs. Lizzie Rossetti and the carryings
on of Mr. Rossetti and that Mr. Burne-Jones and
that Mrs. Ruskin, poor dear thing . . . Her husband
says to her on their wedding day as they drove away
in their carriage . . . A shame I calls it . . . And
the Queen acting so cruel! . . . Fair threw the
President's chain in Sir Everett's face as he knelt
before her, they say she did . . . And her such a
pretty thing when she was Miss Euphemia Grey . . .
But he never forgive your father, Mr. Ruskin didn't
. . . Always thought he connived because, the night
they eloped, your father had him to dinner . . .
Charlotte twice had Queen Alexandra's prize for
having been longest in any family in the kingdom
. . . after sixty years of it and after seventy. . . .
When she was eighty-two she was sitting on a bench
on Primerose Ill and a gentleman sat down beside
er and says e ad the nest and e wanted a little bird
to put in it and ad she any savings? . . . Threw er
bonnet in is face she did 'n' tole im what she thought
v im. . . . I bet his ears burned!

The great seen from the linen room were thus
diminished for me—the awful, monumental, mina-
torily bearded tumultuous and moral Great of those
days. . . . Insupportably moral they were, and I
imagine the sense of original sin that in those days
possessed me in their presences would have overwhelmed me altogether but for the moral support
that the anecdotes in the linen room afforded me.

To stand, say, at the age of eleven between the
painter of the 'Light of the World,' Mr. Holman
Hunt, and Mr. Ruskin would have been an insup-

portable ordeal. Mr. Hunt had a voice like a creaking door, endlessly complaining; in moments of virtuous emotion Mr. Ruskin fairly hissed like an adder. . . . The whole world had conspired to misjudge, vilify, misrepresent, misunderstand, misestimate . . . even to rob, both of them, singly and together. It was as if they were mountainous islands entirely surrounded by villains. Mr. Hunt would creak:

'Gabriel . . . Gabriel was nothing but a thief . . . A common sneak-thief. I could have had him up before the magistrate at Bow Street. At any moment.'

Mr. Ruskin would dither, 'Dear, dear, dear, dear!'

'At any moment,' Mr. Hunt would repeat. 'He borrowed my copy of Browne's *Hydriotaphia* with Flaxman's plates . . . worth three pun ten, at least . . . and never returned it. . . . A common, vulgar sneak-thief. . . .'

I heard Mr. Hunt use those very words not so long after his friend Rossetti's death. . . . If I think about it hard it was perhaps not to Mr. Ruskin but to Lord Justice Ford North, who was the only human being I ever knew who was more disagreeable than Mr. Ruskin. He would, in moments of fury, snatch off his wig and throw it in the face of his clerk of the court. He was a militant churchman and was translated from the King's Bench to the Court of Chancery because he sentenced Foote the Atheist to penal servitude for life . . . for denying in a penny pamphlet the existence of the Deity. . . .

Well, they were that sort of alarming persons for a little boy . . . the members of the pre-Raphaelite circle, and certainly their society would have been an insupportable ordeal if I hadn't been able, when they weren't looking at me, to squint sideways into their faces and say to myself:

'Ah, yes, you're Mr. Ruskin. . . . My grandfather says you look like a cross between a fiend and a tallow-chandler and Charlotte says . . .' Well, I have already adumbrated what Charlotte said of Mr. Ruskin. . . . What she said of Mr. Hunt would not bear even adumbration but it was very fortifying to me. . . . As for the judge I never heard anything worse of him than that he suffered from an internal ulcer, which was what made him so obstreperous. He once cursed Charlotte at the top of his voice all the way from the studio to the front door. . . . But she had seemed rather to like it. Collected burial urns, he did. . . .

But as for Mr. Swinburne . . . Ah, that! . . .

I don't know whether it was Charlotte's adoration for him or whether I worked it out for myself. . . . But he at least was a solar myth with the voice of a Greek god, beautiful and shining and kind so that when *he* came on the scene, drunk or sober, all was gas and gingerbread and joybells and jujubes. . . . Well, he used to give me jujubes, slipping them out of his waistcoat pocket in his beautiful, long, white fingers. . . . And now and then it would be a poem suited to my comprehension and written in his beautiful clear hand, minutely, on valentine paper with lacey edgings and Father Christmas embossed on the reverse, or pink roses. . . . Usually, as far as I can remember, about my dog Dido . . . rhyming 'dog' with 'fog' and 'bog' . . . I think Mr. Swinburne once came on me on Wimbledon Common, which was near my birthplace, on a misty day, immensely distressed because my dog Dido had gone into one of the ponds and would not come out. . . . So Mr. Swinburne wrote me a series of little jingles about the adventures of that faithful hound, and used to deliver them furtively as if he were slipping me little parcels of candy. . . .

He was like that to children—and I daresay to grown-ups. And if you think that his coming home occasionally in four-wheel cabs from which he had to be conveyed upstairs to the bathroom . . . if you think that that made any difference to my—or even Charlotte's—childish adoration, you are mistaken indeed. . . . It didn't make even any difference to me that he was unduly short in stature. When the door opened before him and you looked to see a man's head appear at about the middle of the upper panel, his chin would not be much above the level of the door handle . . . not much. But then it was such a glorious head that you immediately forgot.

And then he was so much the great gentleman . . . which is a thing as to which the servants' hall and the nursery never make mistakes. He was one of the great, ruffian Swinburnes of the Border . . . with the Eliots and Crasters and Armstrongs and Jocks o' Hazeldean, reiving the cattle and burning the towers of the fause Scots, for ever in revolt against the Tudors, giving their lives in defence of Mary Stewart, chronicled in all the border ballads from Chevy Chase to Preston Pans. . . . It was said even to have been a Swinburne who wrote:

> Hey, Johnnie Cope are ye waking yet?
> And are your drums a-beating yet?

You know: it begins:

> Cope sent a message frae Dunbar,
> 'Charlie meet me an you daur,
> An I'll teach ye the arts o' war
> Sae early in the morning,'

to the tune of 'John Peel with his coat so grey.'

Yes, that was Mr. Swinburne . . . of the servants' hall and the nursery, fifty years ago. . . . Sixty, pretty nearly. . . . And it remains Mr. Swinburne to me now, looking at the vengeful evening light under the heavy clouds that are about to discharge their torrents on the drenched fields of West Kent. For you shall not say that I am not conscientious in these undertakings. . . . Having found it impossible in six weeks in Paris to keep my mind down to the *Poems and Ballads,* I imagined that that Gallic atmosphere was unsuited to the products of the Northumberland-Hellenic Muse and so have brought the thousand and a half odd pages of verse over here to within a yard or so of where the gentle Sidney wrote his *Arcadia* whilst the Princess Elizabeth, who was afterwards to hang a Swinburne for defending her cousin, sat under the great oak trees in the Park, being painted by Zucchero and handing apples to the deer.

And, no . . . It meant nothing to me that Mr. Swinburne had occasionally to be carried past between Charlotte and a kebman. . . . For the matter of that Charlotte would have carried him all by herself. . . . And you should have heard her defending him in the linen room.

'That Mrs. Lizzie Rossetti,' she used to exclaim. 'If the poor dear young gentleman wants to drink,

why shouldn't e? . . . Not that e drinks like Mr.
Blank does . . . not to say soak. . . . No, he gits
rearing tearing boosed when e as the mind ter . . .
n calls for pen n paper in the bath n writes n ode.
. . . E wrote two last Friday as ever was. . . . To
Mister Mazzini n against the Emperor of the French.
. . . N why shouldn't e? . . . That Mrs. Lizzie Rossetti. . . . A powerful pernicketty lady *she* was. N
would have things jest so. . . . Why shouldn e git
drunk in er box at Common Garden Oppra if he ad
the mind? If so be s she ed bin faithful to er usband
she might have spoken. . . . But she must go n
take n overdose'v opium. . . . Onreasonable I call
it. . . . Now look here Miss Catherine. . . .' My
mother was Miss Catherine for her until her death
. . . and to her death her Mr. Swinburne was more
sinned against than . . . but no, for her he never
sinned at all. . . . It was all that Mrs. Lizzie Rossetti's fault . . . when it wasn't the indigestion, all
them poor fellows avin no one to look after ther
meals.

For Charlotte took the view that all the woes of
the pre-Raphaelites, as of the world, were born simply of indigestion—an agricultural population having
suddenly become industrial and yet eating food intended for ploughmen staggering over the heavy
furrows. So they had stomachal *malaises* which they
palliated by pouring spirits down . . . to keep their
spirits up, as the song said. Charlotte used to declare
that SREnry Bird, at Bow Street when gentlemen
were brought too often before him for being 'drunk
and' . . . used to reason with them and suggest that
for their own benefits—because it was no trouble to
him to give them ten bob or fourteen days—when

the desire for unsweetened was on them they should drink instead half a wine-glass of Worcester Sauce. That would warm the pits of their stomachs quite as well as would London Particular, itself. And if they made *that* a habit they might rid themselves of the other. Some of them did, some of them didn't. Our Mr. Swinburne, I believe, did . . . at any rate Worcester Sauce entered, I was told, largely into the cure of the shining poet that was ultimately effected by Mr. Watts-Dunton at the Pines, Putney.

Charlotte, however, and I in her wake, did not particularly desire his cure. Perhaps she felt that if he were cured by Mr. Watts-Dunton, at the Pines, Putney, his poetry might suffer. And certainly she considered that his special tragedy, as it had come to her, demanded that he should drink in order to forget. That was part of the fitness of things. . . .

I suppose it to be generally known to the world interested in such matters that Swinburne entertained a passion for Mrs. D. G. Rossetti—the Elizabeth Siddal of earlier days, the model for Millais' *Ophelia*, the Félise of Swinburne's ballad. . . . The famous Miss Siddal, in short. According to Charlotte his interest was reciprocated by the lady to the extent of her being ready to elope with Swinburne. . . . Though, Charlotte used to say, it was astonishing that anyone so cold-blooded and hearted as Mrs. Lizzie, should want to elope with anyone. And on the night before the planned elopement Mr. and Mrs. Rossetti were in a box at the opera and Swinburne joined them in a state of inebriation so insupportable that Mrs. Rossetti went home and took an overdose of some opiate. . . .

There were, of course, in Charlotte's account other

gloomy and harrowing details of miscarriages and misunderstandings in a lugubriously oil-lamp-lit, indigestion-ridden, gin-sodden, always dripping London of the seventies—than which city none other could be imagined less suited for the sports and loves of lyric balladists of origin whether North Country or Italian. . . . On those you can employ your imaginations to any extent or, as to them, read legions of other writers. . . . The reports of the inquest— which Charlotte needless to say attended—state duly that before taking her overdose Mrs. Rossetti had been at the Opera with Mr. Rossetti and Mr. Swinburne . . . and the coroner and jury passed a vote of sympathy for Mr. Rossetti, thus left without anyone to sew on his shirt-buttons. But they say nothing of Mr. Swinburne's intoxication, which you can take or not as you please.

The point is that neither for Charlotte nor for me did any of these lugubriousnesses in the least dim the shine of the figure of Swinburne, the great little gentleman. He remained for us the glorious, reckless Border cattle-reiver, champion of Mary Queen o' Scots and of Liberty, Hellene, near-Godhead, golden in voice, infinitely chivalrous. . . .

One of the most poignant sayings of our time is that of M. Cocteau about Victor Hugo. He exclaimed, 'That man's mad. He thinks he's Victor Hugo.' So when my weary eyes fall on a page that begins:

> Though thy most fiery hope
> Storm heaven to set wide ope
> The all-sought for gate when God or Chance
>   debars . . .

and after a long time ends:

> On me a child from thy far splendour shed
>   From thine high place of soul and song
> Which, fallen on eyes yet feeble, made them
>   strong,

the enfeebled mind, weary of travelling the rivulet
of print between top and bottom of page, exclaims
pettishly: 'Why "thine"? . . . In heaven's name why
"thine" high place?' And then in exasperated protest:
'That page is mad. . . . It thinks it's Swinburne!'
. . . Because the poet that I—and Charlotte—
knew wrote, in the bath or in any other old place,
glorious golden verses, quivering, chanting, bearing
the glorified soul toward Heaven or Olympus's top.
He must have. . . . I tell you he *must* have. . . .
He smote his blooming lyre and the mountaintops
that freeze and the innumerable incarnadined seas
bowed themselves when he did sing. . . . Only—
where are they . . . those *neiges d'antan?*

Well, Time went on; my father died; Mr. Watts-
Dunton became my mother's trustee and my guardian. He also threw his comether over Mr. Swinburne
and took him to live with him in the Pines, Putney.
There they both grew deaf together under the house-
keepership of Mr. Watts-Dunton's sister, the widow
of an attorney who had not made good—in a white,
high, widow's cap, white mittens, and a black silk
shoulder-cape. Deaf, too. . . . You may imagine
all three deaf people sitting together in the dusk of
the Pines waiting for the argand colza-oil lamp to
be lighted, when Mr. Swinburne and Mrs. Mason

would play cribbage whilst the poet sipped his glass of Worcester Sauce and Mr. Watts-Dunton pored over a crabbed volume of forgotten gipsy lore . . . or made pretence so to do.

The Pines, Putney, as its name shews, was no place for the stabling of Pegasus. It was, upon the whole, the most lugubrious London semi-detached villa that it was ever my fate to enter. It was spacious enough, but, built at the time of the 1850-60 craze for Portland cement, its outer surfaces had collected enough soot to give it the aspect of the dwelling of a workhouse master or chief gabler. In the sooty garden grew a single fir that, in my time at least, could have gone as a Christmas tree into the villa's dining-room. In the next garden there had been another, but that had died.

I don't mean to say that the house was poverty-stricken. It was the residence of the highly prosperous family lawyer that Mr. Watts-Dunton was, well staffed with servants, the windows and furniture always kept at a high pitch of polish, the cut steel fire implements always shining. . . . I imagine the walls must have been covered with brown paper in the proper aesthetic fashion of the advanced of the day and that that drank up the light. . . . At any rate the rooms of the Pines, Putney, were always dim. . . . I had occasion to go there pretty frequently . . . once a quarter at least when my mother's dividends were due; and on occasion when she had outrun the constable and needed an advance . . . or when I myself did! . . . So it was pretty often.

Then I would be received with an extraordinary pomp of praise by Mr. Watts-Dunton. He would address to me studied periods of laudation of my

latest published book. . . . I had published I think
six before I came of age . . . and Mr. Watts-
Dunton addressed me as if I were a public meeting.
And Mr. Swinburne would add some nervous phrases
to the effect that he intended to read my book as
soon as time served. . . . He would be floating
somewhere about in the dimnesses like a shaft of
golden light. . . . But when I came seriously to
prefer my request for a cheque and Mr. Watts-
Dunton had exhausted the praise with which he put
me off . . . then, if I was at all insistent, extraordinary things would happen. . . . Loud bells would
ring all over that establishment. Housemaids would
rush in, their cap-strings floating behind, bearing the
orange envelopes of telegrams on silver salvers. And
Mr. Watts-Dunton would start like a ship suddenly
struck by a gale, would tear open an envelope and
exclaim dramatically:

'Sorry, me dear faller. . . . Extraordinarily sorry,
me dear faller. . . . Tallegram from Hazlemere.
From Lord Tennyson. . . . Have to go . . . ah
. . . and correct his proofs at once. . . . M'm, m'm,
m'm. . . . Desolated to be unable to be further delighted by most int'rustin' conversa . . .' And he
would have disappeared, the dimnesses swallowing
him up with improbable velocity. . . .

When it wasn't Lord Tennyson, it would be
Browning . . . or Coventry Patmore or Lewis Morris. . . .

And you are not to believe that Mr. Watts-Dunton
was merely a toady. He was an extraordinarily as-
siduous and skilful family lawyer and adviser as to
investments and solvent of brawls and poets' fallings
out. . . . So that where those poor pre-Raphaelites

would have been without him there is no knowing. . . . His one novel . . . *Aylwin* . . . had the largest sale ever enjoyed by any novel up to that date and for decades after. It was what his friends called bilge, and his innumeral poems seemed to be all devoted to proving that he had once been kissed by a Rommany lal . . . a sort of watered-down Isopel Berners. . . . But what else could the poems and novels of the proprietor of the Pines, Putney, be? . . . And when reading his poems aloud to Mr. Swinburne, he would coyly hold his head on one side as if the better to afford you the view of the spot on the side of his jaw where the gipsy maiden had kissed him. . . . And I really believe one must have done so once. . . . But he did save ever so many of those outrageous poet-painters from the workhouse or the gaol and kept as many more on this side of delirium tremens. . . .

On the less dramatic occasions when Mr. Watts-Dunton really produced a cheque I would be invited to stay to lunch. . . . And owing to the increasing deafness of the two friends and of Mrs. Mason the meals passed in ever deeper and deeper silence. . . . Mr. Swinburne ate, lost in his dreams, with beside his plate, an enormous Persian cat to whom he fed alternate forksful of food. Mr. Watts-Dunton gobbled his meats with voracity. The cooking was exquisite, the wines quite impeccable—though Mr. Swinburne touched none. Mrs. Mason addressed inaudible remarks to the maids. . . .

At a given point she would catch the eye of non-existent ladies and rise stiffly. . . . Immediately, with an extremely jerky movement so rapid as to be

almost imperceptible, Mr. Swinburne would be on his
toe-points, positively running to the door, his coat-
tails flapping behind him. . . . It was the singular
action of an extremely active man. At one moment
he was sitting sunk in his chair; at the next he was
on the points of his toes and in extraordinarily rapid
motion. . . . Mrs. Mason would be passing out of
the doorway with a rigid inclination of the head to
Mr. Swinburne, who had opened the door for her;
and slowly and meditatively the poet would regain his
chair . . . with the litheness of a slow cat . . . and
would begin to talk in long, wonderful monologues
. . . about the *Bacchae* or the *Birds*.

Mr. James when he had occasion to mention Mr.
Swinburne would do so with positive sparks of indignation welling from his dark and luminous eyes,
his face rigid with indignation. . . . I do not know
what the poet of the Pines can have done to him;
Mr. James would be almost speechless with indignation. I never heard him otherwise be immoderate.
And with real fury he would imitate Swinburne's
jerky movements, jumping up and down on his chair,
his hands extended downwards at his sides, like a
soldier at attention, hitching himself sideways and
back again on the chair seat and squeaking incomprehensibly in an injurious falsetto. . . .

No! I never knew what so excited the Old Man,
though I have often reflected on the subject. There
cannot have been any quarrel, for the only time I
heard Mr. Swinburne mention Mr. James it was
merely to observe without any emotion of one kind
or another that he saw from the *Athenaeum* that

young James was still writing books. And I cannot imagine that Mr. James ever cherished a secret passion for Ada Mencken!

I have come to the conclusion that it was the natural antipathy that the indoor man of tea-parties must feel for the outrageous athlete, clean-boned, for ever on the seashore or longing to be there. Mr. James indeed exploded with an almost apoplectic fury when I once raised my voice and said that Mr. Swinburne was one of the strongest—the most amazingly strong—swimmers of his day. I remember recounting, to rub it in, my anxiety on the shores of the Isle of Wight when Mr. Swinburne had disappeared in the horizon on a rough day, amongst the destroyers and battleships and liners and tramps . . . disappeared and then reappeared hours after, walking with his light, swinging step over the sand dunes a mile behind my back. . . . Yes, he could swim . . . and be made a wonder of. . . .

Do you remember the story of Maupassant's in which he recounts how, canoeing miles and miles from the shore at Grasse or somewhere, he was amazed to observe, rising out of the sea, the golden-rufous head of a marine deity who immediately began to discourse on Anacreon and the Greek Anthology. . . . And, so conversing, swam beside the canoe to the shore . . . and up the sands conversing still in golden and glorious French of the glorious, golden Greeks? . . . And when he stood, dripping the sea over the parquet of Maupassant's salon, the author of *La Maison Tellier* exclaimed:

'You are . . . you must be . . . Monsieur Swinburne. . . .'

And Swinburne said: 'Yes, I am Swinburne,' and was not mad.

Perhaps Maupassant invited Swinburne to lunches at which there were many—not merely one—*femmes du monde,* naked and masked. That would be enough to annoy Mr. James. Or he may have heard Turgenev read Swinburne to his Pauline and to Flaubert and Zola and the Goncourts and Catulle Mendès and declare that he was the only great, golden-voiced singer that barbarous Anglo-Saxondom had produced. . . . And the others all agreeing! . . . That would be pretty annoying. . . . And of course Swinburne was the real, right thing in families, the descendant of Admirals and Wardens of the Marches, and hanged men, and cattle-reiving assassins . . . and a real great classical scholar who could write Greek verse faster than Aeschylus . . . and French rhymed Alexandrines to beat Victor Hugo himself. . . . You did not find that particular Real Thing in the *parages* of Washington Square. . . .

And so you come to my sad Paris six weeks and Kentish fortnight. . . . I don't profess to know anything about Verse Poetry. But you would think that, with effort, one ought to be able to keep one's mind down on pages and pages of verse. . . . After all I once passed a quite difficult examination in Sanskrit and Urdu; I can still go on with most of the paragraphs of the Manual of Military Law if you will start me on them! I have read every word of the *Dawn in Britain,* not to mention *Arabia Deserta.* . . . And indeed all—every word and several times over— of Mr. Pound's *XXX Cantos.* But Swinburne I can-

not read; my mind will not stick to his pages; I read
two thirds of a verse . . . and my mind, whilst my
eyes still follow the lines, goes away on thoughts as
to my bank balance or the state of Europe. With a
jerk I remember again my duty and read

> White rose in red rose-garden
> Is not so white;
> Snowdrops that plead for pardon
> And pine for fright
> Because the hard East blows over . . .

The lines already run together. . . . My mind
questions whether, by any possible image, snowdrops
can be considered to plead or to pine. They are the
hardiest of all flowers; pushing through the frosted
earth in the bitterest winters. . . . Well, then . . .
the fellow just stuck in snowdrops because they are
white and 'pardon' to rhyme with 'garden' . . . a
pretty poor sort of conjuring trick. . . . Let us try
another page. . . . Ah, this is nearer it:

> Let us go hence, my songs; she will not hear.
>   Let us go hence together without fear;
> Keep silence now, for singing time is over
>   And over all old things and all things dear,
> She loves not you nor me as we all love her.
>   Yea, though we sang as angels in her ear,
>   She would not hear.

That is supportable. . . . But let us look at it with
the remorseless cruelty of the *prosateur* criticizing his
own words. . . . The first line arrests the attention.
. . . But the second? Why? Why is it there? What

have the man and his songs got to fear? . . . That
of course is stuck in to get the rhyme. . . . Well,
the impetus of the first line may just carry us past it.
The third line may stand; 'now' and 'for' are put in
to make up the eleven syllables of the line. . . .
Line four is rather insupportable. At first sight it
appears to be just jingle. But of course this fellow is
a POET. He arrogates to himself the right to dis-
regard punctuation. If he had put a comma after
'over' the line would at least have been immediately
comprehensible. Line five is unreasonably long . . .
mainly, perhaps, because it is all monosyllables.
Monosyllables move very slowly. . . . Lines six and
seven are not too bad . . . biblical in derivation but
sufficiently arresting to the attention. . . .

If, in short, we had to write that sort of thing it
would turn out:

> Let us go hence, my songs; she will not hear.
> Keep silent; singing time is over with all old
>   things and things dear;
> She never loved us as we love her,
> Nor, though we sang as angels in her ear,
>   Would she hear.

We put the 'nor' to get rid of the archaic 'yea' and
to get the last line into a cadence as opposed to a
metrical rhythm. . . . Then we should probably tear
the whole thing up, as not being very interesting.
. . . The original is no doubt better. There are the
metrical rhythm and the rhymes for those who like
the sort of thing . . . for adolescents and the academic praisers of things past.

Then what? . . . Is it perhaps merely a matter

of fashions and of, as it were, the rhythms of our day? Might Swinburne come again if the Machine Age collapsed and we all became small Producers? . . . along with Tennyson and Dante Gabriel Rossetti and Coventry Patmore . . . oh, and Milton and the author of *Arcadia,* who wrote half a mile from where I am writing. . . . It is perhaps only our ears that are as it were cut to a fashion; those others being permanent. You never know. . . . We hear, I mean —we, today—too many metrical sounds to need them in our literature of escape. . . . We have them for ever with us, in the chopped metre of our railway wheels, in the rhythms of the planes overhead, of our automobile wheels, of the flywheels in waterworks, of dynamos. . . . So it is really no escape from our world to go into the *Hymn to Proserpine:*

Sweet is the treading of wine, and sweet the feet
   of the dove;
But a goodlier gift is thine than foam of the
   grapes or love;
Yea, is not even Apollo, with hair and harp-
   string of gold,
A bitter God to follow, a beautiful God to be-
   hold . . .

because it is with its endlessly returning metre, merely taking a journey in a streamlined train . . . and of that all of us today have enough.

That is less fantastic a statement than it seems at first sight. Man—you, I, and the policeman at the corner—has as definite a need of the patterns of rhythm in his life as he has of salt in his diet. To get it he must dance ceremonial dances, chant in num-

bers, listen to rhymes. But when his normal life of
the street, public conveyance, and suburb is perpetually interspersed with mechanical rhythm he will
have little use for the long onrolling of classical
metres evolving slow and not unusual thought. Swinburne and his contemporaries were already deriva-
tive. They supplied to the public of their unrhythmed
day a facile substitute for the real classics . . . as
it were a piano version of orchestral masterpieces.
Today we need on the one hand the crisp sparks of
immensely artificed prose . . . for it is not easy to
write arresting prose. . . . Either, then, that or the
quintessence of the real classics. For the man who
can get little pleasure out of Swinburne's *Hymn to
Proserpine* can yet get immense, vital, and, as it
were, startled enjoyment out of reciting to himself
for the hundredth time

> Filia consuetis ut erat comitata puellis
>   Errabat nudo per sua prata pede;
> Valle sub umbrosa locus est aspergine multa
>   Uvidus ex alto desilientis aquae

and, oh but immensely more yet from

> εἴπατε τῷ βασιλῆι χαμαὶ πέϛε δαίδαλος αὐλά
> οὐκέτι φοῖβος ἔχει καλυβαν!

And don't believe that these sudden citations of
unusual authors are a gratuitous exhibition of ped-
antry. They are the revelation of secret pleasures that
I have carried about with me for half a century
. . . and perhaps the Greek is the more glowing
because I once heard Mr. Swinburne repeat those

lines after lunch at the Pines, Putney. . . . But above all don't believe that *ouketi Phoibos echei kaluban*. . . . Phoebus has still his cabins in the hearts of a great many . . . and as the pressures of life grow heavier and heavier and our anxieties more dire so the necessity for him grows more and more urgent.

The easy-going Victorian contemporaries of Mr. Swinburne could water Apollo down and down till the diluted fluid was the fit accompaniment for post-prandial club armchairs. . . . It is perhaps what one has most against them . . . that they turned the *Morte d'Arthur* into the *idylls of the King* and the *Greek Anthology* into . . . well, it is not our business to hold up too many works to scorn. . . .

We have today our Agamemnons. . . . But these were the strong men that preceded them. . . . And what shall the revolution of the resounding ages do to us? . . . I rather fancy that, if we last a little better—I don't say we shall, but *if* we do—it will be because we are a little less men and a little more craftsmen than they were. . . . I don't see any of us being adored as was the author of *Félise* . . . but I equally don't see us being carried up to the bath between a cabman and Charlotte, twice a week, through the kitchen. . . .

That is perhaps really it. . . . Algernon Charles Swinburne, descendant of Admirals, rebels and free-booters, desired to be in turn an Admiral. His curiously diminished physical structure forbade that. So he carried his filibustering into the realms of Letters . . . and his aristocratic, snorting contempt for the Established and the tradesman. Unfortunately the profession of letters is also an occupation for crafts-

men: you write a good paragraph of prose or a good
verse as cobblers mend shoes. . . . That was something that, soaring for ever in the empyrean above
Putney, he overlooked. If indeed he had been aware
of it he would no doubt have abandoned the trade
of poet and have taken to waving the red flag over
barricades . . . or, later, the Union Jack on Constitution Hill.

As it is he is a very good poet for the adolescent in
love who can restore to him some of the careless
glory that has faded from his long lines. . . . But
for me—as I hope from now on a little for you too—
he will always remain a male creature of a great
radiance, chivalry, sweetness of voice, and generous
gestures. So that if you desired to think of the Type-
Poet, or to install in some Valhalla an image of the
greatest of all the pages of our Lord Phoebus, you
could not well find any more fitting model.

'THERE WERE STRONG MEN'

THE history of the fifty years of contacts with the Great in letters that I have been telling in these vignettes divides itself sharply, like All Gaul, into three parts. Each runs for some time contemporaneously with the others; they never mingle.

If I go up to the summit of one of the small mountains which ring in the city of my residence I shall see, looking inland, at a great distance, immense white shapes, like gigantic old hags in shrouds, miching and mowing and telling each other evil stories. I don't know them by name and don't want to. There are probably Mont Blanc, the Matterhorn, the Righi. But *I* call them Mr. Ruskin and Mr. Carlyle and Dean Stanley and Mr. Emerson and the rest of the Middle Victorian, tumultuously bearded Great who were a childish nightmare to me. They ringed in my young horizon, miching and mowing and telling each other disagreeable stories, each one about all the others who were out of earshot. Yes, that bitter, enormous, greybeard assembly of the Great ringed in my child's horizon as completely as here, on the top of my little local mountain, you see the great mountains ring in their dark foothills and all the inlands. The pellucid Mediterranean imposes its remorseless barrier behind you so that you can't run away.

And yet I don't know that it was so merely a matter of childhood; it was perhaps an abiding claustrophobia so that, as my eyes take their last glance of the world, I may seem to see myself surrounded by barrier after barrier of the Victorian Academic Great. . . . At any rate, after I was blown up at Bécourt-Bécordel in '16 and, having lost my memory, lay in the Casualty Clearing Station in Corbie, with the Enemy planes dropping bombs all over it and the dead Red Cross nurses being carried past my bed, I used to worry agonizedly about what my name could be—and have a day-nightmare. The night-nightmare was worse, but the day one was as bad as was necessary. I thought I had been taken prisoner by the Enemy forces and was lying on the ground, manacled hand and foot . . . and with the Enemy, ignoring me for the time, doing dreadful stunts—God knows what—all around me. . . . Immense shapes in grey-white *cagoules* and shrouds, miching and mowing and whispering horrible plans to one another! It is true they all wore giant, misty gas-masks—but wasn't that the logical corollary of the bitter-hating age that produced the mid-Victorian Great Figure? Wouldn't, I mean, Poison Gas be just the sort of thing that, could they have invented it, the Ruskins and Carlyles and Wilberforces and Holman Hunts would have employed on their enemies or their blood-brothers become rivals? So their Germanic disciples used it when their Day came. Inevitably! Because the dreadful thing about nineteenth-century Anglo-Saxondom was that it corrupted with its bitter comfort-plus-opulence mania not merely itself but the entire, earnest, listening world. What effect could a serious and continued reading of those fellows have had but 1914? . . . And 193. . . .

It has only just occurred to me that that Corbie-phobia of my middle years must have taken at least its shape from my childhood's dreads. I might well, I mean, have had as my chief dread in those white huts surmounted with the Red-Cross, the fear of being taken prisoner by the Germans—but I doubt if my imagined Germans would have taken just that gigantic miching and mowing shape if it hadn't been for the nature of my childhood's ambience. I was then horribly imbued by those people with a sense of my Original Sin so that I used to have innumerable fears when the candle was put out. . . . But that was the worst of all . . . the dread that Mr. Ruskin or Mr. Carlyle or Mr. Holman Hunt—or even Herr Richard Wagner!—should with their dreadful eyes come into a room where I was alone and where there was no other exit . . . and, fixing me with their dreadful, shining eyes . . . God knows what then. . . .

I set this down here then because the Rhadamanthine Conductor of the *American Mercury* when silencing my objections to writing these particular vignettes used as his final argument: You don't know what it means to Us to know what it felt like to have been in contact with Them! . . . That was what it felt like. Now you know!

Well then, round the extreme of my mountain-top, inland horizon, go those other mountain tops . . . that freeze. But below them are the dark higher-foot-hills, running sinuously like great, jocund breakers— that landscape seeming always in motion to me.

The image has perhaps gone nearly far enough.

But if you imagine the High Alps to be the intolerable Victorian Moralists with, in their crannies, the forgotten, humble novelists of their day, you will have part of a useful pattern. Then consider the foothills below them to be the Conrad-James-Crane-Hudson group of whom I have most lovingly treated. They appear to me to move, to roll like dolphins over a summer sea, to utter jocular 'Ho, Ho's,' like Mr. James when he had got hold of a good joke. . . . .

And below the foothills runs a rolling plateau of champaign country that may stand for Lawrence and his rivals and contemporaries—mostly still existing. And so the ground runs up to ourselves, standing on our little mountain—of another system. . . .

The difference between generation and generation of these writers was not less marked than that between High Alp, foothills and champaign plateau. It becomes most appreciable when you approach it from the point of view of the Moral Purpose. The Middle Victorians professed themselves inspired by that as by a divine afflatus—and the whole world believed them. Victor Hugo appears mad because he believed—he finally kidded himself into really believing—that he was as inspired by the great moral purpose as the *Victor Hugo* that he set before the public. Mr. Ruskin went really mad in the effort to be as moral as the *John Ruskin* of the *Stones of Venice*. He told Mrs. Ruskin in the carriage when they drove away from the wedding service that they were going to live as God's blessed angels lived . . . Carlyle the same.

The next generation of writers sensed the danger. It couldn't, they said to themselves, be good for the World that its chief intellectual compulsion should

come from eunuchs and a tyrannous, elderly widow.
So they were amoral. Probably they came in a moral-
less wave because the world felt that it needed just
that. So neither Conrad nor James, neither Crane nor
Hudson were in any sense major moralists. James
desired to see the world made fit for afternoon tea-
parties with Lady Maud Warrender because he liked
the atmosphere of afternoon teas. Conrad, following
Flaubert, who was in all things his master, declared
rather platonically that every work of art had a profoundly great moral purpose. As if, when you saw
the *Winged Victory* you should feel an urge to go to
Sunday-school. Crane I never heard utter any moral
platitudes whatever—except, I suppose, that if you
jumped blind baggages to Hot Pan or got sunk in the
Caribbean and had to swim ashore, you would one
day come to be able to swat flies with the foresight
of your gun—supposing your gun to have a foresight.
Hudson was equally unlike Polonius. His one passionate item of propaganda was that beauty must be
preserved for the world and that you preserved
beauty for the world by forcing legislatures to pass
bird-protection measures, birds being the only sure-
thing items of beauty in a defective world. Art might
or might not be beautiful; Virtue might or might not
be beautiful . . . or loyalty or love of women. Birds
always were.

Those then were the Impressionists, with of course
behind them the great shades of Flaubert and Turgenev. The one passion that united them all—as
perhaps it unites all great and serious writers—was
that: to leave behind them a creative record of their
time. They said: 'Once we have rendered our day,
with a due vision for the inner truths of it—then the

World can draw its own morals. . . . But the important thing is that the World should have an *aperçu* of itself as it is . . . a passionless reconstitution, not passionate fakings of aspects and of evidence by widows past marriage and eunuchs.'

So, just as Flaubert had created the Norman *moyenne-* and *haute-bourgeoisie* and Turgenev, Russia of the times of the serfs, so James set busily to work rendering—creating, that is to say—English five o'clock tea-time. Crane created outposts of progress or barbarism, whichever you prefer to call it— the life of pioneers rough-riding the lonely wildernesses in reaction at once against the East Side and Washington Square; splendid, be-legginged creatures whose leisure was occupied by swatting flies with their foresights. For Crane, the son, as he preferred to say, of an uptown New York Anglican bishop—or as he actually was, the son of the wife of a New Jersey Non-conformist minister, that life, together with the wagings of the ridiculous little wars of those days, presented the aspects of Romance . . . whilst he remained in Elizabeth, New Jersey. But once he got into that Romance territory, he nailed it down in his impressions as few other lives have been nailed down. Hudson gave you, along with dazzling projections of the pampas, about the best renderings of English life of the agricultural South that have ever been written.

And poor Conrad, if his career was at first warped by the insupportable privacies of the Sea, gave you, when he took his courage in both hands and deserted in his books that trying element, extraordinarily vivid renderings of urban social life from Moscow to Peru —of that life under the incidence of political stresses.

So that, by the time the nineteenth century had petered out and the twentieth was on its way to Armageddon, you had such a set of renderings of the world from Moscow to Peru as had never before existed. It was of a brilliance, a self-sacrifice, a reality that made all the records of previous recorders, analysts, and propagandists seem extraordinarily dim and disingenuous. Given that the method could have spread—and indeed I am not saying that these were by any means the only writers pursuing those methods—given, then that the method could have spread to cover all shades of life on the map and to capture vast numbers of readers, the history of the World might have been very different. . . . You couldn't, if you were any decent sort of man at all, contemplate the murder of the herds and ploughmen of *A Shepherd's Life.* You would order your Ministers of War to be degraded or executed even, before you would permit them to do that.

Let us however leave that—most important—aspect of the case to consider for a moment another, more intimate, side of the Art of Letters. The Flaubert-Turgenev-Conrad-James wave of Impressionism lasted prominently—in Anglo-Saxondom—say, thirty years—from 1893 to the death of Conrad in 1923. Its World Course was longer, lasting, say, half a century, from 1870 to 1920. But in England and America and their Dependencies you may say that the Movement was being promoted and propagandized for by Mr. Edward Garnett in the nineties; publicly adopted by the Intelligentsia between 1900 and 1910, and taken up and pushed by the Trade from 1910 a little way into the twenties, so that by say 1923 the Great, but so quickly tiring, Public was avidly buying its products as wall-furniture and parlour-table decorations. By 1929 the movement died. Furniture was no longer being bought; parlour tables were being hocked. . . . Besides, about ten years is about as long as the Great Public can stand its Greatest Writers. A crisis is a good excuse for jettisoning them; but it will jettison them without excuse if there is none handy.

There is however another side to the matter—it has indeed a hundred sides but we have room for only two or three. The world adopted the Impressionists because it was weary to death of the large-scale Moral Purposists Polonicisms. It wanted some Hamlets. But it was weary not merely of Eunuch-Widow point of view; it was weary of its and their Languages. The unease took visible shapes in various parts of the world. The French got busy about *mots justes;* they could no longer stand the hackney-cab-man styles of Balzacs and Dumas. The Slavophils of Russia expelled Greek- and German-derived words from their manifestos; the English pre-Raphaelites, led by William Morris, determined to use none but Anglo-Saxon expressions; the Germans by law abolished the word *garage* and substituted the more majestic *Kraftwageneinstellraúm*—'power-wagon-standing-in-room.' . . . I myself saw the change being effectuated on the signboard of a hotel on the Rhine under the orders of the General Officer Commanding the Ehrenbreitstein district. . . . And Whitman insisted on adopting for his poems the language of patent-medicine prospectuses. And found followers. Right up to the day and time of Mr. Dreiser. . . .

By the nineties, in fact, not only had the literary language become unusable by the common man the
world over; it had become nauseous when it was not
merely grotesque. . . . In my battalion, after mess,
when they wanted to feel good they would say to me:

'Speak like a book, H. . . . Do speak like a book
for a minute or two.'

And I would begin gravely:

'After mature consideration I have arrived at the
conclusion . . .' There would be already titters . . .
'That his Majesty's Officers of this Unit of the Line,
being in the nature of the case and of their genealo-
gies, dispositions and careers, incapable either of con-
structing a balanced sentence or of comprehending—
much less appreciating—the simplest statement
couched in the said gracious sovereign's impeccable
vernacular—such, I repeat, being their normal and
unchangeable mental and intellectual complexions.'
. . . But all the golden waistcoat buttons would by
then be loosened; the wearers rocking in their seats
and my voice drowned in unceasing salvoes of guf-
faws, so that I never did finish that sentence.

And if that was the effect of presenting standard
forms of their language to my companions in arms
off parade it was nothing to what happened if I tried
to get Battalion Orders expressed with some regard
to, say, syntax. The men could not understand a word
of it, and the resulting confusion was such that I was
threatened with the most unpleasant disciplinary action by Headquarters. . . . And one of my most
carefully written reports on something or other was
returned from Garrison with, scrawled all over it,
the remark of the General: 'The illiterate Officer of

illegible name and rank will rewrite his report in
clear and concise language, leaving one quarter mar-
gin,' and decorated with innumerable hilarious notes
of exclamation in blue pencil from the officers at
Headquarters the English of whose Orders I had
presumed to criticize.[1]

I don't think that either instance is at all exaggerated. The officers of my regiment were certainly
better educated and more literate than the average
civilian of the day—but indeed a similar hilarity
would have greeted 'speaking like a book' in any
mixed gathering on either side of the Atlantic. The
Literary Language of Anglo-Saxondom was really
quite dead, by about 1890, and I am not sure that,
except in the realm of creative writing, it has not
remained dead to this day.

Let me, having thrown the lay reader, for his
amusement, the bone of the story of Violet Heyman
. . . let me, then, say a word or two on a subject
that is very near my heart.

[1] It may interest the reader to know what was the
particular sentence of my Report that so enraged the
gallant Garrison Commander. It ran: 'And moreover the
charge against the defendant Violet Heyman—of *"being
on enclosed premises the property of H.M. the King
for the purpose of committing prostitution"* will not lie
because she did not enter the premises *proprio motu* but
at the instance of the prisoner Lance Corporal Plant of
the 7th Welch Regt so that the offence of prostitution
could not have taken place, the essence of prostitution
being soliciting . . . which she had found unnecessary.'
As a Briton I am proud to think that the General Commanding that garrison was cashiered for the offence of
imprisoning a civilian on a false charge and, being a
gallant old boy, afterwards went out to France as a
second lieutenant.

The Roman master of literature when he had the occasion would say:

> Habeo bonum equum
> I have a good horse.

But the contemporary, say Pompeian, corner boy, groom, cakeseller, professional gladiator and the lower middle classes generally would have put it:

> Ego habeo unum bellum caballum
> I have a fine beast of burden

. . . in a weak sentence, straggling like a long-legged calf, without precision, conciseness, and of diluted interest . . . diluted by the introduction of unnecessary words.

Cicero, Caesar, Livy, the Plinies and even Horace, Vergil, and perhaps above all Petronius and Catullus, who was in our sense the only Roman Poet—all these writers, right down the Augustan Age to the Decline watched and doctored their language fiercely, knowing that, if readers were to be held they must be struck by each sentence as if it were a brickbat thrown at their heads. They invented as they went along—how contrary to our habits!—a vigorous slang. The most vigorous that the world has ever seen! So that it was not the gladiator, and still less the Man in the Street, who could knock you down with his epithets—it was Cicero or Cato the Elder. The latter, as you know, ended every one of his orations in the Senate, no matter what its subject, with the words 'Ceterum censeo, delendam esse Carthaginem'—five words that it takes us fourteen to translate—fourteen words of which eleven are mono-syllables. . . . And monosyllables extraordinarily de-lay the impinging of the sense of a statement on the brain. The Lord's Prayer in French takes 62 words, in English 55, in Latin 47. But of syllables the Eng-lish version takes 80, the Latin 100, the French 106 . . . The Vulgate version takes incomparably less time to appreciate—yet the English version is very fine English, the Latin very indifferent Latin. I use it however as an example because it is the only piece in which you can find universally accepted transla-tions in all three languages. When it comes to trans-lating Classical Latin the difference, try to be as concise and polysyllabic as you will, is much more marked.

Terra tribus scopulis vastum pro-
    currit in aequor   Words 7   Syls. 15
A three-pointed land runs out into
    the vast waters   Words 10 Syls. 13
        Monosyllables: Lat. 1; Eng. 6

Trinacris a positu nomen adepta
    loci   Words 6   Syls. 14
Its name, Trinacria, having been
    conferred on account of the
    shape of the place   Words 14 Syls. 20
        Monosyllables: Lat. 1; Eng. 10

Grata domus Cereris multas Ea
    possidet urbes   Words 7   Syls. 15
The pleasant home of Ceres she
    there possesses many cities   Words 12 Syls. 16
        Monosyllables: Lat. 0; Eng. 5

In quibus est culto fertilis Henna
    solo   Words 7   Syls. 12
Amongst which is Henna with its
    fertile soil   Words 9   Syls. 11
        Monosyllables: Lat. 2; Eng. 5

The whole working out at:

	Lat.	Eng.
Monosyllables	4	26
Words	27	45
Syllables	56	60

The number of English syllables employed is, in fact, nearly equal; the number of words, more than half as many again, and the number of monosyllables, over six times as many. And look at the extraordinary difference in the amount of space taken up on the paper.

And that too makes immensely for the superiority of Latin over English as a means of conveying thought; the eye gets as tired of travelling over lines on paper as do the feet on long roads. . . . But this matter does not end there, for it is not with the eye that the competent reader reads. It is with his brain. It is not letters but ideas that his mind takes in, one by one.

On the face of it and measured by letters the word 'strong' is less long than 'incontestable.' But if you write: 'The proposition is strong' . . . or rather, as for the sake of euphony you probably would write: 'The proposition is a strong one,' you are giving the brain more work to do than if you write: 'The proposition is incontestable,' because of the greater definiteness of the longer word. The mind accepts the statement; whereas when the word is only 'strong' it tires itself a little by asking: 'How strong?' So that, if your page is made up of semi-indefinite statements, the mind, coming to an end of it, is tired like a dog that, instead of keeping to a straight footpath, makes incessant detours out into the field and back. The length or number of letters in a word has nothing to do with it: it is the mind behind the words. A definite, as it were masculine, mind, puts its thought across definitely as if it carved statements with a chisel on stone.

Unfortunately it was the illiterate populace rather than the Masters of Prose that survived the sack and disappearance of the Roman Empire. It was therefore upon their straddling *'ego habeo unum bellum caballum'* rather than upon the masculine and direct *'habeo bonum equum'* that all our Occidental languages have modelled themselves. Until they became, irrevocably, backboneless masses of a sort of plasticine, masses of clay gummed together by superfluous little words—a soft substance in which it was impossible to make any hard statement. Of this language academic panjandrums from time to time took charge enjoining on you perpetually that you must not use any word that had not been codified fifty years or use them in any sequence that had not been sanctified by prolonged overusage.

The natural and inevitable reaction by 1890 had become twofold. The literary Language had grown perfectly unfit for the communication of any kind of daily thought, or indeed for any kind of thought at all. Thus, the practising writer found a necessity for a complete overhauling of the written language; and any member of the lay public who for any reason or another felt the necessity for rapid and adequate communication of his thought took to the invention of words and phrases that might do for him what the Academically legalized vernacular would never permit. And this applied to the normally academic intellectual quite as much as to the corner-

boy or professional gladiator of the day. . . . I
remember asking my Uncle William Rossetti in
1894 what he thought of Charles Augustus Howells,
who had been his brother's friend and Mr. Ruskin's
secretary. And William Rossetti, who, on the face
of him was quite as academic and orthodox as it
was possible to be, answered composedly that after
mature consideration he had arrived at the conclusion
that Charles Augustus was a pretty fishy kind of a
bloke. . . . And Henry James, who, again, on the
face of him was a particularly orthodox, comfortable
gentleman for a polite tea-party, never had the
expression 'if I may permit myself the phrase,' and
then some such colloquialism as 'all was gas and
gaiters,' off his lips. . . . And never, never shall I
forget my astonishment as when in Cambridge, Mas-
sachusetts, in 1906 I asked Mrs. William James where
her son William—the beloved 'Nephew Billiam' of
her distinguished brother-in-law—was. And that
lady, who seemed as if, wearing a helmet and armed
with a great spear, she ought to be guarding the
Groves of Academe and who seemed most herself
when expressing thought suited for her great husband
in the vernacular of Doctor Johnson—that for me
always alarming *grande dame* of the Hill answered
negligently that she guessed that at that hour her son
was probably doing stunts round Trinity Church
spire. . . . I don't know which to me seemed the
more alarming and significant of the passing of an
era—that the favourite nephew of Henry James, of
all people of that civilized globe, should be practising
aviation, or that the lady who seemed to have been
invented by God to be the custodian of America's
muses should have employed the horrificent, brand-

new East Side expression 'doing stunts.' . . . But it will be observed that official language there had broken down. How else could she have expressed herself? Nohow! A plane does stunts and nothing else but stunts once it is off the beaten tracks of its commercial or organized-criminal pursuits. 'Stunts' is therefore the only real, right, incontestable *mot juste* . . . and what other type of word could be used by the guardian of a Nation's Muse?

In the meantime poor Conrad, continuously groaning that the English language was no sort of a medium for a Polish gentleman and *prosateur,* pursued the desperate quest of just words that should make you see the ripples of wind running uphill on the golden russet of a wheatfield's whispering surface, in the sunlight, beneath a blue sky. And Mr. James, too conscious of his ambassadorial position as between two great Republics of letters to say that the language of the country of his adoption was N.B.G. for the *prosateur*-psychologist of a fictional vocation; and pursuing further and further his studies into the conversational methods of my Lady Maud Warrender and her friends, who, since they included our sovereign lord Edward VII, might indeed be considered to speak, if I may use the phrase, the King's own English. . . . Mr. James got further and further from the limpid beauty and simplicity and force and gas and gaiters of his original vernacular. Until, unless you read him aloud, you could not make head or tail of his meanings, though, matchless Impressionist that he was, he succeeded in conveying to you the impression that some tremendous, tremulous, tenuous game was, somewhere in the Index, being played. Crane went on—but for how short a

time!—discharging his granitic phrases as if he had
been a stick of dynamite in a quarry. And Hudson
went on taking little words out of copybooks to substitute for other, more used words, and so achieving
the supreme of beauty of English style. . . . As for
me I went on working beside Conrad, trying, when
his passionate and possessive material, mental and
physical vicissitudes left me the leisure, to evolve for
myself a vernacular of an extreme quietness that
would suggest someone of some refinement talking
in a low voice near the ear of someone else he liked
a good deal. I don't really imagine that I really
influenced Conrad at all. I suggested quite often
colloquial synonyms for words of which he had only
the literary versions—as you might say 'wire' or
'cable' for 'telegram.' . . . Only of course it was not
usually as simple as that. And I corrected the syntax
of his proofs and put in or took out commas. And—
and that is the only reason why I mention the
collaboration at all—Messrs Garnett and Gosse and
Galsworthy and Wells and Havelock Ellis, though
the last rather unwittingly, all in varying degrees
of loudness suggested that I was ruining Conrad's
delicate Oriental style. I may have—but after a great
deal of reflection I am pretty certain that I didn't.
Suggesting that a man write 'like me' instead of
'like I did' or 'different from' instead of 'different to'
can't do him much harm. So that I don't believe I
influenced him at all: he was too set on his own
ways, on his gorgeous cadences and Elizabethan-Slav
mental evolutions. No!

In any case the Movement went on turning out its
extraordinarily vivid renderings of places and frames

of mind. Could it, as I have suggested, have spread further and influenced more people it might have saved the world from Armageddon. You can't really make war on a people whose literature has profoundly and illuminatingly rendered for you its aspirations and achievements. Or, if you like to put it in another way, the great master of Impressionism was Flaubert. And Flaubert asserted that if France would have read *Education Sentimentale* she would have been spared the horrors of 1870-71. That may or may not be true. But could he have lived until 1914 he might have boasted with a truth that was absolutely incontestable that *Madame Bovary* and *Salammbo* and the *Trois Contes* saved France for the world—those works of his and of his learners who carried on his methods. For it is impossible that a World that—so almost universally—read those works, or that in other branches was ready to accept as masters all the Flaubert-derived writers from James and Conrad downwards—it is impossible to consider that such a world would regard with equanimity the disappearance of a civilization that had produced that frame of mind and those works of Art. I can say at least for myself that never, at a too advanced age and having just written the only novel of my own that I considered—and indeed consider—at all to count, so that I might at last have considered myself to have achieved a 'technique' . . . never then should I have done what M. Herriot called *'jeter la plume et cingler l'épée'* if it hadn't been that I could not bear the idea that fresh and posthumous troubles should be added to those of the poor shades of Emma and Charles Bovary. Or that Félicité should be cast from her turfed grave by projectiles hurled from the

North. And if that happened to me so it happened to the thousands—and to millions influenced by those thousands—who went to die among the poppies.

I am not here writing propaganda for France. I am simply making the unimpassioned constatation that the literature—and more particularly the novels, of France saved that country for the world. It is a merely scientific deduction. If your tastes are more Nordic you can go back forty odd years before 1914 and see how the howls of Carlyle and his similarly inspired followers under the auspices of a Teutonic Court saved divine, Protestant, cleanly, industrious, acquisitive Almaigne from intervention when for the twenty-sixth time since the days of Brennus she was engaged in plundering the fields and châteaux of her chattering, vainglorious, negligible Southern neighbour. . . . You can console yourselves with the thought that that is all matter of flux and reflux and that your turn at the cake will come again. The fact remains that the Great Moral Alpine Peaks of mid-Victorianism were Teutonically inspired—inspired by Albert the Good and the goose-step of Frederic the Great and the Great Exhibition of 1850 that was to have given the World universal peace, and Goethe and Lessing and Kant and Richard Wagner and Felix Mendelssohn Bartholdy and Froebel and the Kindergarten. . . . And the succeeding Impressionist Movement in World Literature was purely Gallic in motive power. . . .

Having then, placed my Impressionists in Space, Time, and the Commonwealth, and, reminding the reader that the last words I ever heard Henry James utter were, upon the occasion of my second going out to France—and he laid his hand on his heart and bowed as he said them in French: 'You will tell your comrades of the trenches that I have loved France as I never loved a woman!' . . . having, then, got that over I will return to the more personal note demanded of me by Mr. Palmer.

It didn't, my poor old Impressionist Movement, last such a Hell of a time. The hounds of Youth were upon its track almost before it sat in the saddle. The control of the *English Review*, which I had started mainly with the idea of giving a shove to Impressionism in its literary form was really snatched from my hands by Mr. Pound and his explosive-mouthed gang of scarce-breeched filibusterers . . . before I had really got accustomed to sitting in my own saddle. . . . And for those infants —Mr. Pound and his disciples, Mr. T. S. Eliot, Mr. Frost, Miss Doolittle, and the rest of the London-transatlantic crowd, as for Mr. Norman Douglas, Mr. Tomlinson, or Mr. Wyndham Lewis (Percy), or for poor D. H. Lawrence, the Impressionists were already fairly old stuff. Lawrence merely grunted with absent-minded half-contempt when I suggested that he might with profit read *Bouvard et Pécuchet;* when I mentioned Conrad to Mr. Tomlinson he said he had never heard of the feller; the London transatlantics whooped with delight when they heard that Mr. Robert Bontine Cunninghame Graham had called the Master 'Henrietta Maria' . . . though I believe that it was George Moore who really said it first. . . . That would be already in 1910 when Impressionism had hardly had twenty years of a run and had only just really conquered the Intelligentsia.

And then one day Mr. Lewis who had penetrated into my drawing-room office with all the aspects of a Russian conspirator-spy . . . Mr. Wyndham Lewis (Percy) caught me mysteriously by the elbow, willed me out into Holland Street and, in his almost inaudible voice . . . said it. . . .

'You and Mr. Conrad and Mr. James and all those old fellows are done. . . . Exploded! . . . *Fichus!* . . . *Vieux jeu!* . . . No good! . . . Finished! . . . Look here! . . . You old fellows are merely nonsensical. You go to infinite pains to get in your conventions. . . . *Progression d'effets.* . . . *Charpentes.* . . . Time-shift. . . . God knows what. . . . And what for? What in Heaven's name for? You want to kid people into believing that, when they read your ingenious projections they're actually going through the experiences of your characters. Verisimilitude—that's what you want to get with all your wheezy efforts. . . . But that isn't what people want. They don't want vicarious experience; they don't want to be educated. They want to be amused. . . . By brilliant fellows like me. Letting off brilliant fireworks. Performing like dogs on tight ropes. Something to give them the idea they're at a performance. You fellows try to efface yourselves; to make people think that there isn't any author and that they're living in the affairs you . . . adumbrate, isn't that your word? . . . What balls! What rot! . . . What's the good of being an author if you don't get any fun out of it? . . . Efface yourself! . . . Bilge!'

I often wonder what fun Mr. Lewis has got out of being an author since those old days.

But he expressed no doubt part of a truth. There is a section of the public that prefers Paganini to music . . . or it might be more just to say that all of us in certain moods like to look at conjuring tricks and performing seals. But not all of us, all the time. There is an immense public that really desires 'vicarious experience.' The novel as a form—is probably the best, or indeed the only form—of education because the really conscientious novelist, all out to render his day, will come nearer to the truth than either moralist or pedagogue who have always some *arrière-pensée* with which to stultify their instructions.

The day of the moralist seems a little on the return, that of the novel-writer to be temporarily obscured. I suppose it not to be over . . . but it may be. The exigencies of the Trade; the large crowds hypnotizing themselves into believing that the reading of poorly written and dully composed adumbrations of the sex-lives of Henry VIII, Katherine the Great, Margaret Fuller, Shelley, Emily Dickinson, Keats, or Beatrice Cenci will earn them marks in the Heaven where Culture counts; the natural reaction towards untidiness of mind after the intellectual effort of the late war; the panic-ferocities of the moment; the shortage of cash of the Intelligentsia and their hangers-on—all these things will continue to make the serious novelist more and more the dependant of his natural enemies. . . . I mean toil, envy, want, the patron, and the gaol. . . . Probably. . . .

For there is in these things no certainty of prophecy before the act. You can only look back and observe. Perhaps, even, if you had studied the matter for a long time you could predict roughly what will be happening next June . . . from what people are reading this autumn. Or perhaps it will be in June after next; or in ten years' time; or in fifty. There is no real knowing. But the probability that if there is a great and lasting craze for the immense autobiographies, formless, rumbling Sagas that amongst Nordics take the place of carefully architectured imaginative literature—and if the craze lasts for the fictional biographic excursions that great masses of people take for serious literature—then we may prophesy that the craze for putting people up against walls will gradually grow. Until, once more, we shall be applauding the plundering by Nordic races of the melon fields, orange groves, and châteaux of the races to their South. Or equally if the Trade finds it more profitable to supply shorter books and the great masses of readers should feel surfeited of sagas and ersatz-pulp biography—why, then we might, we just might, decide not to massacre any more people and we might . . . oh, hang up our good luck horseshoes over our doors, not vertically so as to get all the luck that is going but tilted a little to one side so as to leave a little for our neighbours. . . . We probably shan't, we Nordics whose damp civilization is occasionally shot with a little of the sunlight from the deep South as days of dripping rain are sometimes pierced from the horizon by shafts of great light. . . . We probably shan't . . . or shan't soon . . . which is all the same as shan't because we shan't any more be here. It's up to you, partner, really.

I had intended to include in this string of vignettes a picture of Mr. Pound and his young disciples, and another of Mr. Hemingway and the striking flare-up in the literary Middle West in the twenties. But I decided that I would not. That would be to begin a new book not to write a coda to an old one. So it must wait until another Rhadamanthus shall desire to see live those heroes who succeeded the strong men before their day!

That conspiracy to change the literary aspect of the western World was accompanied by an attempt to revivify Verse Poetry too by a lapidary revolution in language. Mr. Pound and his Imagistes and Vorticists made the discovery that was then so impatiently waiting to be made. If Literature was once more to occupy the place that in Anglo-Saxondom it should it must be done by Latinist economy of words and bareness. That was a working out, a lineal descent from the Impressionists' impatience with the literary language of their day. It was warranted enough. You will laugh when, to put it shortly, I say what I am about to say. But consider it carefully: The best training that a young writer could have today would be a year's training in writing headlines for the papers. *That* is writing! Imagine yourself getting up one morning and reading: PRESIDENT HAVELOCK ELLIS CONFER. KING KNIGHTS QUAY WEST PACIFIST. HITLER UNBURNS HOLY WRIT. DUCE READS *DAS CAPITAL*. STALIN STUDIES HEARST-ROTHERMERE PRESS. . . . Wouldn't you know that all was well with Literature? And with the world that only good letters can save. . . . And all done with twenty-one words. That, I repeat, is writing.

But it is all a very tenuous affair . . . this of writing and the life Literary. You can ask yourself so many questions and there are so few sure answers. What makes Literary Greatness? . . . The number of readers you have? The esteem in which you are held by a few picked minds . . . or the amount of misrepresentation you incur or the imprisonments you undergo? Or the fact that you starved before dying, like Villon? Or that like Thackeray you always made a comfortable income? Or that as was the case with Byron you changed the psychology and male tailoring of the adolescent world for half a century? Or that like the Sage of Croisset you saved France? Or like Heine had your works burned by Mr. Hitler, who nevertheless has to quote your poems in his school-readers—as by an anonymous author—because his country refuses to get on without them or to pass the Lorelei Rock without singing '*Ich weiss nicht wass soll es bedeuten*'? . . . That must be a rather pleasant form of triumph.

There is no answer to all these questions. . . . I know one thing only. . . . You are a great writer, say. You recline otiosely somewhere or other and look on your labours. You died either in the workhouse or in a West Kensington mansion or a duplex apartment in the Bronx. You were thrown into a hole; your creditors seized your corpse . . . or to the sound of organs you were buried in the Poets' Corner of Westminster Abbey. Now you take your ease.

You remember your life here in earth. You had an easy career to glory—or a difficult one. You were introduced in the beginning to the world by some sort of *accoucheur*—like Mr. Edward Garnett for my poor dear Impressionists or Mr. Pound for the later and noisier ones . . . by some sort of *accoucheur* and his assistants in the Press and the Trade. Or you got in through the crime-reporter's desk in Toronto or the remoter provinces. You were received with obloquy or you sprang at once, like Musset, into the position of the young Prince of Poets. You toiled obscurely or you went from triumph to triumph. You were early accepted by the

Intelligentsia and through all the drawing-rooms went the whisper proclaiming you It. From the intelligentsia your fame spread to the Great Public and all the accompaniments that Fame bears upon her wings rustled for years round your head. Or you just worked and nobody noticed you and you lie beneath a quite ordinary tombstone in a quite ordinary churchyard. . . . All that is all one.

Or you remember your fame. It arose in the night as did that of Byron; it was a matter of wide diffusion through alcoholic cellars, kings' courts and thieves' meeting-places as were the fames of Villon . . . *and* Shakespeare. Well, one way or the other you had Fame—for a city, for a county, a nation, for the world. Then it knew eclipse. That is inevitable. . . . You will have been too much drummed into people's heads by your fans, parasites, collectors, or mere imitators. Or you will be affected by changes in fashion or the wiping out of your civilization by Nordic hordes. However it come you will suffer an eclipse. Obviously it may prove a perpetual limbo.

But that one can never tell. I in my pride may say that Swinburne is gone for ever, superseded by Mr. Pound, who uses fewer clichés of emotion and a vernacular that will keep one awake while one reads. But I may be perfectly wrong. A day may come when, tired by verbal felicities and explosive progressions, the mind of man may crave once more for the immense, immense *longueurs,* the Greek-derived and outworn poeticisms, the incredible syntax, the superfluous words dragged in to make up a metre. So Swinburne may come back again, and I shall be glad because, as you will have perceived, I loved him and I am none of your incorruptibles. . . . When

I think of these things in terms of my Alpine landscape I seem to see Swinburne, poised in the blue empyrean above Mont Blanc, winged, rose-garlanded, and with bow and quiver, aiming an arrow at the heart of Mr. Ruskin. . . .

Anyone, indeed, might have a comeback staged for him. Tennyson, even, or even Longfellow. Compared to our more brilliantly accomplished workers of today and tomorrow they may some day have the touching aspect and the beloved naïvetés of Primitives, for no one could accuse them of knowing how to write. . . . Yes, anybody. I was brought up to regard Mendelssohn as less than the dust; deader than Ponson du Terrail of whom you never, perhaps, heard. Yet yesterday I was told that in today's Anglo-Saxondom he is considered quite a boy. Few London or New York concert programmes are without a Song Without Words, a Caprice, or something inspired by Ossian.

So there is absolutely no knowing. But one knows this. What brings back a forgotten artist is what I will call an essential honesty—of writing, of purpose, of selection, of presentation. The poor dear Impressionists are, it would appear, today going through a period of eclipse. If you mention them to the Intelligentsia you will be laughed at as someone was laughed at by Mr. Pepys for praising to him the antick stuff of the Swan of Avon. The books of Conrad, James, Hudson, and Crane are difficult to obtain. Few French booksellers stock the works of Flaubert, though, knowing a little of their trade, they will get them for you in a week or a fortnight. I read in a preface by M. Edmond Jaloux—the last elected of the French Academy

—a grumble that he had looked in vain for twenty years for one of the novels of Turgenev.

But I think that those men will surely return—because they had, each, minds fixed only on their work and the methods of their work. So they achieved that certain honesty of purpose that unites all writers who have returned. To say that James resembles Dante or Conrad the great Elizabethans seems absurd until you think about it for a good time. Then a certain shadow of resemblance begins to swim out of nothingness. Dante's work was compounded of gossip about his contemporaries; was propelled by a deep, an almost venomous hatred for what he did not stand for in his civilization. He loved unsuccessfully once and went on to an advanced age like the Master, in the *Wings of the Dove,* idealizing and embroidering the image of the woman he did not attain to. . . . And the resemblance between Conrad and the Elizabethans grows extraordinary when you think of it. He did not have to sue out coat armour because he was born to it; but he was the gentleman adventurer who followed the seas and was possessed by dreams of the golden East until he threw away his compass and seized the goosequill beloved by Raleigh. And he had their intolerances, and prides, and elaborate courtesies and vainnesses and high loyalties and singular fallings away from loyalties and duellists' valours and gamblers' foolhardinesses. . . .

I won't labour these points. They are such as a reader may well work out for himself. . . . But those men distilled truth from their lives, their temperaments, their adventures, their circumstances, their lost loves—and it is an odd coincidence that all those men, Hudson with his Rima, Conrad with his Rita, James with his cousin who died, Crane with his Young Lady from the Oranges who married another . . . all of them had in the backs of their minds a sort of Beatrice Portinari, just as all were impatient of their surroundings. And all expatriates, like Ovid or Dante, crossed or followed the seas, settled in the foreign, lurked in woods, or with difficult implements killed flies. And then, as the spider lets issue from its belly its glutinous and singular web, they drew out truth from their adventures . . . their own truths, with their own colours and shades, and their own integrities. So the betting is that they will come again.

Because in the end, have the true writer what he may or let him go without what perforce Destiny denies him, he has—and oh Great Writer don't you know it!—one thing that is possessed by no other man. That is his integrity . . . of purpose or of achievement. That he has to have, or no one will rediscover him among the shards of ruined Empires. He has to have it because it is what is demanded by mankind as the passport to the seats of the Mighty. And his achievement is his alone; he is the eternal solitary with no assistant. Give him a flint and a block of sandstone and he will confer immortality on Alexander.

It is difficult to see one's contemporaries. You perceive at a quiet tea-party an elderlyish gentleman, rather given to stoutness, of rolling eyes, of Pickwickian jocularity, of extravagant rotundity of phrase, and you say indignantly: 'That man likely to outlast in fame the successful General—or any other murderer; the great financier K . . . or any other sneak-thief; the illustrious sprat-canner L . . . or any other

wholesale poisoner; the world-famous politician M.
. . . or any other confidence trickster. . . . Perish
the thought!'

But he very likely will. . . . And if he doesn't it
is yet sufficient that somewhere there should exist a
fascicle of living words, woven in true thoughts and
capturing beauty in its cobwebby net. For the book
will live, not the reader, even though all the masonry
of a sacked city have fallen on its hiding-place and
the ground be buried beneath the dust of vanished
civilizations. . . . You know that, oh Great One,
reclining wherever it is that you recline.

THE END

Just as I was writing the two words above, it came
into my head to imagine myself . . . But no . . .
that is a cliché. I don't imagine myself places. . . .
I was then wondering what I should do if I found
myself on a desert island midway in the Atlantic.
There should stand before me a serviceable but not
unsurpassably muscular djinn who should offer to fly
to one bank or other of the sea and bring me back
about ten pounds' weight of books. He was not a
first-class djinn or he would have made it Professor
Somebody's hundred-yard shelf. And I imagined
myself saying: 'Go to the British Museum . . . or
no, to New York Public Library with its incorrect
date on its forehead, because they let you take out
books there and bring me . . .' And I imagined
myself reflecting that I should not want immense
classics because I should have a hut to build and a
garden to dig and beasts to slay and capture. So I

should not want the *Decline and Fall.* . . . 'Hurry!' grumbled the Djinn: 'Bring me,' I said then in my haste, '*Pride and Prejudice* and *Mansfield Park* and *Framley Parsonage* and *Mary Barton* and Christina Rossetti and Emily Dickinson and Ezra's *Cathay* and the *Four Visits* and the *Death of the Lion* and the *Real Thing* and the *Spoils of Poynton* in one volume and *Nature of Downland* and the *Open Boat* and *Farewell to Arms* and *My Heart and My Flesh* and *Penhally* . . .' . . .'That's twelve authors,' the Djinn grunted. 'Make it the baker's dozen for luck.'

I said—that is to say I imagined myself so addressing him:

'You understand. I do not say that those are the best authors ever.' I was tired. I had just finished a book. I wanted to get pep and at the same time peace under the sound of the guns dully conversing all day in Spain below the horizon. I wanted to renew friendships; to get rid of the memory of associations. I had left out authors I knew by heart. . . .

'The Thirteenth,' he grumbled.

'Ah,' I said, 'you want to know too much. I think I shall keep that secret locked in my own breast.'

'Do you want *Ethan Frome* or *My Antonia,* for old sake's sake. Or *Flowering Judas* to shew you keep pace with the times. . . . Which you don't. . . .'

'Aha!' I exclaimed, 'I see what the female side of your epicene personality is up to. You want me to name seven women to six men. . . . It was you who, the other day, were grumbling at me because I had not done the portrait of any woman in the whole of this series. But look here. . . . Granted, if you will, that women have done better work than men in the last hundred years, there are certain social difficulties in knowing very intimately a writer of a sex different from one's own. I don't believe I ever knew intimately a first-class woman writer of the decades of which I have treated—outside my distinguished connection, Christina Rossetti. And I never heard her talk about anything but the state of her sister-in-law, my Aunt Lucy's health, or whether it would be advisable to refuse to let her three per cent Consols be converted into Goshen's or buy more Bloomsbury real estate. So you see. I can't of them write personal reminiscences . . .'

But he was already winging his way beyond the storm-tossed Bermoothes.

NEW YORK: TOULON:
PARIS: NEW YORK:
March MCM XXXVI
to Jan. MCM XXXVII